Transactional Analysis for

Transactional Analysis for Depression is the first research-based, transactional analysis psychotherapy manual. Developed from the author's research into TA therapy for depression, the book also draws upon a wide range of contemporary research findings relating to depression and its treatment. Mark Widdowson provides the reader with a solid understanding about the nature of depression and clear guidance about how to provide effective psychotherapy for depressed clients.

The book is a step-by-step guide to therapy, from the point of first contact through to ending, and covers:

- The theory and practice of TA therapy
- Understanding factors which maintain depression
- Conceptualising depression using TA
- Original material on the mechanisms of therapeutic change
- Optimising the psychotherapy process
- Key therapeutic processes in the therapy of depression
- Tailoring the therapy to client needs
- An introduction to neuroscience and the medical treatment of depression

Complete with an additional resources section, including downloadable material designed to be given to clients to enhance the therapeutic process and strengthen the working alliance, *Transactional Analysis for Depression* provides structured, practical guidance to TA theory for therapists in practice and training.

Mark Widdowson is a Teaching and Supervising Transactional Analyst and a UKCP-registered psychotherapist. He is a lecturer in counselling and psychotherapy at the University of Salford and lives in Manchester, where he also has a small psychotherapy practice.

For additional resources and downloadable material, please see: https://www.routledge.com/products/9781138812345

Transactional Analysis for Depression
A step-by-step treatment manual

Mark Widdowson

Routledge
Taylor & Francis Group
LONDON AND NEW YORK

First published 2016
by Routledge
2 Park Square, Milton Park, Abingdon, Oxon, OX14 4RN

and by Routledge
711 Third Avenue, New York, NY 10017

Routledge is an imprint of the Taylor & Francis Group, an informa business

© 2016 Mark Widdowson

The right of Mark Widdowson to be identified as author of this work has been asserted by him in accordance with sections 77 and 78 of the Copyright, Designs and Patents Act 1988.

All rights reserved. No part of this book may be reprinted or reproduced or utilised in any form or by any electronic, mechanical, or other means, now known or hereafter invented, including photocopying and recording, or in any information storage or retrieval system, without permission in writing from the publishers.

Trademark notice: Product or corporate names may be trademarks or registered trademarks, and are used only for identification and explanation without intent to infringe.

British Library Cataloguing in Publication Data
A catalogue record for this book is available from the British Library

Library of Congress Cataloging in Publication Data
Widdowson, Mark, 1973-
Transactional analysis for depression: a step-by-step treatment manual / Mark Widdowson.
pages cm
Includes bibliographical references.
1. Psychotherapy. 2. Transactional analysis. 3. Psychotherapist and patient. I. Title.
RC475.W53 2016
616.89'14—dc23
2015014489

ISBN: 978-1-138-81233-8 (hbk)
ISBN: 978-1-138-81234-5 (pbk)
ISBN: 978-1-315-74663-0 (ebk)

Typeset in Times New Roman
by Swales & Willis Ltd, Exeter, Devon, UK
Printed and bound in Great Britain by
Ashford Colour Press Ltd, Gosport, Hampshire

Contents

Introduction   1

PART I
TA theory and depression   7

1. The theory and practice of transactional analysis psychotherapy   9
2. Understanding depression   20
3. Depressogenic processes   26
4. Conceptualising depression using TA theory   42
5. Basic technique in TA therapy   57
6. Therapeutic processes and change mechanisms   64

PART II
Therapy protocol   75

7. Structure of therapy and the initial phase of therapy   77
8. Key therapeutic processes   105

PART III
Neuroscience of depression and medical treatments   149

9. A primer on the brain and the neuroscience of depression   151
10. Medical treatment for depression   158

Conclusion 170
Appendices 173
  1 Getting the most out of therapy 175
  2 Self-help for depression 179
  3 Basic transactional analysis (TA) theory 186
References 199
Index 214

Introduction

This is the first research-based, disorder-specific transactional analysis (TA) treatment guide to be published, and has been developed from a wide range of research literature and years of clinical experience. The psychotherapy community in general has had a somewhat ambivalent relationship with such therapy manuals over the years (Addis & Krasnow, 2000; Navajits, Weiss, Shaw & Dierberger, 2000). The detailed specification of a particular approach to therapy is considered to be essential to the process of building research evidence about the effectiveness of that type of therapy. Many practitioners, particularly beginners, scour books and journals for information about specific issues and for guidance about how to help their clients overcome their problems. Despite this, a large number of therapists also have reservations about manualised therapies, and have understandable concerns about the prospect of using a rigid and restrictive framework which might limit their creativity and responsiveness to the needs of individual clients. Such concerns are valid; however, the use of a treatment manual does not need to limit a practitioner's repertoire, nor does it necessarily undermine the therapeutic relationship, or turn the therapist into a mere technician. Manuals are often developed by researchers as a starting point for their explorations regarding the effectiveness of a particular therapy. The manuals are then tested in clinical practice to see if they have 'real-world' applicability.

This treatment guide was developed from my research, which examined actual psychotherapy cases as conducted in routine clinical practice (Widdowson, 2013). From these cases, principles of best practice were identified from the participants' feedback about the aspects of therapy they found to be the most helpful. The intention was to create a treatment manual that was suitable for use in 'everyday settings', which could be used flexibly and was capable of adjusting to individual client needs. To date, over 70 therapists (in the UK and the Netherlands) have been trained in the use of this manual, and the feedback and data they have provided strongly suggest that this treatment guide is effective, relatively easy to use and gives them enough freedom to be creative and adapt the therapy to the needs and preferences of their clients. This guidebook has also been developed using recommendations regarding treatment manual design and content (Carroll & Rounsaville, 2008; Carroll & Nuro, 2002; Duncan, Nicol & Ager, 2004) and it is hoped that you will find it to be of immediate practical use in your client work.

It is also my intention to provide you, the reader, with direct access to research findings which are relevant to your work and may go some way to closing the gap that often exists between research and everyday practice (Widdowson, 2012a).

Research has repeatedly shown that the quality of the therapeutic relationship is the most important factor in determining the outcome of psychotherapy (Horvath, Del Re, Flückiger & Symonds, 2011). This treatment guide provides guidance on how to strengthen the therapeutic relationship right from its very beginning and, as such, it is hoped that this will maximise your effectiveness with your clients and reduce treatment failure and drop-out rates.

Research background of this book

The past few years have seen something of a renaissance in TA research. My own research has provided evidence that TA can be effective for the treatment of depression (Widdowson, 2012b, c, d) and for mixed anxiety and depression (Widdowson, 2014a). TA has been demonstrated to be effective in short-term settings for depression and anxiety symptoms (van Rijn, Wild & Moran, 2011) and has been shown to be equally effective as integrative counselling psychology, gestalt therapy and person-centred counselling (van Rijn & Wild, 2013) for the treatment of depression and anxiety. There is also evidence for the effectiveness of TA therapy for the treatment of posttraumatic stress disorder (Harford & Widdowson, 2014) and emetophobia (Kerr, 2013) and for the usefulness of TA therapy for people with long-term health conditions (McLeod, 2013). There is more TA research under way, and I anticipate that within the next few years we will have accumulated a respectable amount of evidence for the effectiveness of TA with a range of presenting problems.

As stated above, this treatment guide was developed from my doctoral research. My thesis is held by the University of Leicester research archive and is available online to anyone who would like to read more, at https://lra.le.ac.uk/handle/2381/28382.

Overview of the book

The book is organised into three parts. Part I covers an introduction to TA theory, and then moves into providing the reader with a solid understanding of depression.

Chapter 1 covers the history and theory of TA and some of the key aspects of TA therapy in practice. The chapter assumes that the reader has a basic understanding of psychotherapy theory and TA concepts. Readers who are completely new to TA might find it useful to begin by reading Appendix 3 to gain some familiarity with TA theory.

The detailed exploration of depression begins in Chapter 2, which addresses the diagnostic features of depression and examines some of the data on the prevalence, course and pattern of recovery of this common mental health problem.

Chapter 3 provides an overview of a wide range of research findings about processes involved in the origins and maintenance of depression (depressogenic processes). This will give you an insight into the experience of depression and will also suggest therapeutic interventions which can address the underlying processes at work in depression. Generally speaking, psychotherapy either seeks to address issues arising from the developmental origins of an individual's distress or attempts to promote change in the client's here-and-now behaviour in order to help the client improve his or her current situation. In this manual, I suggest that both approaches can be used simultaneously, and that effective therapy for depression involves addressing underlying issues as well as interrupting processes which maintain the client's depression.

Chapter 4 moves into a more detailed analysis of depression from the perspective of TA theory, and explores how we can understand depression using TA.

Chapter 5 consists of a brief introduction to some basic techniques in TA therapy.

In Chapter 6, I present a number of proposed change mechanisms and therapeutic processes which underpin the affect-focused, experiential form of TA as described in the next two chapters.

Part II is divided into two chapters. The aim of this part is to provide a detailed overview of the therapy protocol that will be of immediate use to practitioners.

Chapter 7 provides an introduction to use of the protocol, general session structure and format of delivery, as well as providing detailed guidance on client induction, conducting the initial sessions, screening and monitoring and managing risk.

Chapter 8 addresses key therapeutic tasks, empirically derived principles for practice, identifying and addressing core therapeutic issues in the treatment of depression. The chapter also offers guidance on troubleshooting and managing problems in therapy, managing the therapeutic relationship and handling issues of termination and ending of therapy.

Part III is an introduction to the neuroscience of depression (Chapter 9) and medical treatments for depression (Chapter 10). The intention is to provide the non-medically trained reader with a basic grounding in these topics, and it is hoped that this will facilitate dialogue between therapists and medical practitioners.

The appendices are a series of psychoeducational materials which you may photocopy for use with your clients. The first appendix is called 'Getting the most out of therapy', and can be given to clients at the first meeting. In my experience, this gives clients valuable information about some of the tasks of therapy and helps them to manage aspects of therapy they may find difficult (such as strong transference reactions), and encourages them to talk to their therapist about the parts of the therapeutic process they might be struggling with. The second appendix is a brief self-help guide which encourages clients to take active steps to make positive life changes which will support their recovery and enhance their well-being. The strategies suggested are all ones which are supported by research literature. I find that when clients first come to therapy they are keen to get some guidance about simple things that they can do to help themselves to feel better. This document goes some way to meeting this need. The third appendix covers a range of basic TA theory. A key finding from my doctoral research was that clients found that learning about parts of TA theory which were relevant to their situation was helpful (Widdowson, 2013). Learning about TA theory gave the clients a means of making sense of and managing difficult and painful experiences, and also gave them a conceptual framework to understand their own process. Furthermore, it gave the client and therapist a shared language and framework for the therapy. If you are completely new to TA, you might find it helpful to read Appendix 3 before reading the rest of this book.

Using this book

I hope that you will find much of interest in this book, and most of all, I hope you will use it as a practical guide in your work. I invite you to ask yourself 'how can I use this material?' as you read. Do not use this book as an oppressive straitjacket that limits your therapeutic work, but instead use it as inspiration and, by all means, continue to experiment and innovate in your own practice.

Get involved

This book is not only the culmination of my own research and the integration of the psychotherapy research literature and TA theory, it is also a work in progress. I am continuing to develop and refine the approach outlined in this book, and I invite you, the reader, to get involved in this process and contribute to the ongoing development of this material. Your feedback is welcomed, and actively encouraged. If you add your own creative touches to how you use the material in this book, or adapt it slightly, I would love to hear from you.

You may be interested in participating in my ongoing research, which is testing and refining this manual, or of contributing data to a research project. Perhaps you have research ideas of your own that you would like to discuss with me. I also provide workshops on the treatment of depression, held at the University of Salford. Whatever your reason to get in touch, I am not difficult to track down, and you can e-mail me at the University of Salford on: m.widdowson@salford.ac.uk.

Acknowledgements

I would like to thank Alison Ayres for her insightful comments and feedback on drafts of the material in this book. I would also like to thank Rob van Tol for kindly providing technical support in the form of many of the diagrams in this book and Dr Per Svensson for checking the accuracy of the information provided in the chapter on medical treatments for depression. Particular thanks go to Professor Sue Wheeler and Professor John McLeod for their guidance and rigour throughout my PhD process.

On a personal level, I would like to thank Philip for all of his care and support, and also my friends who, together with Philip, provide me with endless sources of fun and connection that keep me sustained.

Thanks, too, to my colleagues at the University of Salford – a lively, creative and passionate group of people who welcomed me into their midst and continue to encourage me to develop my work further. Similarly, I would like to thank my TA colleagues, in particular Ian Stewart and Adrienne Lee who, ever since I started my journey into TA, have never wavered in their encouragement. There are so many colleagues who have been a part of this journey, and I would like to thank them all – they know who they are.

All the people who have attended the various workshops on depression I have delivered over the past few years deserve thanks, and especially the therapists who have provided me with invaluable feedback and data on how this manual works in practice. And finally, I would like to express my immense gratitude to the therapists and clients who have participated in my research and generously let me into the inner sanctum of their therapy, and to my own clients, past and present, who continue to teach me more and more about psychotherapy every day.

Part I
TA theory and depression

1 The theory and practice of transactional analysis psychotherapy[1]

> TA is probably the most comprehensive theoretical framework currently available in the field of counselling and psychotherapy. (McLeod, 1998)

A brief history and context of transactional analysis

The founder of transactional analysis (TA) was Eric Berne, a Jewish Canadian neurologist who emigrated to the USA in 1935 in order to train as a psychiatrist. Between 1941 and 1943 Berne commenced training in psychoanalysis in New York. His training was interrupted for a few years whilst he served as an army psychiatrist during Second World War. After the war, he moved to the San Francisco area and resumed his psychoanalytic training.

Berne was particularly interested in social psychiatry, and ran weekly seminars on the subject from his home. By 1956 he had developed the basic elements of his theory, which he had named transactional analysis. In 1959, his application to join the San Francisco Psychoanalytic Institute as a full member was rejected. This event acted as a catalyst and inspired Berne to develop his theories in conjunction with the colleagues who had joined him in his seminars. Culturally, San Francisco is well known as being a hub of subversion and counterculture and this spirit of rebellion no doubt influenced Berne. By 1961 his first book on TA was published and his theories started to gain popularity.

TA has grown and flourished over the years into an international community of practitioners. The European Association for Transactional Analysis currently has over 7,500 members, of whom around 1,500 are based in the UK.

The theory of transactional analysis psychotherapy

Berne was passionate about demystifying the psychotherapy process and the importance of engaging the client as a collaborative partner in the therapy. This passion was evident early in his career as a psychiatrist. Berne was one of the first psychiatrists to invite patients into case conferences in hospitals, and he actively invited them to participate in choices about their treatment (Berne, 1966). One aspect of the demystifying process that Berne emphasised was his insistence on using colloquial, everyday language for the theoretical concepts of TA. While the use of accessible language and concepts have likely contributed to TA's popularity, some TA professionals have speculated that the colloquial labels typically used in TA theory might give an impression of lack of academic substance or even amateurishness. Despite this, some authors argue that the use of accessible language and the diagramming of internal and interpersonal processes are among TA's strengths (McLeod, 2009; Stewart & Joines, 1987).

The theory of personality – structural analysis

> Parent, Adult and Child ego states were first systematically studied by transactional analysis, and they are its foundation stones and its mark. Whatever deals with ego states is transactional analysis and whatever overlooks them is not.
>
> (Berne, 1972: 223)

Berne's theory of ego states developed from the theories of his analyst, Paul Federn (1952), and those of Eduardo Weiss (1950) and Ronald Fairbairn (1952). Federn was particularly interested in understanding one part of Freud's tripartite structure of the personality – the ego. Federn's definition of an ego state was of the entirety of an individual's internal subjective experience at any given moment (Federn, 1952).

Berne developed this definition of an ego state to include the element of observability (Berne, 1961), which posited that an internal shift of an individual's ego states might be directly observed (or inferred from observations of shifts in an individual's behaviour) by an external observer (in this context, the therapist). Berne developed Federn's theory that an ego state could be a direct response to the here-and-now situation the individual was presently experiencing, or one re-experienced as a regression to a childhood state to include an ego state which the individual had 'taken in' or introjected from external sources (generally, parents or parent figures). Thus, he developed his theory of a tripartite structure to the ego which was both internally experienced and directly observable (Berne, 1961).

Within TA theory, the personality (ego) can be manifested in three ways, known as *ego states*. An ego state is defined as a 'consistent pattern of feeling and experience directly related to a corresponding consistent pattern of behaviour' (Berne, 1966: 364). Ego states are divided into three categories, which are called Parent, Adult and Child. The Parent ego state is a repository of *introjected* 'others' – usually primary caregivers but also influences from the social and cultural environment which were internalised by the infant during personality development (Stewart & Joines, 1987). This internalisation process is shaped by the quality of the relationship with caregivers, which is 'recorded' in the infant's psyche. The Parent ego state is believed to have a powerful influence on an individual's behaviour and internal process (Figure 1.1). Berne defined the Parent ego state as 'a set of feelings, attitudes and behaviour patterns which resemble those of a parental figure' (Berne, 1961: 66), a definition he later extended to include aspects of the individual's personality which were 'borrowed' from others (Berne, 1966: 366).

```
  ____
 /    \
|  P   |    PARENT EGO STATE
 \____/     Behaviours, thoughts and feelings
            copied from parents or
            parent figures

  ____
 /    \
|  A   |    ADULT EGO STATE
 \____/     Behaviours, thoughts and feelings
            which are direct responses to
            the here and now

  ____
 /    \
|  C   |    CHILD EGO STATE
 \____/     Behaviours, thoughts and feelings
            replayed from childhood
```

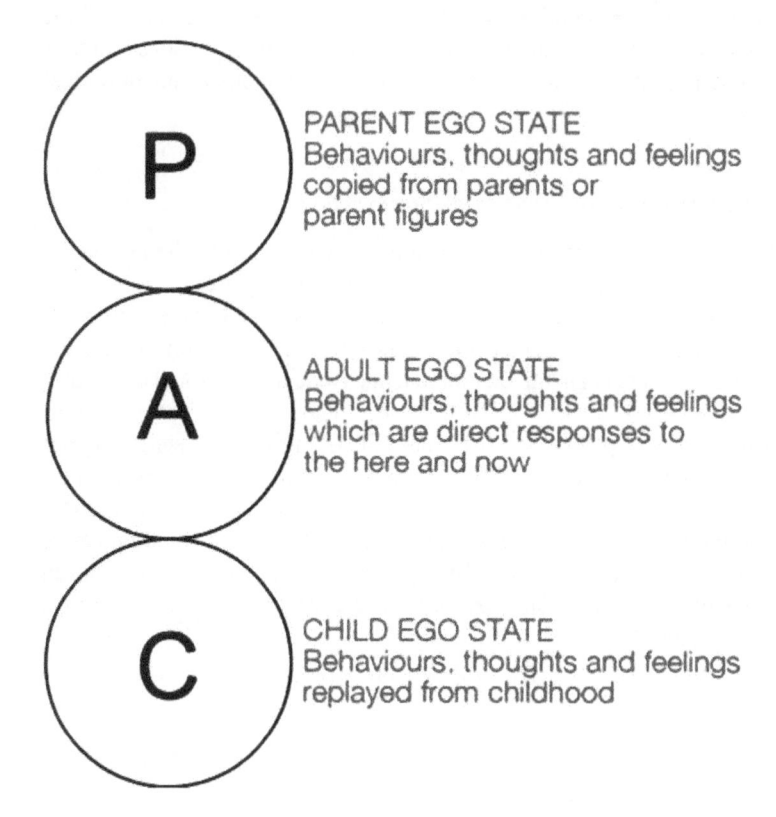

Figure 1.1 The first-order structural model of ego states (Berne, 1961; Stewart & Joines, 1987, reprinted with permission).

The Adult ego state stems from here-and-now reality and was described by Berne as 'an autonomous set of feelings, attitudes and behaviour patterns which are adapted to the current reality' (Berne, 1961: 67).

The Child ego state is comprised of an individual's historical experiences and acts as a source of regression from a repository of subjective memory systems, including the affective components of experiences. Berne defined the Child ego state as 'a set of feelings, attitudes and behaviours which are relics of an individual's own childhood' (Berne, 1961: 69).

Fairbairn's theory of the ego proposed a tripartite structure (Fairbairn, 1952) which Berne described as being 'one of the best heuristic bridges between transactional analysis and psychoanalysis' (Berne, 1972: 134). Fairbairn argued that the ego is composed of an observing 'central ego', an object-seeking 'libidinal ego' and an 'antilibidinal ego' which he described as the internalised persecutory aspect (Fairbairn, 1952). A key difference between Fairbairn's theory and Berne's was that Berne's theory included nurturing and caring functions within the Parent ego state (Clarkson, 1992). Also, Berne's theory asserted that ego states are directly observable phenomena rather than abstract theoretical constructs (Stewart, 2010a).

12 TA theory and depression

TA therapists pay considerable attention to analysis of the content of the different ego states *and* to the internal interaction between ego states, such as internal dialogue (which is often presumed to be pre-conscious or unconscious) (Berne, 1972).

The theory of communication – analysis of transactions

Berne's interest in social psychology led him to explore group therapy as an adjunct or alternative to individual therapy. It is from his experiences as a group therapist that he developed many of TA's theories relating to communication and interpersonal processes. In TA theory, individuals are said to be communicating from a particular ego state at any given moment and these interpersonal communications are referred to as *transactions* (Berne, 1961). The nature of the transactions between individuals and groups is then analysed. Using the ego-state diagram (Figure 1.1) as the basis for analysing transactions, communication between individuals can be diagrammatically represented in terms of the source and recipient of each particular communicative transaction and the subsequent communicative response (Figure 1.2). Berne's model of analysis of transactions can also be used for the analysis of transference and countertransference reactions and responses (Berne, 1972; Erskine, 1991).

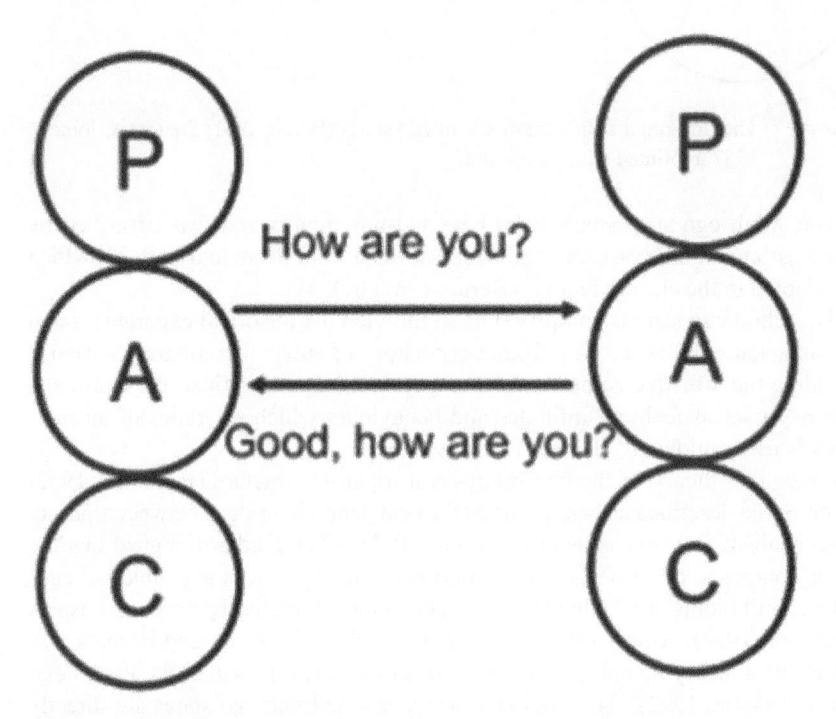

Figure 1.2 Analysis of transactions (adapted from Berne, 1961; Stewart & Joines, 1987).

The life script theory of the genesis of psychopathology

The *life script* is an 'unconscious life plan' (Berne, 1966: 368), or 'a life plan made in childhood, reinforced by parents, justified by subsequent events and culminating in a chosen alternative' (Berne, 1972: 445). Erskine describes the script as 'A life plan based on a decision made at any developmental stage which inhibits spontaneity and limits flexibility in problem solving and in relating to people' (Erskine, 1980: 102). The script determines how an individual experiences and interprets the world, and interacts with others and the environment. Berne's theory of life script was influenced by Adler's (1956) theory of 'style of life', which Adler described as an unconscious and repetitious pattern of living (Ansbacher & Ansbacher, 1956). Berne was also influenced by Erik Erikson (with whom Berne was in analysis for several years), and Erikson's theories of psychological development through the lifespan (Erikson, 1950, 1959). The theory of life script also has clear parallels with the cognitive-behavioural therapy theory of *schemas*, which are underlying structures that determine how an individual experiences self, others and the world (Beck, Rush, Emory & Shaw, 1979; Young, Klosko & Weishaar, 2003).

TA theory assumes that an individual adopts a *life position* which is a fundamental orientation the infant develops, usually in response to very early interactions with his or her caregivers. It establishes the sense of relative worth and value of the self and others. In characteristic TA style, the life position is described using everyday language. The ideal, healthy position is one where an individual develops an 'I'm OK – you're OK' life position. Unfortunately (often in response to interactions in these early relationships), individuals may develop an 'I'm OK – you're not OK', 'I'm not OK – you're OK' or an 'I'm not OK – you're not OK' life position (Berne, 1972). These link to Klein's (1975) concept of the Paranoid, Depressive and Schizoid positions, respectively. This life position is to some extent malleable, but it is largely consistent and 'reinforced' throughout life. Life positions have similarity to attachment patterns (Ainsworth & Bowlby, 1965; Bowlby, 1979, 1988; Hobbes, 1996, 1997; Holmes, 2001).

The *protocol* (Berne, 1972) refers to the very earliest relational (unconscious/preconscious) 'blueprint', which sets out the 'rules of engagement' that individuals determine from their early interpersonal experiences about how self and others interact. There are clear parallels here with Stern's (1985) concept of representations of interactions that are generalised, and to Luborsky's (1984) core conflictual relational themes.

Early TA (during the late 1960s) was particularly concerned with the script and script analysis, and the conscious elaboration of script. However, more recently, TA therapists have turned their attention towards understanding and working with the protocol. This shift in focus has been shaped by an increasing interest in implicit memory and early child development theory (Stern, 1985) that has influenced recent psychotherapy theory.

Life positions, protocol and script can be considered to be satisfying structure hunger (see below), and as part of an inherent tendency amongst people to organise the world psychologically and make meaning. The theory of life script (as well as life positions and protocol, which are subdivisions of script theory) serves to describe how human survival is preserved by the development and maintenance of relationships. The infant is entirely dependent on his caregiver(s) and will adapt very early to the needs of the caregivers to ensure he gains the optimal care. 'Script decisions represent the infant's best strategy for surviving in a world which often seems hostile, even life threatening' (Stewart & Joines, 1987: 101–102).

Life script decisions are, however, often deeply irrational and overgeneralised, which is a direct result of them being developed with a child's cognitive skills. It is postulated that the child's relative lack of power, lack of options and lack of information, together with immature thinking capacity and a neurological inability to handle stress, make him particularly vulnerable to extreme conclusions and sweeping generalisations about self, others and the world (Woollams & Brown, 1979). These script decisions are then stored in the Child ego state and profoundly influence how the child lives his life and interacts with others. Experiences which conflict with script beliefs (generating cognitive dissonance) are frequently discounted (Schiff *et al.*, 1975) in order to preserve the script, and so preserve the internal sense of attachment with caregivers.

Racket analysis: the intrapsychic process of the script

Transactional analysts believe that an individual's script beliefs will be linked intrapsychically to her affective experience and behaviour and her memories in a self-reinforcing cognitive-affective system known as a *racket* (Erskine & Zalcman, 1979).[2] Each racket will have its own emotional content, such as sadness, or anger, or anxiety, which will in some way link to the emotions that an individual was 'permitted' to feel in childhood. It is believed that a racket feeling will cover some repressed emotional content, often related to particular experiences (usually those from childhood). The concept of working with repressed emotions is similar to psychoanalytic theory regarding repression. In both TA and psychoanalysis, the treatment aim is for the client to access and express the repressed affect. In TA, the process of contacting and expressing repressed affect is also known as *deconfusion* (Berne, 1961, 1966; Hargaden & Sills, 2002). Berne described deconfusion as being a psychoanalytic process in his early work (Berne, 1961) in that it requires the discovery and expression of repressed affect. The racket feeling will be connected to a series of beliefs about self, others and the world, and a range of internal experiences (or symptoms) and observable behaviours. It will also have a number of associated memories. All this is interlinked in an associative network known as the script system (Erskine & Zalcman, 1979; Erskine, 2010). A parallel can be drawn between the cognitive-behavioural theory of schemas (Young *et al.*, 2003) and the script system (Figure 1.3).

TA theory of 'games': how the script is enacted

TA theory states that people 'play games' to further their life script (Berne, 1964). 'Games', in this context, are repetitive, predictable and maladaptive interpersonal

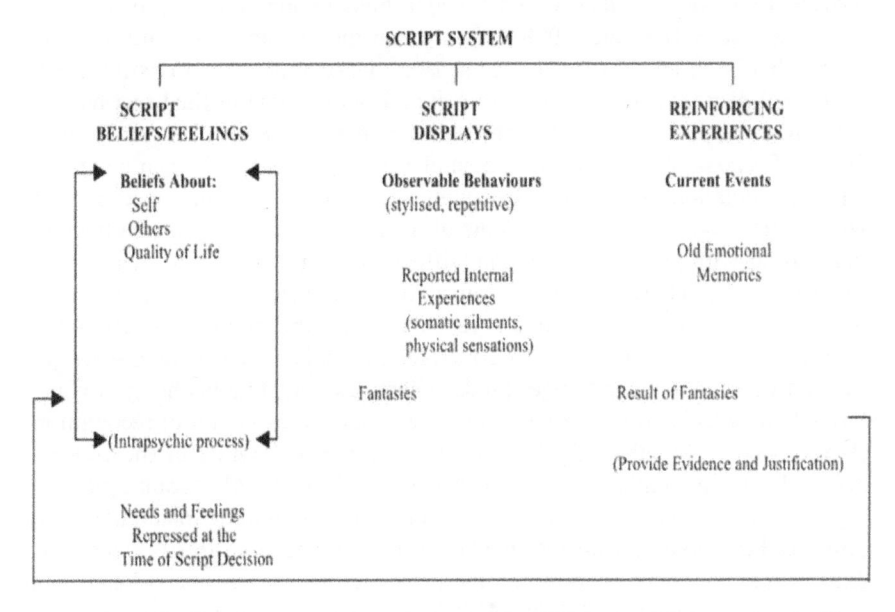

```
                              SCRIPT SYSTEM
        ┌─────────────────────────┼─────────────────────────┐
        SCRIPT                   SCRIPT              REINFORCING
    BELIEFS/FEELINGS            DISPLAYS             EXPERIENCES

     Beliefs About:         Observable Behaviours    Current Events
        Self                (stylised, repetitive)
        Others
        Quality of Life                              Old Emotional
                            Reported Internal         Memories
                               Experiences
                            (somatic ailments,
                            physical sensations)

                               Fantasies            Result of Fantasies

   (Intrapsychic process)
                                              (Provide Evidence and Justification)

     Needs and Feelings
     Repressed at the
     Time of Script Decision
```

Figure 1.3 The script system (Erskine, 2010; Erskine & Zalcman, 1979, reprinted with permission).

patterns, which result in one or both parties feeling bad (Stewart & Joines, 1987). The negative thoughts and emotions at the conclusion of a game serve to reinforce the script and 'confirm' the individual's script beliefs. These unhelpful relationship patterns are thought to be linked to the early experience of the individual, and might be seen as a symbolic re-enactment of some primary scene from the individual's early life history.

This theory accounts for patterns that might ordinarily be thought of as problems of the individual (such as alcoholism) which usually have some interpersonal element to their aetiology, wherein the individual's interactions with others and his or her environment provide reinforcement (strokes) for the problematic behaviour.

Berne's psychoanalytic background and the influence of Freud's (1914) theory of 'repetition compulsion' is evident in the theory of games. From this, Berne created a model for direct observation and analysis of the repetition compulsion (Berne, 1972; Stewart, 1992).

Motivational theory

Berne was inspired by some of the psychology experiments of the late 1950s into sensory deprivation, and also the work of René Spitz regarding 'failure to thrive' amongst children looked after in impersonal orphanages (Spitz, 1946). From this, he developed his theory of *the psychological hungers* (Berne, 1964). The hungers provide a motivational theory to TA which links biology and the social world with psychology (Erskine, 1998). Noting that the human senses are designed to absorb stimuli and that prolonged sensory deprivation leads to extreme psychological distress and even psychotic experiences, Berne posited that humans have an innate need for stimulus, and therefore have a *stimulus hunger*. With his theory of *recognition hunger,* Berne emphasised the fact that human beings are inherently relationship seeking. Recognition hunger leads a person to interact with others, which in turn meets some of his or her stimulus needs, particularly those to do with physical contact and affection. Berne also noted that humans seem to have an inherent need to organise (or make psychological sense) of their world. This extends to the need to organise time and the environment through to the creation of social hierarchies. Berne referred to this need as *structure hunger.* In adult life, relationship hunger (and, to some extent, stimulus hunger) is met through the acquisition of strokes. A stroke is defined as 'a unit of recognition' (Berne, 1972: 447), thus highlighting the interpersonal nature of the concept. Stroke theory has similarities with the behaviourist concept of operant conditioning (Skinner, 1937), in that strokes are considered by transactional analysts to reinforce behaviour. TA practitioners consider that negative strokes can also be used as reinforcement, working on the principle that 'any stroke is better than no stroke at all' (Stewart & Joines, 1987). The view that humans are inherently relationship seeking also links TA theory to the object relations approach within psychoanalysis and in particular the theories of Fairbairn (1952). Thus, the core motivational theory of TA has similarities with both psychoanalytic and cognitive approaches.

These core aspects of theory provide TA therapists with tools for understanding intrapsychic process (structural analysis and racket analysis), and interpersonal process (analysis of transactions and game analysis), as well as presenting a unifying theory which accounts for both intrapsychic and interpersonal processes (script analysis).

The practice of transactional analysis psychotherapy

Contractual method

Berne's belief in client–therapist collaboration was reflected in his theory of contractual method (Berne, 1966), in which clients are invited to set their own goals for therapy, rather than coming to therapy to 'work on' some indeterminate goals arbitrarily and unilaterally decided by the analyst. This acknowledgement that the client does indeed have some insight into his or her needs is congruent with the humanistic values of TA. The client's goals are usually defined by some observable means so that the therapist and client can readily identify whether the goals have been reached or not (Berne, 1966; Goulding & Goulding, 1979; Steiner, 1974; Stewart, 2007). Attainment of the client's stated therapy goals is used to determine when therapy should be terminated. The whole process of TA therapy is contractual. The therapist and client negotiate and seek agreement at each step of the way, agreeing on the focus of each session, agreeing on (and establishing informed consent for) the use of specific techniques, and collaborating towards the ongoing facilitation of the client's goals (Stewart, 2007; Woollams & Brown, 1979). The therapy contract is not a 'static' phenomenon in that it can be, and often is, renegotiated regularly throughout the therapy.

The practice of TA psychotherapy

Traditionally, TA therapy eschews formal treatment manuals and favours a more individualised approach to therapy. However, several key texts do influence the ways in which TA therapists approach therapy and select their interventions (Hargaden & Sills, 2002; Lister-Ford, 2002; Stewart, 2007; Widdowson, 2010; Woollams & Brown, 1979). The influence of Berne's medical training is embedded throughout TA. Traditional medical terms are frequently used in TA – 'diagnosis', 'treatment plan' and 'cure' are medical in nature and suggest a medical model approach to the person and to psychological therapy (Tudor & Widdowson, 2008).

Berne developed the concept of *stages of cure* (Berne, 1961, 1966). Berne's theory was that the first stage of the change process is *social control,* whereby an individual develops control over her behaviour in interactions with others. The next stage, *symptomatic relief,* involves the individual obtaining some subjective relief from her symptoms, such as anxiety. The next stage in Berne's framework is *transference cure,* whereby the individual maintains health by keeping the therapist 'in their head' as an introject (Clarkson, 1992; Stewart, 2007). It is considered that the 'cure' will be maintained for as long as the client can sustain the introject as a significant intrapsychic presence. Berne's final stage of cure was *script cure,* which involved the individual completely 'throwing off' the script, redeciding limiting script decisions and becoming autonomous.

The concept of 'cure' is particularly problematic for many TA therapists, as it is often viewed as being philosophically incongruent with a humanistic approach to the person (Tudor & Widdowson, 2008). Also, the concept of cure suggests that one can be completely script-free and also maintain a disease model – a view that many modern TA therapists are challenging. Recent views consider that, rather than becoming script-free, an individual develops a more flexible script (English, 2010; Newton, 2006).

The goals of TA therapy

Berne (1972) advanced two primary goals of TA therapy: (1) the attainment of autonomy; and (2) the attainment of an 'I'm OK – you're OK' life position. Berne (1964) defined autonomy as being characterised by the release of three capacities: *awareness, spontaneity* and *intimacy*. It is a state in which the individual is adaptive and relates to the self, others and the environment in ways that are not restricted by the negative or limiting aspects of the person's life script (English, 2010).

Preconditions for therapeutic change in TA

The TA therapist seeks to develop a relationship in which the client experiences the therapist's warmth and acceptance towards him. This subjective feeling contributes towards being part of an 'I'm OK – you're OK' relationship in which both parties are valued and in which there is a sense of mutuality (Berne, 1966; Stewart, 2007; Woollams & Brown, 1979). The development of the 'I'm OK – you're OK' relationship has clear parallels with the person-centred concept of 'unconditional positive regard' (Mearns & Thorne, 2007; Rogers, 1951), a therapeutic model which is widely recognised and empirically supported (Norcross, 2002). The development of an accepting therapeutic relationship is augmented by the contract to foster the formation of the client's sense of self-determination and to help form an egalitarian therapeutic relationship with a greater degree of mutuality than approaches to therapy that require the therapist to adopt an authoritarian stance (Sills, 2006). The therapist also seeks to create a therapeutic atmosphere of *protection* and *permission* whereby the client can safely experiment with relaxing his script (Crossman, 1966). This is combined with a stance of therapeutic *potency* which requires the therapist to be a robust and resilient figure who can construct appropriate therapeutic interventions (Steiner, 1968).

Core change processes in TA psychotherapy

The process of TA therapy can be seen as comprising three core change processes, each of which the therapist is seeking to facilitate. These processes are *decontamination, deconfusion* and *redecision*.

Decontamination is a process which is focused on working with the Adult ego state (Berne, 1961, 1966; Stewart & Joines, 1987; Woollams & Brown, 1979). It can involve procedures that are designed to challenge irrational beliefs, similar to the cognitive-behavioural therapy method of disputing negative automatic thoughts (Beck & Beck, 1995), as well as procedures designed to enhance an individual's capacity to be in the here and now. In practice, this tends to be a largely cognitive process.

Deconfusion is often a cathartic process, whereby previously 'hidden' feelings or unmet needs held within the Child ego state are expressed and the individual makes meaning of (and peace with) her past. This also involves developing an internal sense of safety (Clarkson, 1992; Woollams & Brown, 1979). As a process, deconfusion relies on empathic transactions and analysis of the transference/countertransference matrix (Hargaden & Sills, 2002), and is primarily an affective process.

Redecision engages both Child and Adult ego states (Goulding & Goulding, 1979; Stewart, 2007): an individual is encouraged to let go of limiting script beliefs and make a new personal decision and commitment regarding how he will conduct his life from now on. The process of redecision combines cognitive and affective processes.

The majority of TA therapy practice is designed to promote or facilitate one of the three core change processes. Decontamination, deconfusion and redecision have often been considered to take place in a roughly linear fashion, with therapy beginning with decontamination and moving through deconfusion to the final stages of redecision, then followed by a period of consolidation and termination (Pulleyblank & McCormick, 1985; Woollams & Brown, 1979). More recent TA authors (Hargaden & Sills, 2002) have challenged the view that decontamination comes before deconfusion. They argue that deconfusion can often be seen from session one, since the establishment of a therapeutic relationship in which the therapist responds empathically to the client frequently results in the client contacting and expressing some repressed emotion in her Child ego state. Clarkson (1992) and Hargaden and Sills (2002) also argue that it is probable that some deconfusion (as part of the process of forging the therapeutic relationship) *needs* to take place before decontamination can proceed effectively. They claim that, once the client has sufficiently decontaminated the Adult ego state to enable the client to function effectively (and has experienced sufficient deconfusion of the Child ego state to release repressed affect), the individual will often experience a 'loosening' of the script. This will enable her to evaluate her script decisions and, where relevant, engage in redecision, which increasingly replaces dysfunctional script beliefs with more healthy and adaptive beliefs. This in turn brings the client a sense of an expansion of options in living and relating to others; therefore he or she becomes increasingly free to live a relatively autonomous life, unshackled by the outdated constraints of the negative script.

Notes

1 This chapter was taken from Widdowson, M. (2013). *The Process and Outcome of Transactional Analysis Psychotherapy for the Treatment of Depression: An adjudicated case series*. Unpublished doctoral thesis, University of Leicester.
2 The 'racket system' has in recent years been renamed as 'the script system' (O-Reilly-Knapp & Erksine, 2010). Throughout this book, the current term of 'script system' will be used.

2 Understanding depression[1]

Prevalence

Figures in the fourth edition of the American Psychiatric Association's (1994) *Diagnostic and Statistical Manual of Mental Disorders* (DSM-IV) estimate that between 10% and 25% of American women and between 5% and 10% of American men will experience major depressive disorder (MDD) during their lifetime. The UK Office for National Statistics (2000) reported that 9.2% of the British general population experienced mixed anxiety and depression in the year 2000, with 2.8% experiencing a depressive episode (without anxiety symptoms). They estimate that one in ten adults in Britain experience depression at some point during their life, with one in six experiencing mental health problems at any one time. In recent years, we have also seen an enormous increase in the prescribing of antidepressants. In 2011, 47.6 million prescriptions were issued for antidepressants in England, and in 2012 the figure was 50.1 million. By 2013 this had risen to a staggering 53.3 million prescriptions per year. The cost of these drugs to the health service in 2013 was £282.1 million.

Epidemiological studies in the USA suggest that 9% of all adults will experience a MDD in any given year, and approximately 16% will experience MDD during their lifetime (Kessler *et al.*, 2003). Depression accounted for 4.46% of total worldwide disability adjusted life-years in the year 2000 and, globally, depression accounted for 12% of the total number of years lived with disability. It is estimated that, globally, depression is the fourth most common cause of disease burden in women and the seventh most common cause in men (Moussavi *et al.*, 2007; Ustun, Ayuso-Mateos, Chatterji, Mathers & Murray, 2004).

Although there are mixed findings regarding the incidence and prevalence of depression by demographic factors such as class and race, there is some research which suggests that people with lower socioeconomic status are more likely to become depressed and to endure more persistent depression than people with higher socioeconomic status (e.g. Lorant *et al.*, 2003).

MDD has a high mortality rate, with up to 15% of people with MDD committing suicide (American Psychiatric Association, 1994). Considering the prevalence of depression, the figures relating to suicide risk for those with depression are alarming. Anecdotal evidence drawn from informal conversations between the author and psychotherapist colleagues strongly suggests that depression is the single most common disorder for which people seek therapy. Clearly, depression is a significant mental health problem – one that all psychotherapists encounter regularly in clinical practice.

Depression: diagnostic features and symptoms

> Depression is not just a form of extreme sadness. It is a disorder that affects both brain and body, including cognition, behaviour, the immune system and peripheral nervous system. Unlike a passing sad mood, depression is considered a disorder because it interferes with ordinary functioning in work, school, or relationships. Unlike normal grief, which comes in waves, it is constant and oppressive. Depression also differs from ordinary mourning in that the mourner experiences the world as empty or bad, whereas clinically depressed individuals locate their sense of emptiness or badness in the self.
> (PDM Task Force, 2006: 109)

Depression varies in intensity, from mild to extremely severe, and its symptoms can range from subtle to profoundly disabling. The American Psychiatric Association's DSM-IV (1994) provided the following diagnostic criteria for major depressive episode (MDE).[2] These are summarised below.

> Major Depressive Disorder is characterised by one or more Major Depressive Episodes (i.e. at least 2 weeks of depressed mood or loss of interest accompanied by at least four additional symptoms of depression).
> (American Psychiatric Association, 1994: 317)

A. Five (or more) of the following symptoms have been present during the same 2-week period and represent a change from previous functioning; at least one of the symptoms is either (1) depressed mood or (2) loss of interest or pleasure.

1. Depressed mood most of the day, nearly every day, as indicated by either subjective report (e.g. feels sad or empty) or observation made by others (e.g. appears tearful).
2. Markedly diminished interest or pleasure in all, or almost all, activities most of the day, nearly every day (as indicated by either subjective account or observation made by others).
3. Significant weight loss when not dieting or weight gain (e.g. a change of more than 5% of body weight in a month), or decrease or increase in appetite nearly every day.
4. Insomnia or hypersomnia nearly every day.
5. Psychomotor agitation or retardation nearly every day (observable by others, not merely subjective feelings of restlessness or being slowed down).
6. Fatigue or loss of energy nearly every day.

22 TA theory and depression

7   Feelings of worthlessness or excessive or inappropriate guilt (which may be delusional) nearly every day (not merely self-reproach or guilt about being sick).
8   Diminished ability to think or concentrate, or indecisiveness, nearly every day (either by subjective account or as observed by others).
9   Recurrent thoughts of death (not just fear of dying), recurrent suicidal ideation without a specific plan, or a suicide attempt or a specific plan for committing suicide.

Criteria summarised from American Psychiatric Association (1994: 327).

Types of symptoms

Affective symptoms include loss of pleasure and interest in life or activities the individual previously enjoyed (anhedonia); feelings of worthlessness, guilt, inferiority, inadequacy, helplessness and weakness; and an overwhelming sense of sadness, despair, loss of hope and self-hatred.

Cognitive symptoms include impaired concentration and memory, indecisiveness, rationalisation of guilt and sustained and intense self-criticism. Suicidal ideation of varying intensity is common in depressed individuals.

Somatic symptoms are common among people with depression and can include fatigue, lethargy, sleep disruption (hypersomnia or insomnia), restlessness and agitation, headache, muscular pain, back pain, weight loss or gain (and associated appetite changes) and loss of sexual desire. A greater number and severity of somatic symptoms has been associated with treatment-resistant depression (Papakostas *et al.*, 2003).

Depression: patterns of natural course, relapse and recovery

Natural course of depression

It is difficult to generalise about the natural course of depression because it is quite possible that many people experience depression that, due to factors such as felt stigma and reluctance to seek advice and treatment, are not identified in epidemiological studies. The course of depression and prognostic indicators vary considerably according to type and number of previous episodes.

Symptoms of MDD typically develop over a period of between several days and a number of weeks, although early indicators of an impending depressive episode (prodromal symptoms) can occur several months before the onset of a depressive episode that meets DSM criteria. The duration of an MDE is variable, although in most cases it is between 6 months and 2 years. Between 5% and 10% of all individuals continue to meet criteria for MDD for 2 years or more. Despite not meeting diagnostic criteria for MDD, it is probable that many people continue to experience depressive symptoms for a prolonged period of time (American Psychiatric Association, 1994). Forty per cent of people will continue to meet diagnostic criteria 1 year after diagnosis of MDD, 20% will continue to have some symptoms without meeting full diagnostic criteria (partial remission) and 40% will have no mood disorder. Initial severity of the episode appears to be predictive of its persistence, with more severe episodes lasting longer.

DSM-IV criteria for recovery from MDD are that the individual must not have met diagnostic criteria (i.e. depressed mood or loss of interest or pleasure plus four additional symptoms) for a period of 2 consecutive months. Throughout this time, an individual may still exhibit a number of depressive symptoms, in which case the individual is considered to be in partial remission.

Relapse rates

A review of follow-up studies by Piccinelli and Wilkinson (1994) found that 75% of people with MDD would have at least one further episode of depression within 10 years. Ten per cent of patients in their study had experienced chronic and persistent depression for a period of 10 years. The DSM-IV states that approximately 50–60% of individuals who experience a single MDE will go on to have a second episode. Individuals who have had two episodes have a 70% chance of having a third, and individuals who have had three episodes have a 90% chance of having a fourth. Clearly, the number of episodes is a predictor of the likelihood of recurring episodes of major depression. There is a greater likelihood of an individual experiencing another episode of depression when there is only partial remission (i.e. some symptoms remain). While psychosocial stressors (such as relationship problems or bereavement) are often associated with the first or second episode, they are less often associated with subsequent episodes.

People with dysthymia (persistent low-grade depression) have a high probability of eventually having an MDE, with estimates as high as 79% of people diagnosed with dysthymia going on to develop an MDD during their lifetime. People who have had an MDD and who have an underlying dysthymic disorder will also have a much higher rate of relapse for an MDD, with 62% experiencing an MDE within 2 years (Keller, Lavori, Endicott, Coryell & Klerman, 1983).

Patterns of symptomatic recovery and relapse in psychotherapy

In their study of patterns of symptomatic recovery in time-limited (cognitive-behavioural or interpersonal) psychotherapy conducted with a sample of 212 depressed patients, Barkham *et al.* (1996) found that percentages of patients meeting criteria for clinically significant change as measured using the Beck Depression Inventory (Beck, Ward, Mendelssohn & Erbaugh, 1961) ranged from 34% to 89% within 16 sessions of therapy. Kopta, Howard, Lowry and Beutler (1994) examined patterns of symptomatic recovery among a sample of 854 patients in ongoing (not time-limited) outpatient psychotherapy measured using the Symptom Checklist-90 (SCL-90-R) (Derogatis, 1983). The study identified three categories of symptoms: acute, chronic and characterological. As might be expected, acute symptoms demonstrated the fastest average rate of response to treatment, followed by chronic symptoms, then characterological symptoms. The mean ED50 ('effective dose' or number of sessions needed for 50% of the sample to achieve clinically significant change) for acute distress symptoms was five sessions. The ED50 for chronic distress symptoms was 14 sessions, and the ED50 for characterological symptoms was over 104 sessions. Within the acute distress category, which listed 20 symptoms, the symptom dimension showing the largest number of ED50 changes was 'depression' (five symptoms), followed by 'somatisation' (four symptoms) and 'obsessive-compulsive' (four symptoms). Within the 'chronic distress' symptoms category, which listed 27 symptoms, depression was again the symptom dimension showing the largest number of ED50 changes (seven symptoms), followed by 'interpersonal sensitivity' (five symptoms).

These two studies suggest that around 50% of patients will achieve clinically significant symptomatic relief of between 12 and 21 depressive symptoms within 16 sessions of psychotherapy – an encouraging result for those who practise shorter-term psychotherapy. Nevertheless, this still leaves 50% of patients who will require a greater number of sessions to achieve symptomatic relief, and characterological symptoms (which, from a transactional analysis perspective would require script change) may require therapy of at least 2 years' duration. Between 78% and 88% of clients who took part in the US National Institute of Mental Health Treatment of Depression Collaborative Research Program and who had short-term manualised therapy had either relapsed or sought further treatment by the 18-month follow-up (Morrison, Bradley & Westen, 2003; Shea, Widiger & Klein, 1992). Westen and Morrison (2001) also identified that, by 2-year follow-up after short-term manualised therapy, only 27% of patients with depression had maintained their improvement. One possible explanation for such low levels of maintained recovery is that manualised therapies used in research tend to focus on a limited area of the client's presentation, do not necessarily work with the client's other presenting problems (comorbidity), do not account for characterological problems and/or do not provide therapy of a sufficient length to remedy such issues (Morrison *et al.*, 2003).

Comorbidity, recovery and standard length of therapy for the treatment of depression

Morrison *et al.* (2003) conducted a study on a sample of 242 therapists in the USA regarding cases in which both therapist and client were satisfied with the outcome. They set out to test the validity of the widely accepted belief among therapists that a significant proportion of clients present with comorbidity of more than one psychological disorder and that a significant proportion of clients present with a comorbid personality disorder. It is also widely accepted that the presence of comorbidity complicates the therapy and will require extension of the usual expected course of treatment a therapist might deliver for single-disorder depression (to achieve clinically significant change, i.e. change in which the client is considered to have recovered from the disorder). They found that 47.9% of patients in their sample presenting with depression had comorbidity with another psychological disorder and 46.3% had comorbidity with a personality disorder. Comorbidity with characterological issues (not meeting personality disorder diagnostic criteria) was as high as 76.9% of all clients, a finding concordant with many therapists' anecdotal clinical experience.

Notes

1 Parts of this section have previously been published in an article: Widdowson, M. (2011). Depression: a literature review on diagnosis, subtypes, patterns of recovery, and psychotherapeutic models. *Transactional Analysis Journal*, 41(4): 351–364.
2 Although the current diagnostic manual is DSM-V, these criteria have remained unchanged in the new edition.

3 Depressogenic processes

This chapter will examine a range of research findings relating to the characteristics and processes of depression.

Developmental processes and vulnerability to depression

It is extremely difficult to make clear statements regarding causality of depression in relation to developmental factors. The studies that have been done tend to be longitudinal or retrospective and correlational in nature. In other words, research can identify associations or higher prevalence of certain developmental factors amongst depressed people, but these cannot be stated as clear, causal factors. Depression, like all psychological disorders, has a complex aetiology with a large number of interacting factors. The full range of factors and all possible variations of interactions between them are still unknown; however, there is a wide body of evidence that suggests several factors which substantially increase vulnerability to depression in adult life.

Maternal depression has been demonstrated to increase risk of depression substantially. In particular, the experience of severe postnatal and chronic depression increases this risk further (Bureau, Easterbrooks & Lyons-Ruth, 2009; Cote et al., 2009; Goodman & Gotlib, 1999; Sterba, Prinstein & Cox, 2007). Despite this strong link, not all children of depressed mothers go on to be depressed in later life. Inadequate parenting, poverty and high levels of family conflict have also been associated with increased risk of depression (Gilliom & Shaw, 2004; Spence, Najman, Bor, O'Callagnhan & Williams, 2002).

So, why does maternal depression increase risk so substantially? Goodman and Gotlib (1999) posit four explanatory mechanisms. These are: (1) heritability of depression; (2) innate dysfunctional neuroregulatory mechanisms; (3) negative maternal cognitions, behaviours and affects; and (4) stressful context of children's lives.

The first of these assumes that there may be some genetic tendency towards depression. This theory has recently had support in studies which have investigated the role of the serotonin transporter gene in depression risk. It is also possible that there may be some inherited tendency towards negative affectivity and other temperamental factors which confer increased risk. Despite this genetic predisposition, the eventual development of depression or other internalising disorder is substantially moderated by environmental influences (Hicks, DiRago, Iacono & McGue, 2009). The second mechanism suggests that there may be an interaction between genetics, fetal development and infant developmental factors which result in a neurobiological tendency towards increased depression risk. The third mechanism proposes that the mother's negative cognitive, affective, behavioural and interpersonal style has a strong impact on the psychological development of the child. This would likely operate through modelling and social learning processes; effectively, the child 'learns' how to use an internalising style, and be depressed, and picks up depressogenic cognitive, affective, behavioural and interpersonal patterns which are consistently reinforced within the home environment. There is some evidence that more severely depressed mothers tend to interact in ways which are more critical, punitive and hostile towards their children, are characterised by flat or negative affect and struggle to meet the child's emotional and social developmental needs. There is also some evidence that depressed mothers are more likely to be slower in responding to their infants and to be less stimulating in their interactions, and thus have lower levels of emotional attunement. The fourth mechanism hypothesises that there are higher stress levels in families where one or more of the members are depressed. In particular, high levels of conflict (especially marital conflict) are known to be present in families where depression exists.

Although these four mechanisms relate to maternal depression, their influence is moderated by a number of factors. Absent fathers, or fathers who have high levels of psychopathology, increase the level of risk and conversely, involved, supportive and nurturing fathers reduce the level of risk. It would also appear that risk is moderated in children who have higher than average levels of intelligence and high levels of social engagement, suggesting that these are protective factors. It also appears probable that interactive, transactional patterns are established between the child, mother and wider family that mutually support the maintenance of depression. For example, if the children show behavioural problems, this is likely to be stressful for the parents, and therefore contribute to a worsening of the depression, which in turn exacerbates the child's behavioural difficulties (Goodman & Gotlib, 1999).

Despite the established link between maternal depression and increased depression risk, there is evidence that both parents have a role to play in the development of vulnerability to depression. There is support for the theory that

> children may learn their cognitive styles in part by observing and modelling significant others, in particular, their parents . . . [and how] parents communicate their own inferences about the causes and consequences of negative events in their child's life such that the child develops an inferential style consistent with the parental feedback.
>
> (Alloy et al., 2001: 398–399)

Also, negative parenting behaviours such as lack of warmth and affection and high levels of criticism will increase risk. This makes sense: a child growing up in a cold, harsh environment is likely to develop a poor self-image. It is not difficult to see how this can lead to a pervasive sense of 'being bad', a self-critical internal dialogue and persistent negative feelings such as guilt and shame.

Insecure attachment has also been associated with increased vulnerability to depression.

> Individuals who develop stable and secure attachment representations are likely to have experienced responsive, consistent and sensitive caregiving from their primary attachment figures . . . Their desires for comfort, support, and exploration were mostly respected and consistently met leaving them confident that important others are available, accessible and supportive during times of need. They develop a complementary model of the self as valuable, lovable, and worthy of consistent support . . . In contrast, individuals who develop anxious attachment representations are likely to have experienced inconsistent caregiving where the support and affection of the primary caregiver were largely determined by the caregiver's own desires. Through such early experiences individuals learn that the actions of others are not contingent on their own needs and they consequently lack a sense of control over their own environments. . . . fail to develop a competent sense of self; they tend to relinquish their own wishes and desires to comply with the demands of important others in their lives [and] . . . have doubts regarding their own efficacy and worth.
> (Morley & Moran, 2011: 1074)

Also, those with insecure attachment styles are more likely to 'develop a model of others as unavailable and unsympathetic during difficult times; they are unable to look to their attachment figure, are left to deal with emotionally charged situations on their own' (Morley & Moran, 2011: 1074).

Although it is certainly not the case that all depressed people have been maltreated in childhood, as one might expect, childhood maltreatment substantially increases risk of depression (Toth, Manly & Cicchetti, 1992). It would appear that maltreatment results in a negative internal representation of both self and others. Many depressed people report childhoods where they were recipients of high levels of criticism, blame and/or lack of parental interest, and with low levels of praise (Hammen, 1992). Indeed, 'unavailability of adequate caregiving provides a unifying framework for understanding the occurrence of depression' (Toth *et al.*, 1992: 98). Overall, people with depression tend to have 'had caretakers who were unpredictable, invalidating, and critical. Their early home lives lacked adequate warmth, safety and nurturing that would have allowed them to flourish and realize their potential' (Watson, Goldman & Greenberg, 2007: 184).

Affect in depression

Depression can be conceptualised as a disorder of affect dysregulation, characterised by intense, prolonged, negative affect (dysphoria), combined with an associated deficit of positive affect (anhedonia). Affect regulation refers to a range of processes through which people can change the nature, frequency, and duration of emotions. Theories of emotion regulation suggest that through regulation people can maintain, increase, or decrease emotions (Gross, 1998; Parrott, 1993), or attempt to cultivate specific emotions. Emotion regulation can be a conscious or nonconscious process, and effortful or non-effortful (Gross & Thompson, 2007). Emotion regulation can take place intrapersonally (intrinsic regulation) or interpersonally (extrinsic regulation) (Gross & Thompson, 2007).

(Carl, Soskin, Kerns & Barlow, 2013: 345)

The ability both to up-regulate (stimulate) and down-regulate (dampen) emotions according to the situation and circumstances is an important skill for optimal psychological and interpersonal functioning.

Certainly there is evidence that poor affect regulation ability is a risk factor for depression (Ehring, Fischer, Schnulle, Bosterling & Tuschen-Caffier, 2008). This is supported by studies such as that by Fehlinger, Stumpenhorst, Stenzel and Rief (2012), who found that affect regulation skills have a beneficial effect on improving depressive symptoms. Management of affect dysregulation seems to be a transdiagnostic therapy target which has a significant role in the treatment of depression, other mood disorders and anxiety disorders (Aldao, Nolen-Hoeksema & Schweizer, 2010), and is likely to be a significant aspect of successful therapy for a wide range of psychological disorders. Similarly, 'optimizing positive emotional functioning in the treatment of emotional disorders promises to enhance long-term recovery and resilience in addition to promoting acute symptom reduction' (Carl *et al.*, 2013: 344). Increased positive affectivity has well-documented neurobiological and physiological effects, including increased activations of the left prefrontal cortex, increased dopamine release and reduced amygdala activation, all of which are targets in the treatment of depression. Positive emotions are not only related to pleasure, but to the achievement of goals – again, both of which are relevant in depression (Carl *et al.*, 2013).

Reduced positive affect in depression can have a significant impact on behaviour. Decreased positive emotions and increased negative emotions can result in avoidance and a reduction in enjoyable activities, which in turn increase negative feelings and further reduce positive emotions in a self-reinforcing affective system. Depressed people also struggle to imagine enjoyable events (Carl *et al.,* 2013). It has been hypothesised that the dampening of positive affect in depression may maintain a consistent and predictable worldview (Feldman, Joorman & Johnson, 2008). There is, however, some evidence that positive psychology and mindfulness-based interventions can be helpful in reducing dysphoric affect and increasing positive feelings (Garland *et al.,* 2010; Seligman, Rashid & Parks, 2006; Seligman, Steen, Park & Peterson, 2005).

Since the time of Freud (1917/1958), anger and, in particular, 'anger turned inward' has been associated with depression. Although these theories have had some support, simple catharsis of anger does not have any beneficial effect on depression. Indeed, many depressed people have problems with overexpression of anger and hostility, and do not find that such expression results in any relief. Nevertheless, it would appear that there is a kernel of truth in Freud's theory. Depressed people are more likely to feel anger and hostility and have higher rates of anger suppression than non-depressed people (Riley, Treiber & Woods, 1989).

Although it is a cognitive strategy, many people with depression use rumination as an attempt to regulate their emotions. A meta-analytic study found that maladaptive emotion regulation strategies (such as avoidance, suppression and rumination) were associated with increased psychopathology and adaptive emotion regulation strategies (acceptance, reappraisal, problem solving) were associated with reduced psychopathology, and that rumination and avoidance in particular were strongly associated with depression (Aldao *et al.*, 2010). Not only has suppression of negative emotion been associated with depression (Campbell-Sills, Barlow, Brown & Hofmann, 2006), but there is also evidence that depressed people suppress positive emotions (Beblo *et al.*, 2012). It would appear that the suppression of positive feelings by depressed people is connected to fear of emotions, or believing that they do not deserve to feel positive emotions. Overall, suppression is an ineffective strategy for dealing with negative emotions and, although it does reduce expression of emotions, it does not reduce distress, and may actually worsen distress and maintain depressive symptoms (Ehring, Tuschen-Caffier, Schnulle, Fischer & Gross, 2010). It would appear that emotional dysregulation is a risk factor for depression, and is often a persistent characteristic, which may therefore increase risk of recurrence (Ehring *et al.*, 2008). Negative emotional states have a down-regulating effect on positive emotions and positive emotions have an inhibitory effect on negative emotions (Carl *et al.*, 2013).

A feeling of entrapment combined with a sense of loss of control has been associated with depression (Gilbert, 2007; Kendler, Hettema, Butera, Gardner & Prescott, 2003). Finding a way out of the sense of being trapped may become a focus of depressive rumination, and it has been theorised that the desire to escape from entrapment (from physical circumstances, or a persistent emotional state, such as depression) increases risk of suicide (Gilbert, 2007). In milder forms, the sense of being trapped may provoke desires to escape which may lead the depressed person into a range of avoidance behaviours.

Some people (particularly those with chronic depression) may become embittered. That is, they become preoccupied with a persistent sense of hurt and anger and dwell on specific (real or perceived) injustices they have experienced (Gilbert, 2007).

Cognitive processes in depression

Although depression is a disorder characterised by dysregulated and negative affect, it is also characterised by a number of cognitive features (Everaert, Koster & Derakshan, 2012; Gottlib & Joorman, 2010). A number of theories have been developed which have explored cognitive vulnerabilities to depression and cognitive processes which depressed people experience. These theories suggest a series of depressogenic cognitive processes which include negative interpretation of experiences, expectations, memory biases, attention and attitudes, all of which increase an individual's vulnerability to depression or contribute to the maintenance of depression (Everaert et al., 2012; Gottlib & Joorman, 2010; Mathews & MacLeod, 2005).

Negative self-image and interpretive frame

Beck, Rush, Emery and Straw (1979) put forward the theory that the self-image (self-schema) of the depressed person is centred on themes of inadequacy, failure and worthlessness. These themes influence individuals' interpretation of events, and their perceptions of their self, the world and their future. Hopelessness theory (Abramson, Metalsky & Alloy, 1989) posits that, when faced with stressful situations, individuals develop a stance of hopelessness, whereby they perceive that these events are unchangeable, somehow linked to their own inadequacy, and that they are somehow fundamentally flawed or worthless. From a transactional analysis (TA) perspective, it can be seen that the individual's negative script beliefs (and supporting mechanisms, e.g. discounting, frame of reference, contaminations, and so on) all support the view of the self as being inadequate and/ or worthless. Alloy et al. (1999) examined the validity and predictive power of these theories and found that depressogenic beliefs were indeed highly predictive of onset of subsequent episodes of depression. One implication of this conclusion is that preventive therapy which modifies these cognitive styles is likely to reduce future risk of depressive episodes significantly.

'Extensive evidence indicates that depressed individuals hold more negative self-views, blame themselves more than others for negative events, are more pessimistic for themselves than for others, and more adversely affected by self-reflection than non-depressed individuals' (Wisco, 2009: 382). Overall, depressed people are more pessimistic in relation to their predictions about their own future, but not about the future of others. Depressed individuals are more likely to dwell on negative information for longer periods of time than non-depressed people (Wisco, 2009). Furthermore, there is evidence to suggest that depressed people are more likely to interpret ambiguous material as negative (Gottlib & Joorman, 2010; Mathews & MacLeod, 2005; Wisco, 2009). This suggests that the frame of reference of the depressed person interprets information in such a way as to support the maintenance of the depressed frame of reference. Similar processes also occur in anxiety disorders. In the absence of certainty, many people fill the gap by projecting their script.

Another process which has similarities to the negative interpretation of ambiguity and which has a strong relationship to depression, anxiety disorders and obsessive-compulsive disorder is intolerance of uncertainty (Gentes & Ruscio, 2011). With intolerance of uncertainty, the individual experiences uncertainty about the future as a source of threat. Increasing the ability to tolerate uncertainty is likely to be an effective therapeutic strategy with those disorders (Gentes & Ruscio, 2011).

Depressed people tend to have a strong negative attribution process; that is, when things go wrong, they will tend to think, 'It is my fault'. This usually only works in relation to negatively attributing things to the self, and the depressed person is less likely to attribute negatively about others. In effect, people with depression tend to have 'double standards'; however, in this instance, the double standards are negatively stacked against them (Schlenker & Britt, 1996). This also includes a tendency to downplay their successes and positive attributes and overgeneralise from their failures, mistakes and negative attributes. The mechanisms of discounting and grandiosity are evident here.

Attentional bias

Attention and perception are also strongly biased in depression (attentional bias). People with depression are more likely to notice negative stimuli and have a reduced attention to positive stimuli. In other words, they see, and to some extent are primed to identify, negative information quickly and filter out positive information. There is also strong evidence that when some negative information has entered the awareness of depressed individuals, they have difficulty disengaging from it (Gottlib & Joorman, 2010). These cognitive processes have an impact on emotional regulation. As depression is a disorder characterised by sustained emotional dysregulation, these processes are centrally involved in the maintenance of and recovery from depression.

Bower's (1981) theory of 'associative networks' posited that memories, moods and thoughts are stored together. The activation of any single part of the system activates many others and primes the entire network for full reactivation at any point. Each time this network is activated, it is strengthened, and possibly added to, and is more easily reactivated in future. This has clear parallels with the script system. (Throughout the rest of this manual the term 'associative networks' will be used interchangeably with the term 'script system'). Depressed people commonly have problems with memory and concentration (Burt, Zembar & Niederehe, 1995), but also find it easier to focus on negative thoughts and feelings and easier to access negatively valenced (mood-congruent) memories (Mathews & MacLeod, 2005). This has implications for therapy: the client may struggle to remember all of the therapy session and also may require the therapist to assist with the retrieval of positive memories. Fortunately, there is some evidence that depressed people can move out of these mood-congruent, negatively biased memory states when provided sufficient structure which prevents negative rumination (Hertel, 2004).

There is strong evidence relating to the existence of a negative memory bias amongst people with depression. That is, depressed people are more likely to recall negative memories and less likely to recall positive memories (Matt, Vasquez & Campbell, 1992; Wisco, 2009). It is also possible that the greater ease with which negative emotions are accessed in depression has an influence on the avoidance and aversion depressed people experience. The link may be the conscious or implicit recall of negative memories that encourages a larger degree of avoidance than would otherwise be the case in someone with a memory system more balanced between positive and negative recall.

There is also some evidence that the deliberate accessing of positive memories has a beneficial influence on mood and reduces negative mood states (Joorman & Siemer, 2004). This has relevance, not only as suggesting a potential mood regulation strategy, but also has interesting implications for therapy, which tends to be focused on the retrieval of negative memories. Perhaps therapy which over a period of time shifts the client's emphasis towards recall of positive memories might be beneficial. Another way in which cognitive processes may positively influence emotional regulation in depression is through cognitive reappraisal, that is, the use of top-down rational processes to reappraise and reinterpret situations or events which result in a shift in mood.

Rumination

Nolen-Hoeksema, Wisco and Lyubomorisky (2008) have identified that rumination is a central cognitive process in depression. Rumination, as the name suggests, is the repetitive 'chewing over' of recurring and persistent thoughts in an almost obsessive way. Rumination refers to this process, as opposed to the content of the rumination, which in depression is typically negative.

> Rumination is a mode of responding to distress that involves repetitively and passively focusing on symptoms of distress and on the possible causes and consequences of these symptoms. Rumination does not lead to active problem solving to change circumstances surrounding these symptoms. Instead, people who are ruminating remain fixated on the problems and on their feelings about them without taking action.
> (Nolen-Hoeksema *et al.*, 2008)

Due to its prolonged negativity, depressogenic rumination increases a sense of hopelessness and futility and thus impairs problem solving and worsens pessimistic thinking. As rumination tends to be negative in nature, it feeds into and maintains self-criticism, which in turn reinforces and maintains the depression.

There is considerable evidence that not only does rumination confer major risk of depression, but it also predicts higher levels of depressive symptoms (Nolen-Hoeksemam, Stice, Wade & Bohon, 2007). It is also associated with a number of other disorders, including anxiety. Rumination amplifies and maintains a range of other cognitive processes involved in depression, such as negative interpretations, negative memory bias and impaired concentration. For example, once negative memories have been initiated, this would cause a worsening of mood, which would encourage greater negative interpretation and increased accessing of negative memories and decreased ability to access positive ones. Thus, rumination propagates a vicious cycle which maintains the depression. It is important to distinguish between healthy, adaptive self-reflection and rumination. The main difference appears to be in their effect and outcome – reflection has a positive, problem-solving effect, whereas the effect in rumination is negative. Furthermore, whilst reflection is neutral, rumination tends to be negative and evaluative.

Depressed people tend to believe that their rumination is a way of motivating them out of their depression, or helps them to solve problems; however, sadly, it has the opposite effect. Also, as rumination is partly intended to provide certainty and explanations (but which end up being negative about the depressed person's perceived failings), it ends up reinforcing the depressogenic script beliefs. Tackling ruminative thinking is a key therapeutic target in the treatment of depression. In the short term, positive distraction and attention shifting can be helpful; however in the long term these can contribute to avoidance and therefore be unproductive. Positive, productive and problem-solving activities (including socialising, exercise, mindfulness, problem solving, rational analysis and experiential interventions) are known to be beneficial to people who are ruminating (Nolen-Hoeksema et al., 2008).

Summary

There is evidence that depressed people exhibit a negative bias in their perception, attention, memory and interpretation (Gottlib & Joorman, 2010; Mathews & MacLeod, 2005). Depression is characterised by a series of negatively biased cognitive processes which include a greater attention to negative stimuli and a reduced focus on positive stimuli, negatively biased memory and interpretation, an impaired ability to detach from negative material and rumination (Everaert et al., 2012; Gottlib & Joorman, 2010). Therapy which addresses the implicit processes in depression is likely to be helpful (Philips, Hine & Thorsteinsson, 2010).

A maximally effective treatment of depression will involve addressing and rectifying the cognitive processes discussed here. In particular, attentional shifting, work that reappraises negative interpretations and therapy which challenges rumination are all likely to be highly beneficial strategies.

Self-criticism in depression

The relationship of self-criticism to depression has been well documented and is well known as being a significant feature of depression (Bagby et al., 1992). Further research has also supported the link between self-criticism and social anxiety (Cox et al., 2000; Cox, Fleet & Stein, 2004), where the individual is hypersensitive to criticism and has low self-esteem and feelings of inferiority. As the two disorders are commonly comorbid, it seems likely that they share a common pathway of introjective pathology (Blatt, 1991). Blatt's (1974) theory of introjective depression posits that the individual introjects critical 'others' and that this self-criticism is amplified and repeated internally and is associated with intense feelings of worthlessness and guilt. In his model, self-criticism is also characterised by 'the sense that one has failed to live up to expectations and will be disapproved of and criticized' (Blatt, 1974: 117).

In the studies by Cox *et al.* (2000, 2004), severity of social anxiety was predicted by severity of self-criticism, and was particularly severe in those with comorbid depression, suggesting that self-criticism is a key feature of these disorders and supporting Blatt's (1991) introjective aetiology hypothesis. This hypothesis had further support in the study of Sachs-Ericsson, Verona, Joiner and Preacher (2006), who found that parental verbal abuse and criticism of children (e.g. 'You are worthless/stupid') would be internalised into the child's self-image. This would lead to being 'consumed by feelings of failure, worthlessness, inferiority and self-doubt [and is] . . . a vulnerability marker for depression' (p. 72), and this was associated with a greater vulnerability to internalising disorders such as social anxiety and depression. They hypothesised that therapy which addresses self-criticism would be likely to be beneficial in the treatment of internalising disorders. There is also some evidence to suggest that strong self-criticism is a predictor of poorer outcome to psychotherapy, again highlighting the importance of addressing this process in therapy (Marshall, Zuroff, McBride & Bagby, 2008; Rector, Bagby, Segal, Joffe & Levitt, 2000).

Marshall *et al.* (2008) found high levels of self-criticism to be associated with poorer response to Interpersonal Therapy for depression. It was proposed that this was due to Interpersonal Therapy being focused on relationship difficulties and not directly addressing internal process/cognitions. Within the case series this protocol was developed from (Widdowson, 2013), all of the clients experienced high levels of pretreatment self-criticism and this was a repeated focus of therapy. The best outcome cases all reported reductions in their self-criticism and experienced clinically significant changes in depressive symptoms. High levels of initial self-criticism did not appear to negatively impact on outcomes of TA therapy with this sample. It is possible that TA therapy, with its focus on changing internal self-dialogue, has a significant effect on reducing self-criticism, which in turn influences the outcome of therapy.

The positive use of self-reparenting as a therapeutic intervention in one of the cases (the case of Tom: see Widdowson, 2012c) adds support to the study conducted by Wissink (1994), who found that participants in a 6-week TA-based self-reparenting group experienced a significant increase in self-esteem. A control group had no increase in self-esteem during the same time period, suggesting that the self-reparenting method was effective at increasing self-esteem, feelings of self-efficacy and self-actualisation. This would suggest that, as a method, self-reparenting holds promise and that further research which investigates the outcome of self-reparenting is warranted.

Tom made extensive use of two-chair techniques at several points during his therapy and this was highlighted by the judges as a significant intervention which yielded several critical change points. This supports the findings of Shahar *et al.* (2011) who recently conducted a study which concluded that the use of two-chair work with clients who were self-critical was associated with significant increase in self-compassion and significant decreases in self-criticism, depressive symptoms and anxiety. This study is of particular relevance to TA therapists, as it was investigating the use of Emotion-Focused Therapy, an empirically supported therapy which integrates principles of person-centred and gestalt therapy and which extensively utilises two-chair methods. Emotion-Focused Therapy therapists view self-criticism as a key component of several psychological disorders and conceptualise self-criticism as 'a conflict split between two aspects of the self, where one part of the self harshly criticizes, judges, evaluates and blocks the experiences and healthy needs of another, more submissive part of the self' (p. 763). They use a

> two-chair intervention [where] the client is asked to enact a dialogue between the inner critic and the experiencing self using two chairs. The client is asked to 'be' the inner critic and speak to the experiencing self using one chair and then enact the experiencing self and respond to the self-critical attacks from the second chair. During the dialogue, the client switches chairs whenever the roles are switched, using empathic guidance and emotion coaching from the therapist to explore, process and provide space for expressing emotions and needs associated with each part of the self.
>
> (Shahar *et al.*, 2011: 763)

Clearly, this method has direct parallels with redecision methods in TA psychotherapy, and in particular the Parent Interview (McNeel, 1976) and Impasse Resolution (Goulding & Goulding, 1979). This suggests that further research which investigates the outcomes of the use of TA and in particular redecision methods for therapy of self-criticism may prove fruitful in the treatment of a wide range of disorders.

Living with self-criticism and perfectionism is likely to cause a continuous degree of dysphoria and interpersonal distancing as the individual overreacts to minor mistakes or problems and perceives that others are judging and condemning them (Dunkley, Zuroff & Blankstein, 2003). It is reasonable to assume that if you are highly self-critical you would expect others to be equally as condemning of you (Gilbert, 2007). Given the origin of self-criticism in growing up in a hostile and highly critical environment, this is understandable. Self-criticism can also feel to people like they are taking charge of the criticism that they believe is inevitable – no one can do any worse to them than they can do to themselves.

Self-criticism can be unrelenting and vicious, and as it is an internal process, the individual cannot escape from its torment. From a TA perspective, this internal self-criticism can be viewed as an ongoing internal Parent to Child internal dialogue. Gilbert, Clarke, Kempel, Miles and Irons (2004) found that there were two primary functions of self-criticism: firstly, it was intended to push the individual to make efforts to improve, although this strategy is flawed in that the person is not likely to be able to live up to these demands and will eventually feel worn down by the criticism. The second function is to hurt the self 'because of self-disgust or hatred, with a wish to get rid of parts of the self' (Gilbert, 2007: 137). Gilbert states that part of the role of the therapist is to draw the client's attention to the nature and extent of self-criticism, to understand its purpose and origin and to replace this with a more compassionate and self-accepting self-talk.

Interpersonal process in depression

Many clients presenting for psychotherapy wish to address interpersonal problems during their therapy. Interpersonal problems are a feature of a wide range of psychological disorders, many of which have characteristic and specific interpersonal difficulties associated with them. Certainly, the vast majority of people with depression (and associated comorbidities) experience interpersonal problems. Depression can seriously impair an individual's social and interpersonal functioning. Lack of self-worth, feelings of guilt and inadequacy can influence the interpersonal relationships of the depressed person, and some symptoms, such as social withdrawal and isolation, can exacerbate and maintain the depression (Hames, Hagan & Joiner, 2013). Although the mean length of a depressive episode is around 8 months, the most common pattern is that the person experiences partial remission and has substantial persistent subclinical symptoms, and there is a strong chance the depression will recur. Clearly, therapy needs to promote full recovery and act as a preventive for future episodes. As part of this, it is important to address and resolve depressogenic interpersonal processes.

Interpersonal experiences which were characterised by a sense of loss, danger, entrapment or humiliation are common in the histories of people with depression and those with anxiety, and appear to be a precipitating factor in the onset of depression (Brown, Harris & Hepworth, 1995; Kendler *et al.,* 2003).

Interpersonal inhibition, which includes avoidance, withdrawal and tendencies towards shyness, has also been demonstrated to correlate highly with depression (Alfano, Joiner, Perry & Metalsky, 1994; Hames *et al.*, 2013). It is suggested that not only do these processes maintain depression but they also contribute to the sense of loneliness and isolation which depressed people experience. Loneliness and isolation are known risk factors for depression (Cacioppo, Hughes, Waite, Hawkley & Thisted, 2006; Perlman & Peplau, 1984; Segrin, 1998; Weeks, Michela, Peplau & Bragg, 1980). Encouragement to 'look on the bright side', although well intentioned, often increases the depressed person's sense of isolation (Vearnals & Asen, 1998).

The work of Kiesler (1996), based on studies using the Interpersonal Circumplex, verifies what most transactional analysts already know: that interpersonal communications 'pull' for a complementary response. For example, warmth and friendliness tend to pull for warmth and kindness, whereas coldness tends to pull for coldness and interpersonal distance. Ravitz, Maunder and McBride (2008) found that interpersonal problems result from a series of

> maladaptive transactions which contribute to self-perpetuating relational patterns. Depressed patients typically [have] . . . a tendency to become disengaged from their social supports. Complementary and reciprocal interpersonal pulls are innate in all interpersonal interactions. This framework allows us to understand interpersonal problems as recurrent interactions or behaviors which lead to disappointment because they fail to recruit proximity or

support, and instead paradoxically extinguish the interest of others at times of need. The interpersonal course of depression can be formulated as a vicious cycle in which maladaptive interpersonal transactions amplify depressogenic processes. Once suffering from depression, patients become more disengaged from their social network and lose their sense of agency or esteem . . . which perpetuates despair and isolation.

(p. 13)

In light of the considerable emphasis in TA on analysis of communication and improving relationships, it seems reasonable to expect that TA therapy will have a significant impact on changing depressogenic relational styles.

Quilty, Mainland, McBride and Bagby (2013) found that a rigid and dominating client interpersonal style was associated with poorer outcomes to therapy. Conversely, friendly client behaviour was associated with better treatment outcome, probably mediated by its impact on the therapeutic alliance. McCullough (2000) argues that chronically depressed people tend towards an interpersonal style characterised by distancing, submissiveness and hostility. Following on from theories of interpersonal complementarity, this relational style can 'pull' for the therapist to be distant and respond with hostility in communication with the chronically depressed client. This theory was supported in a study by Constantino *et al.* (2008), who also found that chronically depressed clients experienced a decrease in hostile submissiveness and increased levels of friendliness in their communication style during the course of therapy.

Drawing on the Inventory of Interpersonal Problems (Horowitz, Rosenberg, Baer, Ureño & Villaseñor, 1988), Barrett and Barber (2007) identified that people with major depressive disorder (MDD) experienced more interpersonal problems than a non-clinical sample, and in particular reported that they

had more problems with social isolation, avoidance of social situations, lack of assertiveness and being cold or distant; together reflecting a socially avoidant interpersonal style. Interestingly, MDD patients reported significantly fewer problems than the normative sample in being overly nurturant, likely reflecting the withdrawal and isolation inherent in depression.

(Barrett & Barber, 2007: 259)

In relation to comorbid MDD and generalised anxiety disorder (GAD), they found that 'MDD patients with concurrent GAD were more distressed by interpersonal problems than patients without GAD and had a generally cold, distant, unforgiving interpersonal style' (p. 260). Unsurprisingly, their study found that 'depressed patients with a PD [personality disorder] had significantly more problems in being unforgiving, vindictive, distant, avoidant, and non-assertive than MDD patients with no Axis II pathology' (p. 261). Barrett and Barber went on to examine the interpersonal patterns of people with comorbid MDD and depressive personality disorder (DPD) and found that people with this comorbidity were more interpersonally vindictive and intrusive than other Axis II patients but were similarly socially avoidant. Our finding that DPD patients reveal a more hostile–controlling interpersonal pattern is consistent with the characterization of DPD patients as displaying self-reproach, negativism, and pessimism. For example, a personality characterized by negativity and pessimism may so color interpersonal relationships that such individuals are hurt or rebuffed by others leading to either avoidance or anger consistent with a hostile–controlling interpersonal style. Whether avoidant or vindictive, such a response would likely increase the person's vulnerability to depression.

(p. 261)

Lack of social support has been strongly correlated with depression risk and higher levels of social support may be predictive of recovery from depression (Marroquin, 2011). High levels of positive social support also appear to act as a protective mechanism in some people who are at high risk of depression (Joiner, 1997). Marroquin (2011) argues that social support influences depression through its role in emotional regulation. It is possible that some of the affect regulation functions of interpersonal relationships come about by chance; non-negative interactions require a degree of attention which may shift the depressed individual's focus slightly away from rumination and other problematic intrapsychic processes. An alternative mechanism is via enjoyable experiences which interrupt depressogenic avoidance processes that starve the individual of positive stimuli and strokes. Friends and family members may also promote perspective change where the depressed person has taken something badly, suggesting a less negative appraisal of a situation, which may positively influence mood.

One of the features of Lewinsohn's (1974) well-validated behavioural activation therapy for depression is noting that depressed people tend to avoid social contact and thus miss out on positive experiences and positive reinforcement. Although Lewinsohn is using a behavioural model, this concept adds weight to the TA model of stroking. Another feature of Lewinsohn's model is the view that depressed people tend to present with social skills deficits whilst in a depressed episode. Various studies have investigated this and found that many people with depression have problems with rate, volume and pitch of voice, avoid eye contact and have a less animated facial expression (Kazdin, Sherick, Esveldt-Dawson & Rancurello, 1985); essentially, many depressed people often look and sound depressed. Furthermore, depressed people often have a negative emphasis in their conversations (Segrin, 2000). Using the principle of complementarity, it is easy to see that conversations with someone who is depressed may well end up reinforcing the depressed position. Alternatively, others may avoid conversation with someone who is depressed because of the impact it has on them, thus reinforcing feelings of isolation and rejection. Also, there is some evidence that people with depression often push people away, or struggle to put the energy into creating and sustaining social networks. Fortunately, these are all aspects of a depressed person's interpersonal style which can be easily changed.

Psychoeducation and coaching using TA principles regarding behavioural and social diagnosis of ego states, the functional model and transactions may all be helpful in changing these patterns.

Joiner (2000) discussed a number of interpersonal processes in depression which contribute to the maintenance and chronicity of depression and which predispose individuals towards relapse. It is fairly easy to translate these processes into TA-friendly language. The processes Joiner identified were: *negative-feedback seeking, excessive reassurance seeking, interpersonal conflict avoidance* and *blame maintenance*. Negative-feedback seeking, or, in TA terms, seeking out negative strokes by someone with depression makes sense when considered from the perspective that depressed individuals will use these to confirm their script (regarding their own value or their expectations of how others will behave towards them, e.g. rejecting), and thus reinforce their depression. Strokes which do not confirm their script are likely to be discounted. In excessive reassurance seeking, depressed people repeatedly seek out reassurance

> regarding their worth and lovability, regardless of whether such assurance has already been provided . . . the depression-prone person may excessively seek reassurance in response to negative affect or a negative life event. Others may provide reassurance, but the depression-prone person doubts its sincerity, and is again compelled to seek reassurance. A repetitive pattern is thus established, in which increasing demands for reassurance are made, inducing frustration, irritation, even depression in others, and increasing the likelihood that others will reject the depression-prone person. Rejection furthers the shrinkage and disruption of the depressed person's interpersonal environment, which, in turn, maintains or exacerbates the depressed person's symptoms.
>
> (Joiner, 2000: 206–207)

If considered from TA theory, we see a strong need for positive strokes, which are filtered out and discounted. Indeed, it is not unusual for a depressed person to assume that others are only being nice out of pity or obligation (Hames et al., 2013). Not only are the strokes discounted, but the sincerity of the reassurance giver's statements is also discounted. The pattern then repeats until friction occurs, which can be understood as a game. In this, the depressed person's game payoff would be a reinforcement of his script beliefs about his self, and also his script beliefs about the sincerity of others or whether others can be trusted or will ultimately reject. Joiner, Alfano and Metalsky (1993) notice the apparent contradiction in excessive reassurance seeking and negative-feedback seeking. They posit the cognitive-affective crossfire model. In this, the individual seeks reassurance, which is emotionally satisfying, but this generates cognitive dissonance due to its incongruence with the person's self-concept. In order to resume balance, the person then seeks negative feedback, which confirms his negative self-views, but which is emotionally unsatisfying.

The third process highlighted by Joiner is conflict avoidance. People with depression are prone to avoidance in general, but Joiner posits that conflict avoidance means that the depression-prone individual does not express herself out of fear of humiliation or other adverse response. In TA terms, we might also consider that this process contributes to racket feelings of resentment and reinforcing an 'I'm not OK' life position. With regard to blame maintenance, Joiner argues that not only does the depression-prone individual have a negative self-image, but in the course of her depression her associates can develop a negative image of the individual which can persist after the depressed person has recovered.

From a TA perspective, we can understand this as representing a fairly stable imago of the depression-prone individual in the mind of others where improvement is discounted and which triggers ongoing Critical Parent or persecuting transactions, which in turn create interpersonal stress. Clearly, work which changes stroking patterns towards the depressed individual is indicated in this instance. TA therapists working with depressed people are advised to be alert to the operation of these four negative interpersonal processes in their clients' relationships and seek to interrupt them wherever possible, replacing them with healthier ways of relating.

Living with highly critical (actual or perceived) family members is associated with greater risk of relapse (Hooley & Teasdale, 1989; Vearnals & Asen, 1998). Experiences of criticism or hostility from partners and family members towards depressed people are highly likely, as partners and family members will often feel worn down and exasperated with the behaviour and/or mood of the depressed person. This situation can set up a series of self-reinforcing feedback loops, whereby the depressed person feels worse (which may be perceived as 'attention seeking', or as indicating a lack of desire to get better) and potentially argues back, thus fuelling her partner's or family member's hostility (as the person may well feel unheard). Fixed roles involving the partner or family member adopting a caretaking position are common in households or families where depression is common, which may lead to resentment or conflict if this is suddenly stopped.

From a TA point of view, the above behaviours may be viewed as representing movements around the drama triangle (Karpman, 1968). Where such dynamics are present, several sessions of couples therapy may be beneficial to interrupt these problematic relationship patterns (Vearnals & Asen, 1998). Sometimes, people with depression become afraid of improving as they fear that their partner or family members may suddenly start making demands on them or requesting more of them than they feel that they can cope with (Vearnals & Asen, 1998).

Attachment style has also been identified as correlating with depression, with insecurely attached individuals having a higher risk of developing depression (Eberhart & Hammen, 2006; Hankin, Kassel & Abela, 2005). Perhaps unsurprisingly, Jan Conradi and de Jonge (2009) found that those with anxious attachment style tended to have longer depressive episodes, more residual symptoms on remission, worse social functioning and longer use of antidepressants than those with secure attachments. This is particularly the case where interpersonal conflicts were a stressor which precipitated the depression (Hames et al., 2013).

4 Conceptualising depression using TA theory[1]

Renaming TA concepts

This protocol proposes the renaming of several transactional analysis (TA) concepts. From the beginning, TA has placed emphasis on using accessible language to demystify the therapy process and to promote a collaborative use of shared theoretical language. This use of shared language combined with the active use of psychoeducational methods is a unique and distinctive feature of TA. The difficulty we face as TA therapists in applying this feature is that a number of TA concepts were named in 1960s California. Consequently, some of the language used is somewhat dated and does not have the same cultural meaning for clients in the twenty-first century. Below are several TA concepts and suggested alternative names. For example, in TA we talk about 'trading stamps'. Many clients under 35 will have no memory of trading stamps and cannot locate the cultural and historical reference; however, all will be familiar with the use of store loyalty cards. The author has found that the word 'games' has particularly problematic associations for people, as it will often be interpreted as meaning 'conscious manipulation', which misses the subtlety of the concept of a 'game' (see Widdowson, 2010). Similarly, 'racket' does not have any current cultural meaning (certainly within the UK). The concept of 'authentic feeling' conveys the implicit message that some feelings are 'inauthentic', which does not match with a client's subjective experience. Within this manual, 'authentic emotion' will be referred to as 'primary emotion' and 'racket feeling' will be referred to as 'secondary emotion'. The racket system has fairly recently been renamed as the script system (Erskine, 2010) in order to convey the sense that it illustrates the life script in action. The author of this manual believes that renaming the racket (script) system to 'associative network' (or, for ease of use in sessions, 'emotional circuit') more accurately conveys the nature of what it is and how it functions. It is believed that this will also make the concept more accessible and understandable to other mental health professionals.

TA theory has many powerful concepts; however, it must be acknowledged that they have limitations. No existing model fully captures the complexity of the person, and therefore is inevitably somewhat reductive. Nevertheless, the models are valuable and clinically useful for both therapists and clients. It is hoped that the suggested renaming of concepts enhances their clinical utility.

Life positions

The theory of life positions by Berne (1972) and Ernst (1971) is frequently the starting point for transactional analysts in understanding depression. Berne drew on Melanie Klein's theory of the depressive position (Klein, 1975) in the development of the theory of life positions, and linked the depressive position with the 'I'm not OK – you're OK' life position. Therefore, the individual has a pervasive sense that she is 'not OK' and is inferior to others, who are considered to be 'OK'. A strong sense of being 'not OK' will lead the person to conclude that she is somehow inherently 'bad'.

Strokes

Steiner (1974) put forward the theory that depression is linked to stroke deprivation. In Steiner's theory, the individual with depression has a powerful set of stroke economy rules, which limit the seeking of and experiencing of positive strokes. The depressed person is seen as living in an interpersonal world where positive strokes are either not forthcoming due to limited or unsatisfactory relationships and/or the positive strokes are discounted by the individual, maintaining that person's low self-esteem and sense of worthlessness. Patterns of negative stroking are internalised into the individual's Parent ego state, resulting in the negative strokes being internally replayed through the internal ego state dialogue as self-criticism and reinforcing the sense of the self as being inherently 'bad'. In addition to the negative, critical strokes, there is an absence of positive, nurturing strokes, which leads to an undeveloped internal Nurturing Parent. Steiner saw this internalised stroking pattern as a 'loveless script' with a central feeling of being unloved or being unlovable (Steiner, 1974).

Injunctions

The Gouldings put forward the theory that many script beliefs can be conceptualised as powerful, restrictive messages that limit and even prohibit what an individual might do in life, and they named these injunctions. If an individual disobeys his injunctions it is believed that he will experience internal conflict and distress. The Gouldings also suggested that depression is linked to the 'Don't exist' injunction and the presence of a suicidal script decision (Goulding & Goulding, 1979). The depressed individual is seen to have an intrapsychic conflict between Parent and Child ego states, known as an 'impasse' (Goulding & Goulding, 1979; Mellor, 1980) around the Don't Exist injunction and issues of worthlessness. They also supported Steiner's view that people who have depression also do not have a sufficient internal Nurturing Parent (Goulding & Goulding, 1979).

Ego state dialogue

Although a number of depressive symptoms and processes can be understood using TA concepts of structural analysis, several TA writers have used the

44 TA theory and depression

functional model to understand the process of a person with depression. The harsh, self-critical process which is a key feature of depression is considered to be connected to a harsh, critical Parent ego state which dominates the internal dialogue of the depressed individual at the conscious, out-of-awareness and unconscious levels (Kapur, 1987; Maggiora, 1987). This process is described by both Kapur and Maggiora in functional analysis terms as the presence of a strong and overdeveloped Critical Parent transacting internally to the Adapted Child, who in turn responds with guilt, shame, despair and a sense of worthlessness. Additionally, the internal Nurturing Parent is seen as relatively weak, which results in the individual being unable to sustain any positive sense of self-esteem (Kapur, 1987; Maggiora, 1987). As the accuracy of the Parent-driven self-critical dialogue and the 'I am bad' response of the Child ego state is accepted by the depressed individual as the 'truth', the negative beliefs about self, others and the world also can be viewed as contaminations of the Adult ego state.

Structurally, this negative internal Parent–Child dialogue can also be conceptualised as a harsh and attacking Parent in the Child (P_1) to Child in the Child (C_1) internal dialogue. If taken to the level of third-order structure, the earliest Parent (P_0) can be seen to be inadequate in its self-soothing function, whilst the earliest Child (C_0) can be seen as experiencing intense, overwhelming affect that he is unable to regulate.

Transactions and the drama triangle

Interpersonally, an individual with depression may simultaneously seek to counteract her sense of badness, prevent abandonment and treat others as having more value (I'm not OK – you're OK) by transacting from a Nurturing Parent position, or rescuing others (Karpman, 1968; Maggiora, 1987). A person with depression with a sense of helplessness may well also present from a Victim position, inviting the therapist and others to rescue her (Kapur, 1987). Depressed people can also engage in negative transactional patterns, which appear to be based on a Critical Parent process, which may be based on an I'm not OK – you're not OK life position. In this despairing depressive position, the client may well invite the therapist (and/or others) to share their sense of hopelessness countertransferentially.

Combining models

The detailed understanding of an individual's depression using TA theory involves a layering of multiple theoretical concepts which would in turn inform the therapist's treatment approach. This provides the therapist with a subtle and individualised way of understanding how each client experiences depression, both intrapsychically and interpersonally, and an understanding of the aetiology and dynamics of the individual's depression. As has been discussed above, depression is not a single, unified experience, and different theories may or may not be appropriate for understanding the particular client's experience. The therapist is advised to consider how each of these theories (or, indeed, any other TA theory)

Conceptualising depression using TA theory 45

either enhances her conceptualisation and understanding of her client's experience of depression, or can be discarded as not being relevant for that individual, thus tailoring her case formulation and treatment plan to the needs of each client.[2]

Contaminations

A contamination is where some part of the content of a Parent and/or Child ego state is mistaken for Adult ego state content (Berne, 1961; Stewart & Joines, 1987, 2012). These tend to be inaccurate or maladaptive rules, beliefs or expectations regarding the self, others and the world. As a broad rule of thumb, contaminations which the individual took in from his environment tend to be Parent contaminations, whereas contaminations which are internally generated and based on the individual's own process tend to be Child contaminations. As contaminations are mistaken for Adult content, the individual usually unquestioningly accepts the validity and truth of them. In the therapy room, some contaminations are obvious in the client's conversation. Others are less obvious and are either revealed through 'slogans' regarding the individual's expectations or rules which he lives by. Contaminations may also be implied or inferred from what the client is discussing.

Some examples of contaminations include:

'Always expect the worst because then you won't be disappointed'.

'I must put other people before myself'.

'I must be liked by everyone'.

'People will think less of me if I make a mistake'.

Because contaminations affect Adult functioning and are experienced by the individual as true, they act as a filter on reality. Consequently the individual may make note of information which he perceives justifies or confirms the contaminations and may discount information which does not.

Clinically, double contaminations are often present (Figure 4.1). In double contaminations, the Parent and Child contaminations often 'agree' with each other or are mutually supportive in some way. For instance:

Parent contamination: 'Fat people are unlovable', 'Men can't be trusted', 'Women are always irrational'.

Child contamination: 'Yes, I am fat so . . . I'm unlovable'.

Identifying the source of contaminations

It is often very tempting for TA therapists who have a hunch that a client's negative beliefs or internal dialogue has its origin in a specific negative introject to ask the client: 'Who said that?' Unfortunately, the answer to this question is often 'No one'. This response can leave the therapist uncertain of where to go. Instead,

46 TA theory and depression

Double Contamination

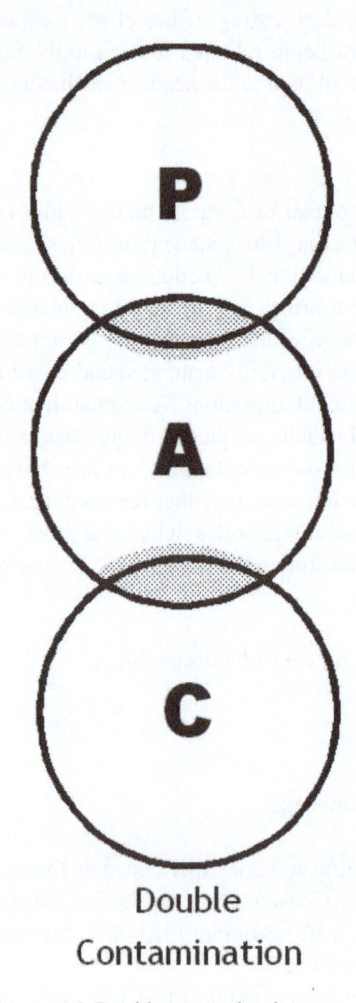

Figure 4.1 Double contamination.

it is more productive to make the open-ended enquiry of: 'I wonder where you picked that up from? Do you have any ideas on what sort of thing happened that might have led you to come to that conclusion?' Alternatively, clients can be asked about experiences they had, or things that they saw or family stories which may give clues as to the source of the contamination.

Biased adult thinking

In the early 1970s the therapists at the Cathexis Institute in Oakland, California identified a series of 'thought disorders' which were common features of a number of psychological problems and were seen to be problems relating to the Adult ego state and the frame of reference (Schiff *et al.*, 1975). All of the Schiffs identified thought disorders involve discounting and grandiosity (Schiff *et al.,* 1975). Around the time the Schiffs were developing their theories, cognitive therapists were also identifying distorted thinking patterns (Beck, 1975). As such, both TA and cognitive therapy share concepts relating to negative and unhelpful thinking biases which result in a negatively oriented interpretation of events. As people become more depressed, these cognitive biases become more pronounced and dominant. These represent a maladaptive frame of reference which interferes with effective Adult ego state functioning and reality testing. These biased distortions are both based on and support an individual's limiting script beliefs about self, others or the world and her script system/associative network. The mechanisms which support these biases are discounting and grandiosity and contaminations of the Adult ego state. As these biases in Adult thinking support depression, it can be helpful to address these in therapy. As with all interventions, it is important to present these to the client in a sensitive manner to reduce the risk of the client seeing the information as being another reason to feel bad about herself. It can be useful to explore with your client aspects of her development from which her biased thinking patterns originate. The list presented below takes the Schiffs' original descriptions and integrates them with aspects of cognitive therapy (Beck, 1975; Burns, 1980).

Examples of biased Adult thinking

Black-or-white thinking

This is similar to splitting and involves thinking in absolutes without subtleties or shades of grey; things are either all good, or all bad. For example, if someone makes a mistake then that person interprets this as meaning that he is 'a failure'.

Catastrophising

In catastrophising, individuals are using both discounting and grandiosity by seeing mistakes, problems or setbacks as being significantly worse than they actually are, and discounting their ability to cope with or manage the situation.

Fortune telling

Here, individuals anticipate unpleasant outcomes of future events (Maggiora, 1987). They will often generate a series of negative scenarios about the future or what will happen in certain situations.

Mind reading

When someone is mind reading she is making negative assumptions about the thoughts and motivations of others, e.g. 'They don't like me', or 'They did that deliberately to upset me'. People who are prone to mind reading can also discount positive strokes; for example, by questioning the genuineness of the person giving the stroke, or by asserting that the stroke was given sarcastically.

Taking things personally

This bias is fairly self-explanatory: the individual takes events or actions of others personally, and may feel offended or upset by actions which probably have nothing to do with him. For example, a friend may not see him in the street, but the client interprets this as 'evidence' that the friend was deliberately ignoring him.

Overgeneralisation

Often when someone is overgeneralising she tends to use the words 'always' or 'never'; for example, 'Everything always goes wrong', or 'I never get anything right'.

Overdetailing

This bias involves excessive and unnecessary focusing on minute detail. The individual can get overwhelmed by such overdetailing and can also struggle to explain things coherently.

Tunnel vision

This involves a selective attentional bias towards the negative, and a discounting of the positive.

Frame of reference

The frame of reference is an enduring organising framework which influences how the individual experiences, perceives, conceptualises and makes meaning of her internal and interpersonal experiences and the world around her (Schiff *et al.*, 1975). It provides a conceptual overarching link between the script and contaminations. In depression, the frame of reference of the individual becomes biased towards perceiving the world from a depressive perspective. Therefore, all stimuli are potentially reinforcing of the (negative) script beliefs. This creates a self-perpetuating loop which reinforces the depressogenic frame of reference. Day-to-day setbacks or normal disruptions in daily life can then become 'justifications' of a negative outlook.

For example:

'See, there is no point in getting hopeful as I always end up disappointed'.

'What's the point in enjoying anything as I'll only end up feeling down/getting punished?'

When such beliefs are held by an individual, it is likely that he will focus on negative stimuli, which build up disappointment or frustration and become a self-fulfilling prophecy. A depressogenic frame of reference may require being repeatedly addressed in therapy, and is particularly influenced by decontamination and redecision processes. The frame of reference of an anxious person tends to perceive the world and other people as somehow dangerous, and experiences the self as unable to cope.

Life script in depression

Depression can be conceptualised as involving the activation or presence of a particularly powerful and negatively weighted life script. When someone is depressed, she will characteristically hold a series of negative script beliefs about herself, other people, the world and her future. Listed below is a selection of typical script beliefs you might expect to be held by someone who is depressed. These lists are not exhaustive, but do cover many of the major themes of depression and are presented as possibilities: the therapist is urged to ascertain each client's script beliefs on an individual basis, although these lists may be used as suggested starting points.

Negative script beliefs about self

I am . . . weak/a failure/useless/inadequate/unlovable/unattractive/defective.

Negative script beliefs about others

Other people . . . don't understand/are uninterested/are inconsiderate or selfish/will reject me/are disapproving and critical/are unfair/are untrustworthy or dishonest/are distant and cold/will not help others/are punishing/are competitive/are unreliable/are irresponsible/are controlling or dominating or aggressive/are weak and submissive/are too needy/are too emotional/are better than me/are more intelligent than me.

Negative script beliefs about the future

I will be rejected/abandoned/alone/disappointed.
The future will be terrible/disappointing.
I will never get what I want.
I will always feel this way.

Script beliefs: early or later development?

A traditional TA view is that the individual would have developed his script beliefs in childhood and that these would be relatively fixed. In the model developed in this manual, it is considered possible that an individual may develop negative script beliefs at any stage throughout the life span (Erskine, 1980, 2010; Newton, 2006; Widdowson, 2010).

Therapy of script beliefs

The therapist is advised to find opportunities to draw on life events in order to challenge the client's core script beliefs. Even if the client does not completely revise her script beliefs but starts to doubt the validity of her negative beliefs, this is a good outcome. It is important to note that deeply held script beliefs can be fairly impervious to change.

Injunctions

In the case series this manual was based upon (Widdowson, 2013), a number of injunctions (Goulding & Goulding, 1979) appeared to be common amongst the clients. These are:

> Don't exist; Don't be close; Don't be you [you're not good enough]; Don't succeed; Don't feel (Don't have needs); Don't belong; Don't be important (Your needs aren't important).

Moving beyond the Gouldings' original list of injunctions, a number of other injunctions appeared to be common amongst the clients in the case series. These were:

> Don't want [because you don't deserve it]; Don't feel successful [inadequacy, sense of inferiority]; Don't enjoy [anhedonia and a lack of a sense of a 'right' to enjoy life] (McNeel, 2010).

The script system and script beliefs

Within TA theory, depression may be seen to be a repetitive and maladaptive coping strategy. 'We find that the [depressed] person has often in the past reacted to stress with depression, sadness, loss of self-esteem, and feelings of being overwhelmed and unable to cope' (Goulding & Goulding, 1979: 182). The view that depression is a repetitive and maladaptive coping strategy is also echoed in the theory of the script system (Erskine & Zalcman, 1979). The script system is used by many TA therapists to compile a diagnosis of the internal dynamics of an individual's depression. The script beliefs about the self that a person with depression experiences might include: 'I am inherently bad/worthless, unlovable/inadequate/inferior,' If things go wrong it is my fault. I won't start things because I will only mess them up. I am a failure' and 'I am helpless'. Script beliefs about others might include: 'Others are better than me' and 'Others will reject me'. Script beliefs relating to the world might include: 'The world is a cruel, unjust and unfair place' and 'Life is pointless and meaningless and hopeless'.

The reported internal experiences on the script system of someone with depression would include a number of their depressive symptoms, and the observable

Conceptualising depression using TA theory 51

behaviours would include withdrawal and avoidance of activities. The individual will have a number of memories which she can draw upon as 'evidence' for the accuracy of these beliefs. The theory of the script system also holds the importance of identifying, understanding and expressing the underlying, repressed feeling as being central to understanding and dismantling the script system (Erskine & Zalcman, 1979). In depression, these underlying feelings are likely to be feelings of anger and grief.

Primary and secondary feelings in depression

As has been stated previously, depression is primarily a disorder of dysregulated affect and is categorised as a mood disorder. Within this manual, what have been referred to within TA as authentic feelings and racket feelings are referred to as primary feelings and secondary feelings, respectively. Primary feelings are those automatic, adaptive and appropriate emotional responses to situations. If these are experienced, expressed and responded to appropriately, they tend to pass naturally. Secondary emotions are those which involve a secondary response, such as a feeling *about* a feeling, or a substitute feeling (see English, 1971), which is learnt or stroked in childhood, is maladaptive, does not resolve when expressed or responded to and leaves the person feeling stuck (Greenberg & Watson, 2006). Consequently, secondary emotions tend to reinforce and maintain an individual's script. The assumption within this protocol is that the major emotional experiences associated with depression are mostly secondary emotions, which become linked to an individual's script via a depressive associative network. This is through his connection with a range of script beliefs, such as: 'I'm bad/I'm lazy/I'm no good/I can't cope/I'm a failure/I'm inadequate/I'm unlovable/I'm losing it/I cannot survive on my own/It's all my fault'.

TA theory has traditionally only considered the four emotions of anger, sadness, fear and happiness as primary emotions. If we take into account modern affect theory, as developed by authors such as Paul Ekman (2003), the list of primary emotions can be expanded to include: surprise, disgust, contempt, amusement, contentment, embarrassment, excitement, guilt, pride in achievement, relief, satisfaction, sensory pleasure and shame.

Some clients struggle to identify their primary feelings because they have not been taught how to identify, name, understand and express their feelings accurately, for example, by confusing the experience of anxiety with anger. Others struggle because they are afraid of their feelings and so need to be gradually taught to experience and regulate them effectively in a process similar to systematic desensitisation and exposure, and as a part of deconfusion of the Child ego state.

Within depression, secondary feelings include a profound sense of loneliness, shame, sadness, rejection, worthlessness, inadequacy, self-hatred, of being unlovable, and of helplessness, hopelessness and despair. These feelings do not provide the individual with information and do not adaptively guide action which results in their effective resolution or in problem solving. Instead, they are self-perpetuating and maintain the depression.

Feelings are also associated with an individual's core script beliefs, such as deep fear of abandonment if an individual's script contains abandonment as a central organising theme. These core script feelings are not strictly speaking secondary feelings and are perhaps best categorised as central script feelings. Certainly, these script feelings are outdated and relate to the individual's earliest experiences and need expressing, re-evaluating and transforming in therapy.

Emotional themes in depression

Greenberg and Watson (2006) identified four major maladaptive emotional themes which are common in depression and appear to be factors in maintaining the depression. These are: shame and guilt, fear and anxiety, sadness, and anger. These emotional themes can be conceptualised as secondary emotions. It is useful to understand these emotional themes as they tend to form the basic emotional experience at the centre of the depressed person's associative network, and therefore suggest avenues for interventions and treatment approach.

Shame and guilt are particularly destructive and pervasive emotions for many depressed people. Whilst the evolutionary origin of guilt is likely to be to preserve social relationships and attachments by motivating the individual to comply with social expectations of acceptable behaviour, a pervasive, intense and persistent feeling of guilt is a common feature of depression. Similarly, shame is often a significant affect in depression. It has been defined as 'a self-conscious emotion, associated with being inferior and socially rejected' (Gilbert, 2007: 124). It has also been defined as where an individual concludes that not only has she failed to live up to her ideal, but she has become something which she dislikes. Furthermore, in shame, the individual feels that she has 'stimulated negative feelings (contempt, ridicule, disgust or disinterest) in the minds of others, and, as a consequence this will lead them either to not wish to form useful relationships with, to disengage, actively reject the self or even attack the self' (Gilbert, 2007: 125). So, we see that shame has both an internal component (I am inferior/bad/flawed/inadequate) and a social component (others will see me as inferior/bad/flawed/inadequate). Dealing with shame in therapy can be particularly difficult, as the client may reject the therapist's acceptance of her, or firmly believe: 'If he really knew what I was like, he would not like me'. Consequently, people who feel like this can be extremely reluctant to be completely open in therapy. Both shame and guilt appear to be dynamically linked in the psyche of the depressed person (Greenberg & Watson, 2006). Both shame and guilt stimulate the intense self-criticism which is part of the experience of depression.

Anxiety is frequently present for people with depression. Greenberg and Watson (2006) report five subcategories of fears which are common in people who are depressed. These are: (1) fear of rejection, judgement and abandonment; (2) fears connected to a sense of the world being a bad and dangerous place; (3) fears of repeating historical emotional experiences (transference repetitions); (4) fear of change; and (5) fear of feelings.

The experience of sadness in depression has been subcategorised as being connected to: disappointment around unmet needs, remorse (associated with guilt) for one's actions, current losses of hopes, ideals, status or relationships and unresolved grief over past losses, particularly bereavements (Greenberg & Watson, 2006).

The 'flavour' of secondary anger in depression is different to that of primary anger. In particular, it often tends to take the form of resentment and bitterness over the past or blaming anger, which may be blaming others and/or strong self-criticism which is a form of anger turned in against the self. At the interpersonal level, people with depression who experience racket anger tend to be irritable and are easily annoyed and prone to complaining, or if the anger is turned in against the self, may be submissive and lacking in assertiveness.

Clearly, these maladaptive secondary feelings, beliefs and their associative networks need to be identified, challenged, re-evaluated, updated and transformed as part of the therapy.

Interrupting the associative network

The associative network can also be interrupted by inviting the client temporarily to access a memory associated with a different emotion. It is possible that the process of state-dependent memory prompts a shift in mood, or that the emotion itself is somehow transformative of the original state (Greenberg & Watson, 2006; Parrott & Sabini, 1990) and may activate neural systems which have a 'dampening' effect on the persistent negative emotion (Levenson, 1992). Similarly, there is some evidence to suggest that adopting physical expressions or postures associated with certain emotions can intensify them (if mood-congruent) or weaken them (if mood-incongruent). The concept of using emotions to antidote negative and maladaptive emotional states is used in Emotion-Focused Therapy (Greenberg & Watson, 2006) and Accelerated Experiential Dynamic Therapy (Fosha, 2000).

Forbidden feelings

Within TA theory, repressed or disavowed feelings are considered to be the driving force 'underneath' the associative network of the script system, again, and also are what is identified and expressed in the process of deconfusion. These feelings are likely to be ones which were either explicitly or implicitly forbidden in the individual's history, or were so unpleasant or distressingly aversive that the individual implicitly learnt to avoid them. This pattern of emotional repression or disavowal becomes entrenched over time. Whenever the individual either starts to experience the forbidden feeling, or encounters a situation which is likely to trigger the forbidden feeling, 'early-warning alarms' are activated (probably via amygdalar activation), producing an almost phobic response to the feeling (McCullough Vaillant, 1997). This in turn keeps the individual from experiencing the forbidden feeling, possibly by even avoiding certain activities, thoughts or situations. This fear-driven system and sustained repression of emotions are considered to be an important mechanism in the development and maintenance of depression, and one which is useful to address in therapy. The therapist is encouraged to help the client to:

- identify which feelings and experiences the client implicitly believes to be 'forbidden'
- identify the (implicit) magical Child belief which goes with these forbidden experiences/feelings
- challenge the belief and encourage the client to feel the forbidden feeling and desensitise from the Child fear of the feeling/experience.

It is possible that the depressed person may feel that positive feelings such as 'feeling good about the self', 'self-care' and 'pride' are forbidden feelings (see section on working with feelings in Chapter 8). Not only is this likely to be a maintaining factor in depression, but it may also be a significant risk factor which causes a vulnerability to depression.

Another area many people with depression seem to struggle with is taking good care of themselves and prioritising their own needs. Such people often feel that doing so is somehow 'selfish'. These people tend to have had early life experiences where they were told that being selfish was particularly undesirable, and they learn to associate self-care and taking care of their own needs as selfishness. Such fears of self-care can be repeatedly addressed in therapy by therapist statements, such as:

> Taking care of yourself is not selfishness. Taking care of yourself does not mean you have to treat other people badly, although it might mean that sometimes you can't do what they want. That might upset them a little, and they may even call you selfish for not doing what they want. Realistically, in such situations, you could even ask yourself: 'Who exactly is being selfish here?' or 'How is me taking care of myself being selfish?'
>
> Each person is responsible for their own happiness and fulfilment in life. There is no virtue in neglecting your own happiness to suit other people.

Prototype combined associative network/script system

In TA therapy, the therapist will compile an associative network/script system diagram for each client which takes into account the client's unique life experiences. It is, however, possible to identify a series of similarities in associative network items amongst people with a shared diagnostic category. In Table 4.1, a series of items are suggested which appear to be common themes for people with depression. This can be used to give the therapist a starting point for treatment, and as such may save time and be an efficient way of making initial interventions and also compiling diagnostic material. Some therapists may wish to read this prior to their initial session with a client for use as a starting point for questioning;

Table 4.1 Prototype combined associative network

Script beliefs (intrapsychic system)	Script displays (behavioural interface)	Reinforcing memories (interpersonal system)
Self	**Observable**	**Childhood**
I will never be good enough (IIII)	Avoidance of activities/ withdrawal (IIIII)	Bullying (III)
I am inadequate (IIII)	Being 'invisible' (IIII)	Bereavement/loss (III)
I've done something wrong/ It's all my fault (III)	Passivity (IIII)	Lack of praise (III)
I cannot have needs or get what I want (III)	Silent and unemotional/ lack of emotional expressiveness (II)	Repeated criticism (III)
I must put other people before me (II)		Being given too much responsibility (II)
I am not important (II)		'Traumatic events' (II)
I cannot say no (II)		
I am powerless (II)		
Others	**Internal**	**Adult life**
Are selfish and uncaring (IIII)	Despair (IIIII)	Redundancy (III)
Are better than me. Will reject me (III)	Strong self-criticism (IIIII)	End of relationship (II)
Will criticise or reject me if I express my feelings or make independent decisions (II)	Lack of energy/feeling 'run down' and loss of interest (IIII)	Conflict (II)
Are unreliable and untrustworthy (II)	Tension (III)	Bereavement (I)
	Poor concentration/ memory (III)	
	Rumination (III)	
	Guilt (II)	
	Low self-confidence (II)	
The world	**Fantasies/expectations**	**Social/environmental**
Life has no meaning (II)	Paranoid – expects criticism/attack/ rejection (IIIII)	Isolation (III)
The world is a cruel and unfair place (II)	Isolation (IIIII)	Stress at work (II)
Life is shit and then you die (II)	My future is bleak and hopeless (II)	Other people at work or in family taking advantage (II)
Life is confusing (I)	I will never be heard, taken seriously and respected (I)	Current 'critical' family environment (II)
Life is to be avoided (I)	I want to be rescued (I)	
Life is difficult (I)		
Repressed feelings/needs		
Positive feelings about self (IIIII)		
Anger (IIII)		
Self-assertion (III)		
Grief (II)		

Adapted from: Erskine and Zalcman (1979) and Erskine (2010), with additional materials from Widdowson (2013).

Note: numerals after each item indicate the number of clients this item applied to.

however, this is optional. It is recommended that the therapist reviews this list after the first session to check which of these items are present in the client's associative network. It is important that the therapist includes individualised items for each client, and does not simply produce a 'mass-market' and generic associative network which could potentially miss out much of the subtlety of an individualised approach.

Notes

1 Some material in this chapter was taken from: Widdowson, M. (2011). Depression: a literature review on diagnosis, subtypes, patterns of recovery, and psychotherapeutic models. *Transactional Analysis Journal*, 41(4): 351–364.
2 End of material taken from Widdowson (2011).

5 Basic technique in TA therapy

A full and detailed description of the basic technique of transactional analysis (TA) therapy is beyond the scope of this book. Readers who would like to learn more about the techniques used in TA psychotherapy are recommended to read:

> Lister-Ford, C. (2002). *Skills in Transactional Analysis Counselling and Psychotherapy.* London: Sage.
> Stewart, I. (2014) *Transactional Analysis Counselling in Action.* London: Sage.

Readers who would like to gain a greater insight into the use of two-chair or empty-chair technique will find the following text to be invaluable reading:

> Goulding, M.M. & Goulding, R.L. (1979). *Changing Lives Through Redecision Therapy.* New York: Grove Press.

Readers who have a solid grounding in TA theory and method, and would like to take their understanding a little deeper, are advised to read:

> Widdowson, M. (2010). *Transactional Analysis: 100 key points and techniques.* Hove: Routledge.

The therapeutic operations

Berne's (1966) therapeutic operations provide the transactional analyst with a range of interventions which form the basis of TA therapy. This model is remarkably flexible and sufficiently detailed to provide the therapist with a good toolbox of techniques which are applicable to all clients. The majority of interventions a TA therapist might make can be classified into one of Berne's eight techniques. Recently, Hargaden and Sills (2002) have adapted Berne's list and have reframed them as *empathic transactions*. This slight change in emphasis reminds the therapist of the importance of sustained empathic dialogue with the client.

Interrogation (enquiry)

An enquiry can take one of two forms. The first type of enquiries are simple, direct questions which are intended to gain information, for example, 'How long have you felt like this?' The second type of enquiry interventions are intended to deepen clients' awareness into their phenomenological experience, for example, 'What do you feel as you say that?' Enquiry is best done from a position of genuine, sensitive curiosity.

Specification

Specification gathers together, identifies, categorises and clearly (re)states information which the client has previously mentioned, perhaps in a scattered and random fashion. Specification may include making summary statements and pulling together strands both from within the session and across sessions. It may also include highlighting repetitive patterns, such as 'You know, as you're talking about how Sarah was rude to you in front of your friends, it's reminding me of similar instances in the past. I'm left with the impression that this happens quite regularly. Would you say that's true?' Specification can also include identifying the subtlety of the client's unexpressed or implicit meaning and can be 'a type of accurate empathy, which can include the more advanced empathy of hearing what is just under the surface of the client's awareness' (Hargaden & Sills, 2002: 120). Statements which are tentative, or which include checking out with the client the accuracy of our understanding are particularly helpful (for example, 'It sounds as though . . . , is that right?'). Frequent use of such specification lets clients know whether we understand them or not, and gives them an opportunity to correct the therapist's accuracy.

Confrontation

The word 'confrontation' can be quite loaded, and can give the impression of a harsh intervention. Within TA, confrontation is used in a broader sense and refers to 'any move you make that invites your client to test his script beliefs against here-and-now reality' (Stewart, 2014: 38). Hargaden and Sills (2002) emphasise the importance of confrontation being delivered in a way which is empathic and understanding of the client's position and can be heard and experienced by the client as validating rather than potentially shaming.

Another way of thinking about confrontation is that it could also be classified as a crossed transaction (Berne, 1961; Stewart & Joines, 2012). The intentional use of a crossed transaction can be a powerful and timely confrontation which is particularly suited when the client is transacting from either Parent or Child ego states and the therapist wants to invite the client into the Adult ego state. In such cases, the therapist needs to make clear Adult–Adult transactions for this to be effective. For example, a client may believe he is helpless and be transacting from his Child ego state, to which the therapist could respond with a statement such as, 'You have all the resources and capability you need to make changes.'

In *Principles of Group Treatment,* Berne (1966) described confrontation as pointing out an inconsistency so that the client's Adult ego state can become aware of and resolve it. This is best done somewhat carefully, as there is potential for the client to feel 'caught out', or criticised, which would likely increase his defensiveness and reduce his receptivity to the therapist's interventions. Berne also noted that an effective and sensitive confrontation will often be followed by the client spontaneously and freely laughing, perhaps at the absurdity of his original position.

Most clients want their therapist to challenge them, sensitively and appropriately. Despite this, clients who have high levels of self-criticism or who have grown up in critical and invalidating environments may find it difficult to hear confrontations or may experience them negatively. It is recommended that the therapist checks in with the client after a confrontation is made (for example, 'How do you feel when you hear me say that?') or even beforehand, where it can take the form of a contract for confrontation (for example, 'I have something to say which I realise might be hard for you to hear. Would you be willing to hear the challenge?').

Explanation

Explanation is an attempt to support the strengthening of the client's Adult ego state, to stimulate reflection and/or to provide the client with Adult information. The intention is to enable the client to understand some maladaptive intrapsychic or interpersonal pattern, to help the client make sense of her current situation and its relationship to her past, and to increase her self-awareness or to help the client make new meaning. The ultimate aim is that this increased insight supports the client's movement out of script-based unhelpful processes. Explanation at its best can be considered to be a form of individualised psychoeducation, and indeed may draw upon more generalised psychoeducational materials relating to either TA or the client's specific symptoms (see appendices for psychoeducational resources).

TA therapists are often very good at providing explanations to their clients and draw on a range of TA theories and concepts to help their clients understand their own process. This, then, gives both therapist and client a shared language not only to make meaning, but also to conceptualise the work of the therapy. This feature of TA therapy was specifically mentioned as a helpful factor by all clients in the research study from which this manual was developed (Widdowson, 2013). If you are offering theory explanations to your clients, it is best to introduce the theory as and when it is immediately relevant to the material that is currently being discussed in the session. This allows the client to understand and integrate the concepts that are introduced one by one and also prevents the therapy session from turning into a lecture.

Illustration

Illustration involves the use of stories, metaphors, analogies, images, and so on.

> Illustration can be a way of utilizing the imagination and building on the power of metaphor and analogy. It can be used as a specification, a form

of accurate, advanced empathy . . . It can also be a very economical use of time, as perhaps a confrontative point can be made by a humorous remark or an anecdote that might take hours of painstaking specification and explanation.

(Hargaden & Sills, 2002: 126)

As can be seen in the quotation above, a well-timed and well-chosen illustration can efficiently make a point, or convey deep understanding, or can invite the client to challenge some aspect of her process, or can encourage the client to make new meaning. Sometimes it can help with clients who feel alone with their problems or to highlight some aspect of the human condition that they are currently grappling with.

Confirmation

Confirmation involves a re-emphasising of previously made points or drawing attention to examples. As an intervention, its aim is to support and reinforce the change process. It is used to block a retreat or 'backsliding' into some aspect of script or some unhelpful pattern. It can also be done by stroking changes to support the change process and interventions which strengthen the client's Adult ego state. It is important that this is not done in a 'gotcha'-type way, where the therapist is 'cleverly' pointing things out to the client, who may well feel shamed by the experience, but is done in a compassionate and supportive way. Although there is a danger in labouring the point when a client has gained an insight, there is value in ensuring that the essence of the insight is captured and 'noted' to facilitate the insight being retained in the client's long-term memory.

Interpretation

The therapist is involved in trying to find a voice for the Child. It is an attempt to 'decode and detoxify' (Berne, 1966/1994) her communications . . . Interpretation is not simply organizing what is known between therapist and client, it is giving a voice to a part of the client that seems to her to be literally unspeakable, thus deepening the Adult's understanding of her own self

(Hargaden & Sills, 2002: 125)

A good interpretation results in a cognitive-affective shift for clients where they experience some insight or increased awareness combined with some kind of emotional release or integration (Gilbert & Orlans, 2011).

The use of interpretation is particularly powerful when used to promote deconfusion of the Child ego state. Deconfusion is essentially a process whereby the client accesses, becomes aware of, expresses and resolves some hitherto unexpressed or repressed feelings.

Crystallisation

A crystallisation is a summary statement that describes the client's position and emphasises the choices he can now make and is designed to prompt active effort in the direction of change. It is often a decisive intervention which can precede or follow from a significant shift. The shift may be a social control shift, but ideally, is a 'deeper' shift which reflects some kind of change in the client's script or some potential for movement out of script. Crystallisation can also make a script belief or some undesirable behaviour ego dystonic[1], and thus increase the client's motivation for change.

Crystallisation interventions are made less frequently than other therapeutic operations and tend to be the culmination of a transactional sequence based on other types of therapeutic operation in a systematic build-up towards change. For example: 'Is it still true that if you do (or don't do) X, that you won't survive?' A statement such as this in effect 'crystallises' the original script belief ('I mustn't do X or I won't survive') and also challenges the client to test this old script belief against here-and-now reality. In the example given, if the client responds positively, such as, 'No, it's not true. I can do X and still survive', then this should be followed up by a supportive and confirming transaction. This can also be taken further to invite the client to think how he is going to maintain his movement out of script. So, to use the example, the therapist might respond by saying: 'That's true. You will survive . . . If you find that old fear of not surviving popping back for a visit, how will you respond to it? What will you say to yourself to manage it?' In this example, we see a contingency management technique being used – that is, anticipating future obstacles and inviting the client to explore how he will deal with them.

Crystallisation needs to be carefully timed, and not used prematurely. The client needs to be receptive and the use of crystallisation is best done when there is sufficient Adult thinking available to process the intervention and sufficient affective charge to make the intervention maximally impactful. The section in Chapter 6 on the memory reconsolidation process is particularly relevant to crystallisation, and can help the therapist in designing and delivering such interventions.

Additional interventions

Amplification

Amplification is where the therapist actively seeks to stimulate and intensify the client's level of experiencing, generally by inviting the client to heighten a particular affect. Amplification also includes the use of 'heighteners' (Goulding & Goulding, 1979; McNeel, 1976), which are interventions which intensify the client's experience of 'stuckness' in order to encourage the client to mobilise energy for change. The use of amplification promotes the experiential nature of therapy and invites the client to maintain a moderate level of affective charge throughout the session, which enables optimal change to take place.

Soothing

Soothing is a response which is used to help the client down-regulate intense and overwhelming affect. Usually, this tends to involve the therapist seeking to soothe the client's Child ego state and to encourage the client into Adult ego state. Many clients come to therapy with an impaired ability to self-soothe and may need to be taught how to do so as part of the therapeutic process.

Metacommunication

Metacommunication (Widdowson, 2008) refers to a range of interventions which draw upon the here-and-now process of the therapy to promote experiential change. This can include the use of immediacy, which involves a direct discussion of the here-and-now interaction of the therapist and client in the session and may make use of process comments relating to what is happening in the therapy room, such as comments about closeness/distance, sudden change in topic/avoidance of an issue/depth of emotional processing/shift in the client (McLeod & McLeod, 2011).

Dual awareness

Effective therapists need to develop the capacity for dual awareness, or awareness that shuttles back and forth between the client and the therapist's own internal experience. This can include attentiveness to the therapist's shifting emotions, train of thought, physical sensations, action tendencies (e.g. moving closer to or further away from the client), fantasies, memories and metaphor/ imagery (McLeod & McLeod, 2011; Widdowson, 2010).

Contractual process

TA therapy is based on contractual process, and contracting can be considered a key aspect of effective TA therapy. In my research, the cases which had the clearest contracts had the best therapeutic outcomes. This may have been purely coincidental, but there is considerable research evidence to support the value of consensus and agreement between client and therapist on the issue of goals and tasks of therapy and the advantageous effect that such agreement has on the overall outcome of therapy (Tryon & Winograd, 2002). For an overview of the role of contracting in therapy, see Sills (2006) and Widdowson (2010).

There are two broad types of contracting which are particularly relevant to the day-to-day practice of TA therapy. These are *outcome contracts* (Stewart, 2006) and *process contracts* (Lee, 2006). Outcome contracts refer to the agreement between the therapist and client on the overall goals of the therapy, and specifically what the client wants to achieve from coming to therapy. Whilst many clients attending therapy often begin with no clear sense of what they want to get out of the sessions, they usually come wanting to feel better in some way.

This can be the starting point for discussion around their goals for therapy, and lead to a clear and well-defined outcome contract. Process contracts (Lee, 2006) are particularly relevant to the type of therapy presented in this treatment guide, as they are focused on the here-and-now experiential process of therapy, and on the unfolding tasks of therapy. When process contracting, the therapist is seeking the client's permission to intervene in a particular way (for example, 'Is it OK if we stay with this for a while?') and is also inviting the client to deepen her awareness about her internal flow of experience and to make active changes in the here and now (e.g. 'What would you like right now?' 'Are you getting what you want right now?' 'What does this experience mean for you?'). The ideal situation in TA therapy is one where both client and therapist are in clear agreement about what they are trying to achieve (the outcome contract) and how they are going to achieve it (the process contract). In situations where such agreement and clarity are not in place, then this would become one of the prime objectives of the session(s) until such time as consensus has been reached.

Note

1 Ego syntonic refers to thoughts, feelings, urges, values and behaviours which are acceptable to the client's self-image. Ego dystonic refers to thoughts, feelings, urges, values and behaviours which are unacceptable, or in conflict with some aspect of the client's self-image.

6 Therapeutic processes and change mechanisms

Domains of experience and change

An examination of the wider psychotherapy literature seems to suggest that different therapeutic approaches tend to have a primary mode of action based around a maximum of two domains out of four. These four domains are *cognitive, behavioural, affective* and *relational* (Figure 6.1).

Effective transactional analysis (TA) therapy works with all four of these domains in order to promote maximum client change. Within most therapies, change is promoted through the emphasis on changing two of these domains, which then results in change in other domains. For example, cognitive-behavioural therapists promote change through their emphasis on changing the cognition and behaviour domains of their clients' process. Similarly, emotion-focused therapy and psychodynamic therapy (although different in theoretical basis) promote change primarily through the affective-relational domains. Whilst these different approaches do include the use of interventions from other domains, they are primarily based on their focus in two areas. In contrast, TA, as evidenced in the case series (Widdowson, 2013), both conceptualises the client and promotes change in cognitive, affective, behavioural and relational domains using an integrative and coherent framework which is capable of being flexibly applied to each case according to the presenting problem(s) and client preferences.

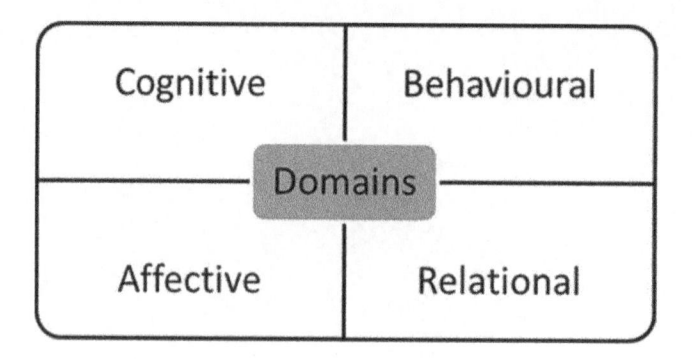

Figure 6.1 Domains of experience and change.

It would appear that this is a unique and significant contribution that TA makes to psychotherapy.

Affect-focused, experiential therapy approach to TA

The approach presented in this manual emphasises two rules of thumb for TA therapy which are considered vital to its successful implementation:

1   Keep the therapy affect-focused, and keep returning to the client's emotional experience.
2   Wherever possible, make the therapy experiential.

The reason for this is that sustaining optimal levels of moderate emotional arousal promotes change. If there is too little or too much emotional arousal, then change is less likely to occur. The experiential focus both enhances and deepens the process of increasing self-awareness in a real and tangible way that the client can make use of and also enables direct implicit and explicit relearning to take place. An effective experiential approach will encompass awareness and change on all four domains.

Psychoeducation and shared language

TA therapy actively promotes the use of TA theory as a collaborative and shared framework for assisting clients in making sense of their experience. All of the clients in the case series study (Widdowson, 2013) reported that the use of TA language and concepts in their therapy had been helpful. It appears that not only did this enable clients to understand what was going on for them, but it also provided clients with a rationale for treatment and a framework for promoting further growth and change. In particular, it would appear that the framework of TA theory gave the clients in the case series a way to reflect upon and identify their internal and interpersonal experiences and enabled them to take charge of and direct their own process of change. This interesting aspect of the cases would appear to be a distinctive feature of TA therapy.

The case series documented each client's use of TA to conceptualise his own process and manage his internal and interpersonal experiences. In theoretical terms, TA holds that this can be understood as enabling clients either to stay in or return to their Adult ego state. From a more general psychotherapeutic perspective, it might be thought that this process enables clients to develop a systematic approach to self-reflection that was then used to self-generate options in how to respond – both internally and externally – to different situations. The use of TA theory also gave the clients a way of making sense of frightening or distressing experiences by helping them to gain insight into their reactions and increase their sense of self-efficacy. This engagement with the language and theory of the model appears to be a distinctive feature of TA and is unusual compared to many other therapies. There is no existing research on the engagement of clients with theoretical material and so further investigation of the impact of this is warranted.

Changing implicit patterns

It is proposed that a central change mechanism is the changing of implicit beliefs and relational patterns – the life script and protocol. The use of TA theory and psychoeducational strategies supports this process by helping clients to bring problematic implicit learning into awareness and give them a framework for changing these. Also, the therapeutic relationship is intended to be a space where these patterns are broken.

Script analysis: deconstructing narrative

> This personal story is based on one's unquestioned faulty assumptions about oneself and what to expect from others, misreadings of others' intentions, and behaviour that often functions in a self-defeating way to make negative expectations into self-fulfilling prophecies. The resulting narratives that one creates to describe interpersonal experiences are filled with contradictions, inconsistencies, ambiguities, and missing connections that preserve the individual's self-protective ways of presenting oneself and seeing others, but that limit possibilities for more fulfilling relationships.
> (Binder & Betan, 2013: 428)

From the initial contact, the therapist is listening out for the client's central narrative themes which form his script. Once the therapist identifies a theme, she then offers this to her client for verification. The therapist teases out and co-constructs with the client a rich and vivid summary of the client's main script themes. These include the client's script themes relating to his self, to his expectations of other people and to his fantasies about the future and the world. The client is supported in examining how these themes run through and influence different aspects of his life. Throughout this dialogue, the therapist encourages the client to examine, deconstruct and re-evaluate this narrative. Thus, the entire process is therapeutic. In short-term therapy, the therapist identifies the core script themes which are at the very heart of the client's depression, and uses this as the central focus in the case formulation, diagnosis and treatment plan.

The client gains insight into his script narrative and, as he brings it into awareness, through the examination and re-evaluation process he begins to deconstruct and change it into a more flexible and adaptive narrative. This process of narrative deconstruction must integrate the cognitive, affective and relational domains. This is then implemented in specific behavioural change.

A detailed and comprehensive client case formulation will draw on many aspects of TA theory. Each aspect can be considered to support other aspects synergistically. Thus, TA therapy aims to interrupt this process by changing these mutually supporting systems. Each small change has a cumulative effect and can have wide-ranging impact throughout the individual's psyche and system.

The principle of systematic experiential disconfirmation

TA therapists tend to pay close attention to the client's life script and its manifestations. In the research, the therapists in the three best outcome cases all actively and deliberately managed the therapy to avoid inadvertently reinforcing the client's life script in the therapy process. Instead, the therapists appeared to focus on challenging their client's life script. The evidence here suggests the therapists were working with an implicit principle that could be described as *'systematic experiential disconfirmation'*. This is a process which has not previously been articulated in TA theory and again constitutes a proposed additional extension to TA practice as a therapeutic strategy. In practice, experiential disconfirmation appears to integrate cognitive, affective, behavioural and relational aspects within a perspective informed by TA developmental theory. For the clients in this study, interpersonal learning and changes in their ways of communicating and relating to others were important parts of their change process.

(Widdowson, 2013: 329)

Memory systems

Memory involves three processes: encoding, storage and retrieval. Memory encoding is where data are registered and processed, storage is where the memory is stored and retrieval is the recall of memories in response to some cue. Memory is commonly thought of operating like recording equipment (such as audio or video recordings); however, research into memory shows that this is not the case. It would appear that memories are actually highly malleable and can be distorted. This is of particular relevance in considering psychological disorders whereby memories can be distorted negatively to support the maintaining mechanisms of the disorder. In TA terms, this can be thought of as a frame of reference which distorts or reconstructs memories to support the script.

High levels of stress cause the release of stress hormones and certain neurotransmitters, in particular cortisol and acetylcholine. These chemicals have a negative impact on memory and can in effect 'jam' the memory-encoding and retrieval systems in the brain. The amygdala has a particular role in memory. Experiences which are perceived as threatening in some way will trigger a fear response. The amygdala will attach salience to aspects of this situation in order to prevent future danger, thus influencing the laying-down of fear-associated memories. All strong feelings will influence memory encoding and storage, and similarly will influence memory retrieval. This is called the *memory enhancement effect. State-dependent memory* is a well-known phenomenon whereby emotions can trigger memories with similar emotional content (for example, in remembering numerous hilarious events when reminiscing with friends). This is highly relevant to understanding depression: depressed mood will trigger the recall of memories which have a similar emotional tone to them, and effectively impair recall of memories associated with other moods. In TA terms, this has relevance to the associative network/script system and how memories become associated with particular feelings and beliefs. When the associative network/script system is activated, a whole range of memories which have similar emotional content will be more available for recall and thus reinforcing the limiting script beliefs.

Existing memories can both be adjusted to accommodate new memories or can affect the learning of new memories. This can work positively in the case of transferable knowledge, such as when learning a language similar to one already known. Conversely, pre-existing memories can interfere with the development of new memories.

Explicit and implicit memory

Explicit or declarative memory is the type of memory that is explicitly stored and retrieved and is available to conscious retrieval. Explicit memory includes memory relating to specific facts, chronological sequence, the learning of abstract knowledge and the memory of events. In explicit memory, the individual is consciously aware that she is recalling information. As explicit memory is linked to the hippocampus, which is not fully formed until around 3 years of age, explicit memory is not present from birth. The explicit memory system would play a part in those aspects of script which are readily available to conscious awareness, including specific and explicit memories and our feelings and thinking process at the time.

Implicit or procedural memory is not based on conscious encoding, storage or retrieval of memories, but on implicit learning and involves behaviours, sensations and emotions (Allen, 2010). Implicit memories do not contain a temporal sense of time or chronological sequence. When an implicit memory is activated, the individual does not have any conscious sense that she is remembering anything. As implicit learning and memory involve the amygdala, it is present from birth. A range of actions such as driving or tying one's shoelaces draw on procedural memory. Implicit memory is of great relevance to TA psychotherapy, as it is assumed that, during development, individuals amass considerable implicit learning about their self, others and the world which forms the basis of the protocol, script decisions and script beliefs (Cornell & Landaiche, 2006). A key aspect of psychotherapy involves the experiential challenging of limiting implicit memories and replacing these with new helpful and adaptive implicit memories.

Memory consolidation and reconsolidation

Memory consolidation is the process whereby memories become 'stable'. There is a period of between a few minutes and up to 6 hours after new information is 'learnt' when the memory is fragile and when synaptic connections are being strengthened. This is of relevance to psychotherapy in that rumination or such like after an unpleasant event means it is more likely to be 'fixed' in an individual's memory. Also, new memories laid down through experiential processes in therapy are equally fragile and therefore the period after sessions is important in ensuring that the new learning is reinforced. For entire memory systems, the process of consolidation is slower and may need repetition, for example, learning a new skill (such as driving) requires repetition to 'fix' the memories. Similarly, widely elaborated aspects of an individual's script (such as the protocol) will likely need time and repetition for these to change permanently.

Memory reconsolidation is of particular interest to psychotherapists. Recent discoveries relating to memory reconsolidation show that memories become labile and malleable when they have been recalled. This is especially the case when there is an accompanying moderate level of emotional arousal. Therefore, if implicit memories can be brought into awareness with some emotional arousal, then the implicit learning can be changed (Ecker & Toomey, 2008). Memory reconsolidation provides a neurological basis to how an individual can make a redecision of an implicit script decision. This theory also highlights the importance of providing opportunities for reinforcement of a redecision after the redecision has been made.

Changing implicit memory

Recent developments in the field of memory reconsolidation and its application to psychotherapy (Ecker, Ticic & Hulley, 2012) are of direct relevance to this model, and provide a powerful framework for facilitating therapeutic change.

The therapist needs to begin by ascertaining as much detail about the problematic symptom as possible. This includes the thoughts, feelings and behaviours which occur when the symptom is present. The therapist will also pay attention to her countertransference and her intuition in listening to the client's account and also inquire into the historical origin of the symptom to see if any clues can be inferred regarding its underlying basis. This enables the full behavioural, social, historical and phenomenological diagnosis of the symptom (Berne, 1961).

In order for the implicit learning to be changed, the symptom-producing implicit learning needs to be activated and brought into awareness with an accompanying degree of moderate emotional arousal. This implicit memory retrieval, combined with moderate affect arousal, generates a degree of lability and malleability, which means that the implicit learning can be changed. Once this has happened, a new learning which contradicts the existing implicit learning needs to be brought into awareness so that a mismatch can occur. That is, an experience that 'deviate[s] saliently from . . . what the reactivated target memory expects and predicts about how the world functions . . . the mismatch can be either a full contradiction and disconfirmation of the target memory or a novel, salient variation relative to the target memory' (Ecker *et al.*, 2012: 21–22). This mismatching happens most effectively when the individual's experiences are drawn upon for disconfirming evidence. Where no existing experience can be drawn upon, the therapist can create an opportunity to 'test out' or generate a disconfirming experience. 'In other words, it must be experiential learning as distinct from conceptual, intellectual learning, though it may be accompanied by the latter' (Ecker *et al.*, 2012: 27). This process of mismatching and new learning is crucial to the change process. It is worth prolonging the mismatching experience either in the session or by using behavioural contracting to support the client in seeking confirmation of the mismatch between sessions. The most effective approach is likely to be a combination of in-session and between-session experiential learning.

Summary of the resolution process: activation and retrieval + emotional arousal + mismatching

Once this process has taken place, the symptom-producing implicit learning has effectively been uncoupled and deactivated.

It is likely that this process begins to dismantle the client's negative associative network (script system), and also challenges his script beliefs and/or protocol and promotes new relearning.

Memory reconsolidation-based therapeutic process

The following therapeutic process is based on the principles developed by Ecker *et al.* (2012), but has been adapted by the author to fit a TA therapeutic framework, in particular by integrating these with the redecision therapy methods of Goulding and Goulding (1979). This method also conforms to the principle of *systematic experiential disconfirmation*, as explained in this manual.

To develop a sense of the implicit learning, the therapist is advised to ponder some of the following questions:

- What implicit learning made it necessary for this client to have this symptom?
- How might this symptom protect the client in some way?
- What does the client feel s/he is not able to do?
- What implicit learning is blocking this client from doing [insert description of what s/he is not able to do]?
- If this client did [insert name of what s/he is prevented from doing], what would s/he fear would happen?
- If the client did not have this symptom, what prohibited action might s/he do?

Once the implicit learning is identified, the client's symptom 'makes sense'. Indeed, the symptom will always make sense and will always have a positive intention at its heart. In this respect, the symptom can be considered to be a 'little professor', or A1 strategy. The client can be asked to complete the following sentence: 'If I were to [thing s/he cannot do] I would feel/what would happen is. . .' It is not unusual for symptoms to be connected to several chunks of implicit learning, so it is wise for the therapist to be attentive to this possibility.

> **Case example**
>
> One of Alastair's presenting problems was a lack of confidence. It quickly became clear in therapy that he was concerned that if he was confident this would make him arrogant and therefore disliked by others. Therefore, Alastair's low confidence 'made sense' when considered from the perspective of Adult in the Child magical thinking, and protected him from rejection.[1]

It is important that the therapist is attentive to the client's level of emotional arousal during the process of uncovering the implicit learning connected to symptoms and presenting problems. Too little arousal and there will not be sufficient emotion to generate the level of implicit affective change needed, too much arousal and the client will feel overwhelmed and may well experience the emotion as retraumatising and reinforcing of the original learning. In order to enable optimal levels of emotional arousal to be sustained, the therapist is advised to ask the client frequently: 'How do you feel as you/I say that?' or 'How does it feel to be in touch with this?', and to introduce affect regulation strategies accordingly.

During the identification of the original implicit learning process, the therapist is advised to make use of heighteners (McNeel, 1976), empathic responses and evocative language to increase the client's level of emotional arousal to moderate levels. Unless the client is getting overwhelmed by emotion, the therapist must not rescue the client and must resist the urge to introduce permissions or strokes which counteract the emergence of the implicit learning. Such premature resolution effectively blocks the transformation in the implicit learning.

Once the implicit learning has been retrieved and brought into awareness, the therapist should write this down on an index card (in first-person language) and ask the client to read it to 'verify' its emotional significance, and then re-read it at least several times during the week between sessions (ideally daily), and in particular whenever symptoms arise. The intention here is to facilitate the process of bringing the implicit learning into awareness. If more than one statement is associated with the symptom, write them all down.

If we return to the example of Alastair, the index card read: '**If I** am confident and speak up **it will mean** I am arrogant and people will dislike me. **So I must never** feel confident **to make sure that does not happen.**'

As the client completes this homework, he will automatically (without any prompting from the therapist) start to question the validity of the implicit learning, or will start to notice examples in everyday life where someone 'disobeys' the implicit learning the client has carried and does not experience any negative consequence. This is an important part of the process, particularly as this challenging has been generated by the client, and not at the therapist's request. This means that the client 'owns' the challenge of this learning.

In the following session, the therapist checks in with the client what his experience of being in touch with the implicit learning has been like. It is helpful to ask the client to say the implicit learning statement out loud and to ask him to pay attention to (and express) what he experiences as he does so. The therapist can then ask the client if he has noticed any 'exceptions to the rule' or if he has 'found any evidence which refutes this learning'. If the client has, then the therapist can ask the client to elaborate on and describe this. Where the client does not describe any experiences which contradict his implicit learning, it can be useful for the therapist to be attentive to any experiences (or to refer to ones discussed in previous sessions) which might act as such evidence.

Following this, the therapist can take the process forward by using methods developed in redecision therapy as part of early scene work (Goulding & Goulding, 1979). The therapist can ask the client to visualise a scene (real or imagined) where the client experiences his symptom and then verbalise his implicit learning statement. It is helpful to use heighteners to increase the level of emotional arousal. Following this, the therapist creates a juxtaposition experience by asking the client to bring to mind the experiences which contradict the original implicit learning. Then, the therapist asks the client what it is like for him to have both sets of knowledge simultaneously. This process of simultaneous activation of old and new learning is a crucial part of the process and is important for the 'old' memory to be uncoupled and for the new learning to be integrated into memory. Effectively, the new short-circuits the old. Sometimes, clients will have done this process automatically in between sessions by reading their old implicit learning statement when experiencing some discomfort and noticing evidence which contradicts the old learning.

> *Case example*
>
> *Alastair had been re-reading his index card daily, and during a meeting at work noticed how several of his colleagues were very confident, and were also well liked by other members of the team. He also noticed that these people were not arrogant, but instead were self-assured whilst being respectful towards others. Alastair realised that it was possible to be confident and that this did not automatically equate to arrogance.*

The change can be verified by asking clients what their internal reaction is as they verbalise the old statement. They will tend to be either puzzled or amused, making statements such as 'Why on earth did I think that was true?' or 'It's a bit silly, isn't it, really.'

To reinforce the new implicit learning, or the redecision, the therapist is advised to write the new positive decision on a card for the client to take away and read throughout the week. The client will usually report that the symptom or problem has not recurred, or that his problematic emotional response has not been triggered. This will happen without any significant effort on the client's part. In cases where there is some residual symptom, this is indicative of another old implicit learning which is holding on to the symptom and which needs to be identified and replaced for the symptom to be resolved.

Note

1 See Widdowson (2014a) for a full description of the case of Alastair.

Part II
Therapy protocol

7 Structure of therapy and the initial phase of therapy

Introduction

Historically, many therapies have been investigated which have been based on the application of a standardised treatment manual. Once initial evidence for their efficacy has been established, these therapies are then tested in routine practice settings to determine their effectiveness in typical clinical settings where variables are not controlled. This present study has reversed this process, by first of all testing a therapy for effectiveness in routine practice and, through examining the process factors associated with positive outcome, has suggested a series of principles for practice which have then been developed into a treatment manual for efficacy testing.

A commonly discussed frustration amongst therapy researchers is the poor rate of take-up of research by therapists (Morrow-Bradley & Elliott, 1986). Many therapists cite that all too often the findings of psychotherapy research are not relevant to their clinical practice (Widdowson, 2012a). Arguably, the production of manuals which are developed from practice-based evidence may be more suitable for use in routine clinical practice and therefore have a higher rate of implementation.

Effectiveness of the manual

This treatment manual was developed from doctoral research conducted by the author. The research investigated the process and outcome of short-term transactional analysis (TA) psychotherapy for treatment of depression (Widdowson, 2013). Several cases from this research have been published, and have demonstrated that TA therapy can be an effective treatment for depression (Widdowson, 2012b, c, d, 2014a). This research investigated 'treatment as usual', and followed a naturalistic protocol with the type of clients who frequently present for therapy in community-based routine practice settings. TA therapy demonstrated effectiveness that was comparable to other therapies which are recognised as empirically supported for treatment of depression (Widdowson, 2013). These findings have been supported by the effectiveness studies conducted by van Rijn, Wild and Moran (2011), who found that brief TA therapy (up to 12 sessions) was as effective as brief integrative counselling psychology in reducing depression and anxiety symptoms. This finding was confirmed in a subsequent study (van Rijn & Wild, 2013), which found that TA therapy was as effective as gestalt therapy, integrative counselling psychology and person-centred therapy for depression and anxiety symptoms and global distress. Their analysis included a benchmarking strategy which demonstrated that TA had a recovery rate comparable to cognitive-behavioural therapy for anxiety and depression symptoms.

This manual has been subjected to preliminary testing using case study research, and has demonstrated effectiveness in preliminary trials (Widdowson, 2014a). It is currently undergoing further testing, the results of which will be published as soon as they are available.

The principles for practice and guidelines in this manual are based on the author's doctoral research, and as such are research-based. A range of evidence-based best-practice principles and guidance taken from the wider psychotherapy research literature has also been incorporated into this manual. It is anticipated that this will increase the effectiveness of the protocol.

To conclude, the existing evidence supports this treatment manual and suggests the methods outlined are as effective as other therapies. As this manual is based on and integrates numerous methods and practices which have been demonstrated to be effective in other trials, there is reason to anticipate that the results from using this manual will be positive.

Participation in active testing of this manual

Users of this manual are strongly encouraged to participate in active testing of this manual by conducting systematic case-study research relating to its implementation. Effectiveness and efficacy trials are also encouraged. Please contact the author for guidance and support relating to how you can develop the evidence base for this manual.

Clients for whom the methods in this manual are suitable

This protocol has been specifically developed for adult clients with depression who have a score of higher than 50 on Global Assessment of Functioning (GAF) scale of the *Diagnostic and Statistical Manual of Mental Disorder*, fourth edition (DSM-IV) (American Psychiatric Association, 1994). The GAF scale is a subjective rating scale where the individual's level of overall functioning is assigned a numerical value between 0 and 100. A score of 50 indicates either serious symptoms or serious impairment in occupational, social or educational functioning. Readers who are not familiar with the GAF are advised to search online for resources about how to assess and score a client using this scale. Clients who score below 50 on the GAF scale are likely to need medication in conjunction with therapy, and should be advised to see their general practitioner. When clients score lower than 40, they are likely to need psychiatric/medical input. In such cases clients should be advised to obtain the agreement of their medical practitioner to continue with therapy.

Specifically, this manual has been designed for the treatment of mild to moderate depression, although the research this manual was based upon demonstrated that TA had some effectiveness for more severe variants of depression (Widdowson, 2012b, c).

The treatment specified in this manual is also likely to be helpful for anxiety disorders, including panic disorder, generalised anxiety disorder, social anxiety, health anxiety and obsessive-compulsive disorder. Initial testing suggests that this manual is also suitable for clients with comorbid anxiety (Widdowson, 2012d, 2014). At present this treatment protocol has not been tested for its suitability for clients with comorbid posttraumatic stress disorder or eating disorders. As this manual is developed and tested by practitioners using it in routine practice, it is anticipated that further data will emerge regarding its effectiveness with a range of comorbid disorders.

Clients for whom this manual is not recommended

This protocol is not recommended for people experiencing current psychotic illness or those with active drug or alcohol addictions. Clients with a GAF score of less than 50 are likely to need a more intensive and longer therapy than the treatment described in this manual. Also, clients with this level of impairment may require medical attention and drug treatment to manage their depression.

Response to treatment and outcome indicators

Research suggests that the largest gains in psychotherapy for depression take place within the first 8–10 sessions, and at least 18 sessions are needed for treatment response in chronic depression (Cuijpers *et al.*, 2010). As a rule of thumb, if a client has not responded to therapy as determined by improvement on outcome measures by session 12, then consider referral for medication or to another therapist or type of therapy. Similarly, if a client with chronic depression or dysthymia has not responded by session 25, then consider onward referral.

Perhaps the exception to this is the case where there is significant characterological pathology/comorbid personality disorder and where the client is happy to continue in therapy. This is because the presence of comorbid personality disorders significantly complicates treatment and increases length of therapy. In this instance, it is advisable to bear the general rule of thumb in mind and seek supervision to discuss the implications of the client staying in therapy and the potential for the depression to improve with longer term in therapy. In line with the findings of Kopta, Howard, Lowry and Beutler (1994), a response time of up to 1 year may be necessary to see improvement in chronic and characterological problems.

Use this manual flexibly!

This manual is not intended to be used in a rigid or prescriptive manner. A skilful and effective therapist can distinguish between times when it is useful to follow the manual and times when the manual can be forgotten in favour of staying with 'where the client is at'. Examples of such times include responding to extremely difficult life circumstances, such as trauma or bereavement. At these times, the therapist is probably wise to suspend using the manual for the time being and instigate a temporary contract with the client to help support him through the difficult time and help him manage his feelings effectively, and resume using the manual when things are more settled. Of course, therapeutic input at such times can be extremely transformative and helpful and can result in significant and lasting change. Nevertheless, therapists are advised to trust their therapeutic judgement and intuition and to use this manual in a flexible and responsive manner.

> The therapist is a disciplined improvisational artist, not a manual-driven technician. 'Therapy' consists of engaging in an ongoing co-constructive dialogue with the client. As the dialogue progresses, specific techniques may emerge as relevant at given points, but these cannot be specified or anticipated in advance. The important skills of the therapist are the ability to (a) empathically enter the world of the client and engage in a genuine 'meeting of persons,' (b) engage in co-constructive dialogue, and (c) be exquisitely sensitive to what's happening 'now' and to the potential for productive interaction and emergent new directions in each moment.
>
> (Bohart, O'Hara & Leitner, 1998: 145)

It is recognised that

> different therapists can practice in widely different ways, use widely different techniques at given choice points, and still be effective if they are implementing certain fundamental humanistic principles. Thus, uniformity of therapist behavior is neither expected nor desired. What is desirable is that therapists individually 'be themselves' in their own idiosyncratic 'healing ways.' Therapists will not necessarily even be consistent from one moment to the next, as they flexibly adjust to the emerging flow of interaction between themselves and the client.
>
> (Bohart et al., 1998: 145)

General format of delivery

The general format of this protocol is based on 16 sessions of weekly individual therapy. Therapy sessions are the usual 50–60 minutes in duration.

Supervision recommendations

As this protocol is based on short-term therapy, it is recommended that therapists have supervision on their client work at a minimum rate of once per month and, ideally, once every 2 weeks. In particular, the therapist is strongly advised to have supervision on each client before the third therapy session. This is to ensure that the therapist has some supervisory input during the crucial initial stage of therapy and to ensure that this treatment protocol is suitable for the client. The recommended minimum supervision time allocated for each client on this protocol is 15 minutes at each supervision session. Therapists are advised to take audio recordings of sessions regularly to supervision.

Use of adjunct treatment approaches

Medication (see Chapter 10)

Many clients who seek psychotherapy for depression have already been prescribed medication by their physician, although it is also very common for people to try therapy prior to medication. A lot of people have a very negative view of medication, and may see that taking medication somehow means that they have 'failed'.

The use of combined therapy and drug treatment for severe depression has been demonstrated to have a high level of efficacy. The efficacy of medication for mild or moderate forms of depression is questionable. Within the UK, the National Institute for Health and Care Excellence (NICE) guidelines indicate that psychotherapy is the treatment of choice for mild or moderate forms of depression (National Collaborating Centre for Mental Health, 2009).

During the course of therapy, some clients wish to discontinue or reduce the dosage of their medication. It is recommended that this does not take place until the client has achieved a clinically significant response, i.e. no longer has scores within the clinical ranges on the outcome measures. It is wise to continue therapy for a while during the medication withdrawal period to ensure that the client does not deteriorate back into depression. Furthermore, dose reductions or complete cessation of medication need to be done under medical supervision. Clients who express their desire to reduce or stop their medication must be advised to speak with the prescribing doctor before adjusting the dosage. When medication dosages are altered during therapy, it can be hard to tell what is causing the effect; therefore it is advisable to suggest to clients that they wait a few weeks until the main part of the therapy is completed.

Use of couples or family interventions

Although it is not a standard part of this protocol (which is based on an individual therapy format), research seems to suggest that the *positive* involvement of partners and family members in someone's treatment can have a *positive* effect. Research has also shown that high levels of conflict or hostility within a client's family can be predictive of poorer response to treatment (Chambless & Steketee, 1999; Zinbarg, Lee & Yoon, 2007). It can be helpful for partners and family members to learn positive, healthy ways of interacting and how to avoid inadvertently reinforcing or supporting the client's depression. Also, the communication between clients and their partners can be facilitated in a session with the therapist and this may have a positive effect on the relationship. If clients report poor relationship, or request a couples session, it is possible that the therapist can do this for a maximum of two sessions before resuming individual work. In this matter, therapists are advised to follow their own clinical judgement and the advice of their supervisor.

General session structure

Establishing a structure for sessions is helpful, and it is useful to do this from the initial sessions and to keep to a similar format throughout the therapy. Clients will quickly pick up on the pattern. This is helpful to prevent the therapy from drifting and being unproductive.

Ask client to complete outcome measures

Some time during the initial session, the therapist should invite the client to complete several outcome measures. It is useful to explain to the client that this is to enable the therapist and client to get a sense of 'where the client is at right now', and also to monitor the client's progress through therapy. Explain the different measures used to the client and provide brief instructions on how to complete them. Some clients feel inhibited completing these in the therapist's presence, so it can be helpful to let the client know you are going to leave the room for a few minutes whilst she completes the forms. When you return, ask the client about what it is was like for her to complete the forms and ask if she has any reflections on the process of filling out the forms or any questions. In subsequent sessions, it is recommended that the therapist leaves the weekly outcome measures, a pen and something to rest on, such as a clipboard, ready for the client and as the client arrives, ask her to complete the forms. The completion of such forms does not take much time and it is possible to review the client's responses quickly at the beginning of the session and to incorporate data from the measures into the content of the session (see section on screening, assessment and progress monitoring using outcome measures, below).

Initial mood check, establish contact

Begin sessions by establishing contact with the client and checking the client's mood by using a gentle, opening enquiry, such as; 'So, how are you today?' or 'How have you been since our last session?' This may also give an initial indicator of the client's progress.

Session bridging

It can be helpful to support a sense of continuity between sessions. To some extent this is achieved by the opening question of 'How have you been since our last session?' It can also be useful to ask the client: 'What was most important for you about last session?' or 'What did you take away from our last sessions that has been useful to you?'

Other possibilities include:

'Last time you were quite upset; I was wondering how you felt after the session.'

'You made some big shifts/gained some important insights last time – how has it been for you since?'

'Is there anything from last session that you want to follow up on today?'

Sometimes clients can't remember the previous session. If you notice this as a pattern, or if your client experiences problems with memory and concentration, it is useful to suggest strategies to help her remember, such as making notes during or at the end of the session or even suggesting that the client may audio-record the session. This may support the client to form a coherent narrative of her experience (Stuthridge, 2010).

Identifying goals for session and session contract

Allow the client to 'get comfortable' and settled into the session for a few minutes, and then establish a session contract or session goals. This can be done gently by asking: 'Is there anything you would like to focus on today?' Alternatively, this can be done by picking up on the content of the client's discussion by checking: 'Is this what you want to focus on today?'

If the client goes into 'story telling', gently interrupt. Say: 'I just want to pause you there. You seem to have got stuck into this story. I'm wondering if this is what you want to focus on today?' If the client says yes, say: 'How shall we structure that? How can we make it so that doing so will be helpful to you and in line with your goals for therapy?'

If the client says that she doesn't know what to focus on, ask: 'What feels most important for you right now?' or 'Are there any specific obstacles or issues which you feel are important to address as part of your recovery?'

If the client is really unsure where to focus, the therapist may allow the session to continue for a little while, until the discussion suggests a particular issue. At which point, the therapist can ask: 'Do you want to focus on this for a little while?'

If the client repeatedly reports that she hasn't got anything she wants to discuss, it can be useful to raise this with her, and check that she is OK with how the therapy is working. The therapist may decide to suggest to the client that she spend some time before sessions or throughout the week thinking about what she wants to cover or get out of the forthcoming session. Clients often find it helpful to keep a notepad handy and to jot down ideas as they come to them throughout the week.

The therapist can suggest a focus for the session if the client doesn't offer one. In such cases, the therapist might raise issues he thinks are important to discuss

84 *Therapy protocol*

or may return to items from previous sessions or matters he has highlighted as potential avenues for exploration in his notes. Getting into the habit of regularly checking the client's treatment plan and reviewing it immediately prior to sessions can be helpful with this.

Occasionally, clients raise a very long list of items they want to discuss in the session. In this instance, the therapist can see if there is a 'theme' which runs across the items, or can explain to the client that it might not be possible to cover the whole list and ask which items they want to prioritise.

It is important that the therapy stays focused and has some structure, but that this structure is flexible enough to be responsive to client needs and to allow the client to deal with day-to-day problems. Finally, do not be rigid with session contracts – it is fine to change direction and recontract during the session.

Review of homework completion

To maintain the emphasis on an active client approach to therapy, the therapist is advised to follow up on the client's homework completion. Straightforward questions such as 'How did you get on with the homework from last week?' are sufficient. Take time to discuss the client's experiences fully, and take note of any difficulties. This can be useful to consider when discussing future homework tasks.

Empathic enquiry

The therapist should remain empathic throughout the therapy. There are two interventions which are correct and suitable for almost all situations: empathy and enquiry.

Attending to the therapeutic relationship

The therapist must remain attentive to the overall therapeutic relationship and addressing any unrepaired alliance ruptures. This is crucial to the effectiveness of the therapy, as unrepaired ruptures will not only adversely affect the therapeutic relationship, but they are also likely to reinforce some aspect of the client's script. At the point of an alliance rupture, there is scope to disconfirm aspects of the client's script and to support the client in making new meaning of the event.

Covering session contract items

The therapist stance should be empathic, balanced with appropriate levels of challenge, and promoting collaboration. The therapist should be aware of the use of potency (Steiner, 1968), protection and permission (Crossman, 1966) throughout, and is advised to make considerable use of enquiry to gather information and promote client awareness.

As you listen to the client, see if TA theory can be used to make sense of or understand the problems he discusses. The therapist may gently intervene, if relevant, or may opt to wait to find out more information or to allow the issue to unfold further.

If the client moves off from the original session contract, quickly recontract by saying something similar to: 'I notice that you've moved on to this. Do you want to shift the session focus to this for a while?'

Sometimes new items emerge towards the end of the session and there is not enough time to explore them fully. In this case, ask the client if you can come back to that another time, or suggest that the client discuss the issue at the start of the next session and make a note of the item. It is worth raising this in subsequent sessions to see if the client wants to include that as part of their session contract.

Summarising and carrying items forward

As and when a piece of work feels complete, or at the end of the session, it can be helpful to ask clients what they are taking away from that discussion or what they are going to do differently. Similarly, at the end of the session, ask clients what they are taking away from the session, or what the most important parts of the session were. Ask if there is anything they are going to do differently and briefly run through any homework/behavioural contracts agreed during the session.

If there are items which are unfinished or which have arisen during the course of the session, ask the client if he is OK with discussing them another time, and make a note of what they are. It is important that the therapist does come back to these items, even if the client does not raise them.

Using process measures

The regular and routine use of process measures is an integral part of this treatment protocol. It can be very useful to allocate a few minutes at the end of the session for the client to complete a process measure, such as Helpful Aspects of Therapy, the Session Rating Scale, Working Alliance Inventory or the Session Evaluation Questionnaire. The use of such process measures can reveal considerable amounts of information which would not otherwise have been raised in the session, and can highlight any strain or rupture in the therapeutic relationship.

It is useful for the therapist to have a number of these available, and to select one or more according to which she thinks the client might find most useful or according to her own preferences. If the therapist wants to use a very quick and simple form, the Session Rating Scale takes less than a minute to complete and can be easily interpreted from sight. Where process measures are used in the session, the therapist can either allow a few minutes to discuss the client's responses, or can score these after the session and, where relevant, come back to them in the next session.

Some clients prefer to take process measures away with them to complete after the session. It is fine to do this. In this case, ask the client for the completed form at the beginning of the next session and do a simple visual scan of the responses to see if anything stands out which may need addressing. If the client takes the form away but doesn't bring it back, ask if the form highlighted any problems or difficulties with the therapy or in the relationship between you.

Managing distress

If the session has been particularly emotional for the client or the client is very distressed, the therapist has to make a judgement as to whether it is in the client's interests to stay with her feelings (for example, where the client usually tends to avoid or shut down feelings, or where the distress will be a motivator, or where the distress seems to be a breakthrough of a primary emotion), or whether some time needs to be allocated to get the client grounded and soothed before leaving. It is useful to explain to the client what the therapist's thoughts are on this, and to explain why the therapist thinks this way. In situations where the client is leaving a session in a state of high emotion, ask what she is going to do to manage her feelings after the session.

Clients who are prone to high levels of emotional distress may ask whether they can contact their therapist between sessions. Generally, this is to be discouraged. Karen Maroda (2010) reminds us that when we go into a session with a client, we are psychologically prepared, whereas, between sessions, we are usually going about our business and so may not have the time or emotional energy available to provide support for our clients reliably, and that frequent between-session contact may be counterproductive to the therapeutic process. In particular, she warns that an overly empathic stance to a distressed client on the telephone will likely lead that person into deeper distress. Maroda also highlights how the dominance of e-mail as a mode of communication means that clients may e-mail instead of (or as well as) telephone their therapists. She advises clients that she will read all e-mails sent to her between sessions but will not reply and will respond to them in the next session. My own preference is to advise clients that they may contact me during normal office hours between sessions for the purposes of scheduling appointments. When clients have a concern about 'needing' between-session contact, my experience is that they are usually highly anxious, and that addressing their anxiety in sessions is likely to be more effective than between-session contact. Also, some clients need to learn how to distinguish between an 'emergency' and a state of chronic distress. In such cases, therapeutic work which focuses on affect regulation is indicated.

Reinforcing change

If any major breakthroughs have occurred during the session, it is worth explaining to the client that the following few hours after the session are important in maintaining and reinforcing these changes. Ask clients what they are going to do (or not do) to keep the momentum going and to make use of this window of opportunity.

Responding to fear of change

Some clients report feeling afraid of changing or, more specifically, feeling afraid of changing and 'becoming a selfish, horrible person'. In these situations, clients can be reassured that people going through therapy will usually become *more* empathic and develop a greater sense of appropriate interpersonal boundaries. Of course, improved boundaries can mean that your client becomes more assertive, and may encounter resistance to his change process from his family and friends. This needs to be handled sensitively, and the client can be supported to work out for himself if his changes are reasonable or not. Other concerns regarding fear of change relate to a general fear of the unknown. This is perhaps more likely to be an issue for anxious clients, who tend to struggle with tolerating uncertainty and ambiguity. Developing such tolerance is indeed a useful therapeutic focus with clients who experience anxiety.

The initial phase

The initial phase of therapy covers the first one to three sessions, and is focused on:

1 client role induction for therapy
2 conducting an assessment of the client
3 building the therapeutic alliance
4 problem formulation, establishing the goals and contract of the therapy
5 promoting insight and understanding into the nature and origin of depression
6 TA diagnosis, and treatment planning (case formulation)
7 motivation and expectation enhancement.

This covers the tasks, goals and bonds of the therapy, thus building the working alliance.

Firstly, it is important to highlight that the therapist should remain empathic throughout the therapy, including from the very first meeting with the client. Be sensitive but probing in your use of enquiry. Your stance should convey the three Ps of protection, permission and potency (Crossman, 1966; Steiner, 1968; Widdowson, 2010) to the client.

Role induction: setting the scene

There is evidence that clients who engage in pretherapy preparation regarding what to expect from treatment and their role may have a better response to therapy. Also, clients who have a realistic idea of what to expect (including being prepared for therapy to involve experiencing difficult and painful feelings) are less likely to drop out and more likely to use sessions productively (Constantino, Ametrano & Greenberg, 2012; Constantino, Glass, Arnkoff, Ametrano & Smith, 2011; Widdowson, 2012b, c, d, 2013).

Preparation can take place by giving clients the 'getting the most out of therapy' document, which has been designed for this purpose (see Appendix 1). It is advisable that the therapist also raise the issue of expectations about the therapy process and roles with the client during intake to clarify any misconceptions and promote a collaborative stance. This can be done quite simply by asking the client: 'What do you imagine happens in therapy? What are your expectations about what we do here?'

Suggested wordings

> There's a good chance you will make considerable improvement during this therapy, and possibly even completely resolve your depression in 16 sessions. One of the major determining factors is how much effort and work you are prepared to put in between sessions. I can't stress enough how helpful it is for you to be really active in your recovery process. The problem may be if you're depressed, you won't feel much like doing anything, and might feel hopeless and that doing something won't make any difference, so think it is pointless. That's part of the trap of depression. If you wait until you want to do something, there is a good chance you won't improve very much. The point is that you actively have to make changes, even if you don't feel like it. With a bit of effort, you'll start to feel better and so making these changes will get easier. It certainly won't be easy at first, but it will pay off within a couple of weeks.

> Therapy sessions are only 1 hour a week, and this represents about 1% of all your waking hours. What you do with the remaining 99% of your time, or 167 hours, is critical to the success of the therapy. To get the most out of the sessions, you will need to be really active in doing things which will help your recovery every single day. At a bare minimum, I would say that you'd need to put in at least 20 minutes each day. If you can put in between 40 and 60 minutes each day that would be even better. If you don't have a lot of free time, then make sure that the time you do put in is good quality. That means putting in a lot of effort into getting the most out of these additional activities.

In order to give the client some preparation about the use of therapeutic enquiry, a statement such as the following can be helpful:

> I'm going to ask lots of questions, some of which might seem like they have an obvious answer, but it's important that I don't make any assumptions, so please do bear with me. Sometimes I might ask questions that I've already asked before, but am doing so in order to deepen where we go with a particular issue at that moment in time, or to connect up particular aspects of your experience. It can seem a little strange at first, but you will soon get the hang of it.

Preparing the client for future sessions

Most people find it helpful to keep a notepad handy to jot down ideas as they come to them throughout the week for things they want to cover in sessions. If you haven't got one, I'd recommend getting a writing pad as soon as you can. Alternatively, you can use the notes app on your phone. Some people find that suits them better.

Problem identification in initial sessions

Ask the client what are his presenting problems, main symptoms and reasons for coming to therapy. Also, ask the client about what his main, consistent emotional experiences are. For example, does he feel down, depressed, anxious, guilty, ashamed, angry or irritable? Ask how these feelings affect him on a day-to-day level and how these feelings are affecting his functioning. For instance, he may find that these feelings limit him in some way, or prevent him from engaging in certain activities.

At this stage, the therapist should facilitate the client in developing an internal focus for problem identification; that is, framing his problems in terms of internal changes he can make. This can be difficult, especially with clients who have particularly bad external circumstances (for example, poverty). Nevertheless, it should be emphasised that the therapy cannot change external circumstances, but can help a client to feel more active and engaged in the world and manage things better. This in turn may help the client actively to change his external circumstances.

Ask the client what strategies he has used so far for managing his feelings and for problem solving. 'I've tried everything' is usually not accurate, or might mean 'I've tried lots of things, but only half-heartedly and only for 5 minutes'. Ask if the client thinks that the strategies he has been using have been completely or partially successful or not. It is possible that strategies have intermittent effect – that is, they work sometimes, but not at others. It is helpful to find out what circumstances or situations they work best in.

Initial contract

Contracting is a central part of TA therapy. At the outset the contract should be fairly loose and flexible and focused on the tasks of therapy, until sufficient exploration has taken place in order to generate a full and final treatment contract. The therapist can suggest the following as an initial opening contract:

> I think there are a number of things we need to address as part of this process. The first is looking at what is currently going on for you, both internally and in your day-to-day life that have contributed to you getting depressed. As we do that, we'll no doubt come across things which you can change. Another area we'll need to look at is what are the things that have made you

vulnerable to having depression in the first place and where did they come from? It's like finding the Achilles heel and sorting that out. How does that sound to you?

Or:

What I propose is that we meet for a few weeks to see how we get on. We can explore and start to understand what's going on for you and how you got to be where you are at. I will probably ask a lot of questions, which might seem a bit obvious, but it's important I don't make any assumptions and instead focus on your perspective. Along the way, we might find areas you can experiment with or find new ways of doing things in order to start the change process off. How does that sound to you?

Both of these contracts address the tasks of therapy and suggest an initial way forward for the therapy.

In relation to contracting for therapy goals, the therapist can also use the client's presenting problems as the basis for an initial contract. For example:

OK, so what I'm taking from all of this and want to check out with you is that you want the main focus of the therapy to be on helping you overcome depression. You've also mentioned that you feel nervous in social situations and haven't been handling things well. Is that right?

Allen and Allen (1997) offer an interesting constructionist perspective on wording interventions, which they describe as 'transformative dialogue' (p. 95). They recommend referring to problems in the past tense, and using wording which suggests expectations of change, such as: 'So you've come to therapy to work out how to lay the past to rest'. They emphasise that such positive dialogue helps clients to move out of their existing negative and limiting narrative into one which is more flexible and adaptive.

Initial case formulation

It is vital that the therapist rapidly develops a sense of the client's core script themes, in particular script beliefs about the self and beliefs about others.

Screening, assessment and progress monitoring using outcome measures

There are many outcome measures available which can be used both for screening and assessment purposes, to monitor client progress throughout therapy and to provide evidence which can be used for the purposes of evaluation of the therapy and also for research. There are dozens of outcome measures: here I present three which are easy to score and which yield clinically useful information. They are

CORE Outcome Measure (CORE-OM), Patient Health Questionnaire-9 (PHQ-9) and Generalised Anxiety Disorder-7 (GAD-7). All are freely available on the internet. It would be useful to download them before proceeding with the remainder of this section.

The measures take the form of client-completed questionnaires. It is recommended that all new clients are routinely screened using these measures at the very first session and at the beginning of each session for at least the first six sessions. At a bare minimum, the measures should be used at least once every four sessions. The initial score provides a baseline score together with a means of monitoring progress, and subsequent use of the measures can give the therapist and client a clear indicator as to whether the therapy is on track or not. When the therapy is going well, the client's scores will drop, which can give the therapist and client confidence that the therapy is working. Where scores deteriorate or do not improve, then this indicates that the therapy needs to be adjusted in some way to address the client's problems better.

Although the three measures discussed below have good validity and are useful for screening, assessment and monitoring purposes, it is important to bear in mind that they are not a substitute for clinical diagnosis and ongoing assessment and monitoring of the client.

CORE Outcome Measure (CORE-OM)

The CORE-OM has four subscales. These are: four items relating to subjective well-being (W); 12 items relating to problems/symptoms (P); 12 items relating to life functioning (F); and six items relating to risk/harm (R).

Full scoring

To calculate the clinical score, add up the numbers for each question and then divide the total number by the number of completed questions (assuming the client completed all items, this will be 34). Then multiply this number by 10 (this will shift the decimal point one space to the right) to give the CORE clinical score. For example, a score of 1.8 becomes a clinical score of 18. Working out the score for each subscale is not necessary, although you are free to work out the subscale scores if you wish.

Recommendation for a therapy priority procedure

When scoring the client's CORE-OM forms, make a note of the items for which the client has scored 3 or 4 using key words on a sticky note which can then be attached to the front of the client's session notes. As these items are ones which are most problematic to the client, they can be considered to be 'therapy priorities', so it is useful to raise them with the client at the first opportunity as something to discuss in the session. This can be done by saying something such as: 'I have read through your scores and notice that there are some issues which seem to be giving you a lot of trouble. Is it OK if we talk through these right now to see if there is anything we can do to help you manage these better?'

CORE clinical score severity bands

0–10: Healthy/non-clinical

10–14: Low level/subclinical

15–19: Mild

20–24: Moderate

25–29: Moderate-severe

30+: Severe

Patient Health Questionnaire-9 (PHQ-9)

The PHQ-9 is a nine-item self-report tool which measures depressive symptoms. The items are based on the DSM-IV criteria for major depressive disorder. As a measure it has good validity and reliability and is simple and easy to administer, score and interpret. The client is given the questionnaire and asked to circle the number on each scale which best describes how things have been over the past 2 weeks. The scores are simply added together to give an overall score (Table 7.1).

Generalised Anxiety Disorder-7 (GAD-7)

As the name suggests, the GAD-7 is a measure based on the DSM-IV diagnostic criteria for generalised anxiety disorder. In practice, it encompasses the main

Table 7.1 Severity bands and treatment indications with Patient Health Questionnaire-9 (PHQ-9)

PHQ-9 score	Depression severity	Proposed treatment actions
0–4	None	None
5–9	Mild	'Watchful waiting' Initiate psychotherapy
10–14	Moderate	Initiate psychotherapy. Consider medical referral for pharmacotherapy
15–19	Moderately severe	Immediate initiation of psychotherapy. Discuss option of medical referral for pharmacotherapy with client
20–27	Severe	Immediate referral for initiation of combined pharmacotherapy and psychotherapy. If severe impairment or poor response to therapy within 4 weeks, request psychiatric referral

symptoms of anxiety and can be used to measure a client's anxiety levels and has a good level of correspondence to other anxiety disorders.

The GAD-7 is scored very simply by adding the scores for each item together. This will yield a score of between 0 and 21.

GAD-7 severity bands

    0–5: Mild anxiety

    6–10: Moderate anxiety

    11–15: Moderately severe anxiety

    15–21: Severe anxiety

Realistically, a score of up to 3 is not a cause for concern and it may be related to transient or situational stressors. For scores in the 1–3 range I recommend 'watchful waiting', as a score this low is unlikely to cause any significant distress or impairment to the client. It is worth discussing any scores above 6 with the client to find out if she thinks that the score represents a transient or situational response, or if this is indicative of her more usual state of anxiety. Scores over 10 are clinically important and worthy of further investigation.

Outcome monitoring criteria for CORE, PHQ-9 and GAD-7

Check the client's progress using these outcome measures at least once in sessions 2–5, and ideally every session. Where scores worsen by 2.5 points or more, there may be problems in the therapy, which could indicate that the client is at risk of deterioration or of dropping out of therapy prematurely. In such cases, it is recommended that you seek supervision at the earliest opportunity to discuss how you are working with the client. Also, it is fruitful to ask the client how she is feeling about therapy and if she feels that your approach is working for her or if she would like you to take a different approach to her therapy. Sometimes clients experience a temporary worsening as they come into greater contact with their emotions. Your client will know if the intensification of the symptoms is a part of the healing process or not, and it is wise to listen to her and to change how you are working if she feels that the increase in distress is not helpful.

Recording client scores

It is useful to develop a simple method of recording the client's scores in a way that is easily viewed to see progress over time. This can be done using a simple table format. It is easy to keep the table in the client's notes, and this enables the therapist quickly to see any progression or deterioration over time.

Motivation

Assessing aspects of motivation

There are several indicators the therapist can use to assess the client's motivation for therapy. These include:

- psychological mindedness (see Widdowson, 2010);
- capacity for reflection, introspection and honesty (frankness);
- willingness to participate in therapy actively;
- curiosity and interest in developing self-understanding;
- realistic expectations of therapy and realistic goals;
- willingness to make reasonable sacrifices as part of the process of change (Sifneos, 1980).

Motivation and commitment

It is vital that clients feel motivated to change and committed to the therapy (Woollams & Brown, 1979). This gives the change process the very best chance of success from the start; indeed, if the client is not motivated, therapy is unlikely to be successful. It is normal for clients to feel ambivalent or uncertain about the process of change. Realising how much needs to be done, or how much work needs to be put into making changes, can feel very daunting. The material below draws on Motivational Interviewing (Miller & Rollnick, 2002), which has been demonstrated to be an effective approach and a useful adjunct to the initial phases of therapy for many different problems and disorders. It can be helpful to draw on these principles periodically throughout the therapy: the entire change process needs consistently high levels of motivation and commitment to succeed.

Five principles from Motivational Interviewing

Express empathy

Motivational Interviewing draws heavily on the work of Carl Rogers and person-centred counselling. Essentially, the view is that the client needs to experience the therapist as empathic in order to promote the change process. Clients feel that changing is hard, and usually when they come to a therapist they are feeling stuck and in need of professional help. They often feel afraid and vulnerable and embarrassed. It can be helpful for the therapist to let the client know that such feelings are very common and normal and are nothing to worry about. This often very quickly puts the client at ease. An empathic, non-judgemental therapist will help to create a positive climate for change and help establish a positive, collaborative working alliance. The therapist needs to ensure that she is using all of her basic listening skills and conveying to the client that she is making a real attempt to understand the client and his situation.

Avoid argument

Sometimes therapists inadvertently contribute to resistance by attempting to persuade the client into changing or arguing with him by talking him into a different perspective. By accepting the client's ambivalence towards change, and offering new perspectives that the client is free to accept or reject, the therapist avoids getting caught in unhelpful arguments, or games.

Support self-efficacy

Having some self-belief that one is capable of making changes has been demonstrated to play an important part in the amount of effort a client will put into the change process. Clients who come to therapy – especially those who are depressed – often feel demoralised and hopeless. They often feel lacking in any sense of personal effectiveness and that their attempts will be useless. By supporting the client's self-belief and ability to change without being overly cheerful or unrealistic, the therapist can gently support a client to make changes. One way of doing this is to highlight areas of the client's life which are going well, or to draw his attention to past successes or challenges he has dealt with effectively and to indicate that you believe that the client already has the resources he needs to change. For example,

> It sounds as though you've had a tough couple of years, one way or another, and even though it probably doesn't feel like you've handled it that well, you've managed to get by and keep going, even when you've really felt like giving in. This tells me that you have more of a fighting spirit than I think you're giving yourself credit for. It also tells me that things can indeed be better for you.

There is a good amount of research to suggest that setting clear, small, achievable goals helps enhance feelings of self-efficacy. The goal-setting process overall can be helpful, but when small goals are set, the client can be asked: 'Do you think you can do that?'

Roll with the resistance

Clients generally feel some ambivalence about the change process. It is not unusual for clients to feel afraid of the level of work they may have to put in, which can inhibit their engagement with therapy. Also, the Child ego state may perceive the therapy as representing a threat to the continuity of its sense of self. It is fair to say that many clients want things to be different, but also do not want to have to change. It is useful to raise this with clients and let them know that as a result of therapy they are likely to enjoy a greater sense of alignment with their 'best self'.

Develop discrepancy

Clients are often attached to the strategies and methods they have been using to help manage their feelings, even if these are problematic or contributing to the problem. Also, clients can feel afraid of the consequences of changing. There is always a balancing act between the argument in favour of changing and the argument against. With developing discrepancy, the therapist helps the client develop the argument in favour of changing, but also acknowledges the other side which is reluctant to do so. It is not unusual for clients to feel daunted by the amount of work that is involved in changing, yet overlook how much energy their problems are taking up. By highlighting this, the effort involved in making changes can seem less daunting. This might take the form of normalising how they are feeling, such as:

> Given how depressed you've been feeling, I think it is only to be expected that it might seem like too much of an up-hill struggle. It's as if the depression has clouded your thinking, leaving you feeling deflated and hopeless. Of course, that type of thinking is common in depression and the trick is to learn how not to treat such thoughts as if they were facts, and to see that change is possible, even if someone is in the darkest of places.

Building the therapeutic relationship

A strong therapeutic relationship is essential to effective TA psychotherapy and indeed is a vital prerequisite for all effective therapy (Horvath, Del Re, Flückiger Symonds, 2011; Norcross, 2011).

Humanistic foundations of TA

The philosophy of TA proposes that the therapeutic relationship should be built on the formation of a relationship grounded in an 'I'm OK – You're OK' life position (Berne, 1972; Stewart & Joines, 2012). Firstly, this places the humanistic stance of valuing the fundamental humanity of the client right into the heart of therapy and in what it means to practise as a transactional analyst. Secondly, it guides the therapist in her manner of relating to the client. Another humanistic assumption at the heart of TA is the view that human nature is essentially oriented towards growth, development and health. Within TA theory, this constructive drive towards growth is referred to as *physis* (Berne, 1972).

Holding on to this stance can be profoundly challenging. Many severely depressed people cannot see that they have any worth or value. This can become part of the transference–countertransference matrix, thus shaking the therapist's humanistic stance. Holding on to the belief in clients' humanity can also be challenging when they describe shocking or unpleasant things they have done. Sometimes these can be held up by clients as 'evidence' that they are a bad person. Here, the therapist can help the client to acknowledge these actions, and see beyond them to a person in pain who is worthy of fundamental human compassion.

Emotional functions of the therapeutic relationship

It is absolutely crucial that the client experiences the therapy as a safe space. In experiencing the therapy as a safe, supportive space where it is not only permissible

Structure and initial phase of therapy 97

but encouraged to explore their thoughts, feelings and way of relating in an exploratory dialogue, clients will often 'hear' their own process (sometimes for the first time) and begin to re-evaluate their thoughts, feelings, behaviours and relational style. This supports the development of the client's 'observing self', which can operate in tandem with his 'experiencing self'. The observing self can be considered as a function of the Adult ego state which promotes change and growth in therapy.

The therapist's patient exploration of the client's emotional reactions to past and current events deepens the client's level of processing and allows the therapy gradually to 'go deeper' and contact pain held in his Child ego state, and also enables the client to identify and re-evaluate his script. The empathic relationship facilitates the expression of emotions which have been deeply held within the Child and thus promotes deconfusion. By being attentive to the client's gradually changing emotional state in the session, and in exploring his emotional reactions to past and present events, the therapist promotes a reflective stance in the client. The therapist's use of affect-regulating interventions promotes the restructuring of the client's ego states.

Part of the experience of therapy is that clients feel that the therapist emotionally supports their Child ego state and validates their emotions. The therapist's empathy and understanding are critical for the client to be able to receive challenge without feeling shamed or criticised. Over a number of sessions, clients will hopefully begin to internalise the therapist's warmth, acceptance and validation and draw on this as a resource to overcome their feelings of worthlessness. It is possible that this helps to build the client's Internal Nurturing Parent. When the client feels understood and accepted by the therapist, this can assist the depressed client to counteract feelings of isolation and worthlessness. The therapeutic relationship can go some way to temporarily meeting the client's relationship hungers (Berne, 1970). It is useful for the therapist to help clients explore ways of meeting these hungers in their other relationships.

The therapist's support and encouragement of the client and her confidence in the client's ability to use his resources to change is crucial. This is particularly the case for clients who are strongly self-critical and who are likely to have had many past (and possibly present) experiences of being criticised, humiliated and invalidated. This support and encouragement can help clients to contact and increasingly rely upon their own strengths and abilities, thus enhancing their sense of self-efficacy, agency and mastery.

Role induction: agreement on the tasks and goals of therapy

The therapist provides some rationale for the therapy and helps the client to learn both explicitly and implicitly how the therapy process works. Although this is a component of the contracting process, it can have a beneficial effect on the formation of the therapeutic relationship. The therapist can also engage the client in a loosely educational process, which may include providing information about depression, how therapy works, the different roles and expectations of client and therapist (see 'getting the most out of therapy' document in Appendix 1) and key concepts of TA (see Appendix 3). This role induction process is a key feature of this protocol and is a valuable part of the therapy. In addition to seeking clarification and agreement about the tasks of therapy, another aspect of the role induction process is to assist clients to articulate and clarify their problems, and engage in a collaborative contracting process regarding the goals of therapy. This emphasises a clear direction and purpose to the therapy and also helps to strengthen the therapeutic relationship.

Affect-focused therapeutic relationship

A sustained, empathic focus on the client's internal and interpersonal world is desirable. This is primarily relating to the client's reactions, actions and self-focus (that is, a focus on what the client needs to change, internally, as opposed to what needs to change in his environment, even though changes in his environment may be desirable and perhaps even essential to a positive outcome).

The therapist is advised to keep the focus on the client's internal exploration and on enhancing his emotional and meaning-making awareness. Questions such as 'What are you feeling as you say that?' are helpful in this regard. Wherever possible, encourage awareness, approach and acceptance of emotions instead of avoidance of them.

> Therapist and client attempt to articulate the client's unique experience. This painstaking form of co-constructive exploration ensures that together they capture the real quality of the client's feelings and meanings. This particular and idiosyncratic rendering of the client's subjectivity enables him or her to evoke experience as well as to understand it. For example, this type of exploration of the client's subjective experience may reveal not just that the client is sad, but that it is a desperate, abandoned feeling captured in the words 'I feel like a motherless child'.
>
> (Greenberg & Watson, 2006: 102)

Relational positioning: 'the Goldilocks zone'

The therapist is advised to be conscious of her 'relational positioning', that is, how she relationally positions herself in her relationship with the client. In effect, this means that the therapist repeatedly has to work out what is 'too little', what is 'too much' and what is 'just right' in how she relates to the client, to keep track of the changing and fluid nature of this and adjust her stance and intervention choice accordingly.

Complementarity and managing countertransference

Some people with depression can be very hostile in their interpersonal style. According to the theory of complementarity, this can 'pull' for a negative or hostile response from the therapist. In these instances, the therapist is advised to notice and contain her own negative countertransference reactions.

Immediacy and metacommunication

High levels of immediacy and the use of metacommunicative transactions (Widdowson, 2008), whereby the therapist focuses on the present and what is happening 'right now' in the therapeutic relationship and helps the client to change his present relationship experience, can be very helpful.

Systematic experiential disconfirmation

Many aspects of the therapeutic relationship promote change. It is proposed that an important change mechanism is *systematic experiential disconfirmation*. In order to make use of this mechanism, the therapist must be aware of the client's life script and wherever possible seek to ensure that the therapy: (1) should be systematic; (2) is most effective when it is experiential; and (3) should seek to disconfirm the client's script repeatedly and systematically at both explicit and implicit levels. In other words, the therapist makes use of experiences both within the therapy and in the client's reports of events outside therapy which in some way disconfirm aspects of the client's script.

> Within systematic experiential disconfirmation, the client's attention is drawn towards some experience which disconfirms an aspect (or more than one aspect) of their script. This is not, however, a solely cognitive process, but rather one which combines observation, attention, cognition and moderate levels of affective arousal with reflection and (co-) construction of new meaning based on the experience.
>
> (Widdowson, 2014b: 204)

Mistakes, ruptures and enactments

It is not unusual in therapy for the therapist, inadvertently, to repeat some aspect of the client's script. It makes sense for you to be attentive to this potentiality, and frequently reflect on whether the therapy or your way of being with the client might in some subtle way be reinforcing the client's script or repeating some aspect of the behaviour or approach of a person from his past. As and when script reinforcement or repetition happens, acknowledge it, and also when the immediate 'sting' has eased a little, comment on how this was in all likelihood especially painful for the client because it had features that made it similar to a particular event or dynamic from the past. For more guidance on this subject, see Widdowson (2008) and Little (2013).

Enactments

An enactment is essentially another word for a game which occurs between the therapist and client. An enactment provides an opportunity to repair some archaic hurt, in that the situation will be emotionally charged and significant in some way for the client. Another way to consider enactments are points where the client's script interlocks with the therapist's in some way. It can be very difficult to identify an enactment when it is taking place, and it is most commonly only identified after the event.

It is important that enactments are dealt with thoughtfully and carefully and with deep exploration which does not avoid difficult emotions. It is vital that the therapist hears the client and responds non-defensively and openly. Skilful repairs of the alliance ruptures and processing of the enactment can provide a unique opportunity to heal some aspect of the client's experience which has been brought into focus. As such, enactments can provide an opportunity for systematic experiential disconfirmation. In this situation, the therapist as a participant in the enactment has in some way repeated the past, but responds now in a way that is different from the original situation. The therapist is both the 'old object' and the 'new object' (Little, 2013), and therefore has the opportunity to help the client take healing and fresh meaning from a situation that is familiar in some way.

Transferential aspects

Transference reactions are an aspect of the here-and-now interaction which has some relationship to the client's past. It has been described as having four distinguishing features:

1. the client's sensitivity and selective attention to certain behaviours in others;
2. a tendency towards making certain sets of interpretations over possible others;
3. the client's responses are determined by and related to his (script) beliefs;
4. a tendency to behave in such a manner as to invite responses which are consistent with and confirm his expectations.

(adapted from Hoffman, 1983, cited in Little, 2013)

Thus, the client will, due to past experiences, have a particular sensitivity to some behaviour, manner or characteristic. This can be understood as an implicit memory. The transference reaction is the elaboration and projection of the implicit memory on to the therapist who is (perceived to be) exhibiting some behaviour or characteristic that is reminiscent of the original problematic situation. The therapist is advised to keep an open mind as to how she is repeating some aspect of the client's past, which role she is taking (or being transferentially cast in) and which roles she is avoiding (such as avoiding being the 'bad parent' by attempting to stay in the 'nurturing, rescuing good parent' role). The therapist is also advised to consider how she may be inadvertently repeating some aspect of the client's past, or some problematic relationship dynamics in the course of therapy.

Case example

Jane was enjoying working with her client, Audrey, but had noticed that Audrey had seemed distant, defensive and disengaged in the last few sessions and Jane wondered if Audrey was considering leaving therapy. Jane commented on this and asked Audrey if she had any concerns about the therapy. Audrey blurted out that she had been feeling that Jane's repeated encouragements for Audrey to be active and make behavioural changes were not accounting for how bad her depression was, and that she had found it hard to keep up with them, which had left her feeling a failure and inadequate. Jane was horrified and apologised to Audrey for her blunder. She also commented that she realised that her behaviour had probably at some level reminded Audrey of her pushy, intrusive and competitive mother.

Optimal neutrality and unconditional positive regard

As therapists, we value our clients and like to believe we value all of them. The person-centred concept of the importance of offering unconditional positive regard to the client (Rogers, 1957) is a complex and difficult matter in practice. In reality, it is extremely challenging for a therapist to value the aspects of the client which are 'not for growth' (Mearns & Thorne, 2000), or the aspects of them which are problematic (including their symptoms and resistances) and this can lead us towards not offering true unconditional positive regard to all of them, or of being less 'regarding' towards their stuck points or problems. This is further complicated by the fact that the client ostensibly arrives at therapy seeking change and the eradication of symptoms. Little (2013) describes the process of unconditionality as 'optimal neutrality'. In this sense, neutrality means that the therapist is not invested in one aspect of the client over another. The intention here is for all aspects of the client to experience our acceptance. This 'warts and all' acceptance is therapeutic and assists the therapist in not inadvertently reinforcing the client's self-critical or self-rejecting processes, which ultimately contribute to his problems.

Potency, permission and protection

Potency (Steiner, 1968) protection and permission (Crossman, 1966) (sometimes referred to as 'the three Ps') are considered to be central to the effective practice of TA therapy, and are concepts which provide a framework for the development of the therapeutic relationship.

Potency

A central theoretical concept in TA therapy is therapist 'potency', which relates to a psychological strength of the therapist which is experienced by the client and facilitates the client's change process. This is a concept which is difficult to grasp accurately, and yet is one which appeared in the case series as an important factor of the therapeutic relationship (Widdowson, 2013). Potency can perhaps best be identified by a grouping or clustering of certain interpersonal qualities combined with a therapeutic stance. Each of the clients in the case series described aspects of their therapist's way of being which indicate that their therapist was warm, 'present', 'contactful', humorous, 'on their side', perceptive and willing to hold the client to account.

A further aspect of this is the client's sense of a 'strength of character' in the therapist, which includes the therapist having the capacity to accept whatever the client may tell her and also the ability to tolerate intense feelings in the therapy. Linked to this has been the client's sense that the therapist was willing to accompany him on his therapeutic journey and would not emotionally abandon him. In this sense, the clients in the case series felt that they had a resourceful ally who was familiar with the terrain of the therapy process. The clients described their confidence in their therapist's competence and skill. There is also a sense of the therapist being a real, vibrant, emotionally open and responsive person. It would appear that the client's perception of the therapist as having potency is an essential prerequisite for change in TA therapy.

Key features of potency

- therapist credibility
- commitment/ passion
- 'walking the talk'
- emotional capacity: for example, processing, metabolising and regulating emotions
- strength of character
- can 'hear' and 'bear' the client's story
- having a treatment rationale and coherent theoretical and practical frame.

Permission

A number of the clients in the case series also either explicitly or implicitly referred to 'permission' in their change interview. The theme emerged of therapy being a space where clients are given permission to be themselves, to explore their thoughts and feelings, to express these thoughts, feelings and experiences and share aspects of themselves, they feel ashamed about in an accepting and non-judgemental space. Experimenting with new behaviours and new ways of being with others seems to be an implicit subtext throughout the accounts of the clients in the series.

Key features of permission

- largely implicit
- absence of judgement
- encouragement to 'go there'
- acceptance
- encouragement to feel and to express and face pain/shame
- encouragement to experiment both in the therapy room and in everyday life.

Protection

Protection was not explicitly discussed by the clients in the case series, but was mentioned in the therapists' notes. Aspects of protection included:

- options
- regulating feelings
- risk assessment
- having a treatment rationale
- following best practice
- monitoring using outcome measures
- effective use of supervision.

Case formulation

A case formulation is a brief narrative that ties together mechanisms that cause and maintain problems, their origins and any interrelationship between problems. Considerable research shows that therapy which is guided by and focused on a clear case formulation is likely to be more effective. From a TA perspective, a case formulation ties together diagnosis, contracting and treatment planning. Case formulation should be completed no later than the end of the third session and before the fourth session. Once you have generated your case formulation, use it as the main focus for the therapy, and keep it at the front of your client's case notes.

- Begin by making a note of the client's key problems and problem domains (e.g. 'symptoms', 'interpersonal relationships' or 'problems at work'). Make a note of the scores from the outcome measures and provide an indication of the severity level of the client's symptoms using each (for instance, CORE-OM scores were 20, indicating moderate functional impairment and PHQ-9 scores were 12, indicating moderate levels of depression). Then compile a full DSM multiaxial diagnosis: include main or most problematic diagnosis in your formulation.
- Make a note of any sociocultural and demographic factors which may be relevant to the client's presenting issues, as well as the client's current and historical family relationships.
- After this, start to identify the client's primary symptoms. In doing this, be as specific as possible, so for example, if the client reports 'poor communication', make a note of the ways in which his communication is impaired and in what situations. Consider how the client's main symptoms relate to or contribute to his identified problems.
- Consider the client's history to identify potential causative factors and the origins of his problems. Also, consider what might have triggered the client's problems and/or symptoms and how they are maintained and reinforced.
- Think about the client's problems and symptoms using TA theory. How can you use TA theory to make sense of and understand what is going on for

104 Therapy protocol

the client? Which mechanisms might be maintaining the client's problems or symptoms?
- Next generate a statement of around two paragraphs in length which summarises and links together all of the above information. This is your case formulation.
- It can be useful to consider how the case formulation predicts and understands problems that might occur in therapy as replays of some aspects of the client's script.
- Systematically plan therapy and use interventions targeted at different aspects of the case formulation and review the case formulation at intervals throughout the therapy.

8 Key therapeutic processes

This chapter focuses on a number of issues in the therapy of depression. It starts with an outline of the key therapeutic tasks in transactional analysis (TA) therapy for depression and moves on to the research-based principles for practice. Then the chapter discusses several key areas of focus, which can be used to guide the therapy and address significant factors which may be maintaining the client's depression. Whilst addressing underlying issues is desirable, firstly, it is not always possible to identify and resolve causal factors. Secondly, in time-limited therapy, the work needs to be efficient and actively promote change in a short period of time. Thirdly, even if clients do resolve underlying script issues, whilst they are engaging in behaviours which maintain their depression they are at significant risk of relapse. These suggested areas of focus are also based on a synthesis of the author's research findings and existing research literature on factors and processes associated with depression.

Key therapeutic tasks in TA treatment of depression

These 12 therapeutic tasks constitute the essential core TA treatment plan for depression.

1 Create an 'I'm OK – You're OK' relationship where the client feels safe enough to explore her thoughts, feelings and experiences and begin to internalise the experience of being accepted.
2 Identify, reflect upon the origins of and re-evaluate self-critical ego state dialogue. Replace this with an accepting and self-compassionate internal dialogue.
3 Identify, re-evaluate and challenge contaminations and script beliefs which negatively impact on the individual's self-concept and expectations of others and life.
4 Support the individual to recognise, re-evaluate and challenge self-limiting systems of thinking, behaviour and experience which maintain the depression (script system).
5 Explore, reflect upon and change stroking patterns (accepting positive strokes, giving self positive strokes, reduction in negative self-stroking/self-criticism).

6   Identify and challenge discounting and grandiosity (e.g. 'If things go wrong it is my fault' which discounts external factors and is grandiose about role of self).
7   Support the reflection upon and re-evaluation of life experiences that have contributed to a sense of worthlessness.
8   Support the individual to make new decisions about how she will view herself, relate to others and engage with the world.
9   Support the deconfusion process whereby the individual identifies, expresses and reflects upon repressed feelings (including repressed anger and working through of grief and loss).
10 Support the individual to explore and experiment with new ways of relating to others which enhance self-worth.
11 Design and negotiate behavioural contracts such as awareness exercises, homework, self-care contracts, exercise, diet and sleep hygiene contracts.
12 Facilitate the client's attachment to and engagement with life, others and the world.

Principles for practice

As psychotherapy is a complex activity which involves making a series of decisions about how best to intervene, and for which prescriptive rules are usually inappropriate, Heidi Levitt and her colleagues recommend the use of *principles for practice*, arguing that 'principle-guided "judgments" emphasise expert discretion, intuition, more "organic" appraisal processes, [and] personal knowledge' (Levitt, Neimeyer & Williams, 2005: 119). They have championed the development of such principles for practice, and they present a persuasive case for their use by stating that:

> empirically derived principles ... could be useful in training therapists to make reasoned moment-to-moment treatment decisions and to consider the principles underlying their work in relation to the context at hand ... In this way, beginning and practicing therapists are not encouraged to mechanistically mimic therapeutic interventions without context; rather, they are taught to use contextually sensitive principles to make decisions on how to guide the process of therapy. These intentional and empirically derived principles allow therapists to consider their interventions in a flexible manner that shifts depending on relational or situational factors, invoking new strategies to maintain treatment coherence.
>
> (Williams & Levitt, 2007: 181)

These principles for practice were derived from the author's case series (Widdowson, 2013) and, as such, are research-based principles which are intended to guide the implementation of the therapeutic process.

- It is helpful for therapists to facilitate clients' understanding about the origins of their problems and to 'go deeper' than the surface, symptomatic level.

This includes helping clients to contextualise their feelings, reactions and implicit learning which influence their current experience and the relation of this to their past experiences.
- Judiciously 'teaching' clients about accessible models which are relevant to helping them to understand their experiences and process can be helpful. This approach works best when the emphasis is on helping the client to reflect upon, understand and manage problematic internal experiences, to make sense of difficult or painful reactions and to understand maladaptive patterns. It can also be helpful to promote change in interpersonal relationships and to enhance the client's sense of agency.
- The use of relevant theoretical concepts in the therapy can be helpful to assist clients in taking charge of their own process of change, in demystifying the therapy process and in giving them tools to promote extratherapy changes. The presentation of theoretical concepts is less effective when it is not clearly matched to the client's presentation or issues, and/or when delivered in a strongly didactic and dogmatic fashion.
- It is important that these concepts are presented to clients as 'potentially useful ways of understanding things', and to explain that these are theoretical models and not absolute truths.
- The use of the ego state model can be helpful to assist clients in identifying, understanding and changing their (implicit) internal dialogue and in helping them to work out what they can do independently to change their internal state when distressed.
- Clients who are keen to engage in 'homework activities' can be encouraged to use the concepts discussed in the session to engage with the change process creatively, for example, through the use of visualisation, reflection or writing techniques. It is recommended that homework activities are simple to implement, and that complex or lengthy tasks are avoided. Where 'homework' is used as a treatment method, it is advisable to check in with the client in subsequent sessions what the outcome of this was.
- Clients who have a strong and clearly identifiable self-critical process can be invited to engage in two-chair work both to address the self-critical process and to develop self-compassion and nurturing.
- Therapists should be attentive to clients' implicit narrative, in particular the narratives which relate to their self-concept and those which relate to their experiences of self and others in relationships. Once the therapist has identified a potential narrative theme, this can be checked with clients that this 'makes sense' to them. The therapist and client can then work collaboratively to seek ways of challenging this narrative. In particular, the therapist needs to be attentive to the manifestation of this theme in the therapy in order to engage the client in a process of systematic experiential disconfirmation and re-evaluation/rewriting to a less limiting narrative, or the creation of a narrative which contains greater potential for growth.
- Where possible, the therapist can help clients to identify specific events from their past and the implicit learning/narrative that they draw from these events.

Once these events and the associated learning/narrative have been identified, the therapist can engage the client in experiential cognitive-affective work to re-evaluate and change any negative or limiting aspects.

- It can be useful to explore with clients their interpersonal relationships and how these (perhaps inadvertently) reinforce their problems. Helping clients reflect upon and change their ways of communicating with others can be productive. This can be facilitated by active coaching, educational approaches which develop the client's communication and relational skills. Providing direct interpersonal feedback can also be helpful in supporting the client's change process.
- It is helpful to facilitate clients in articulating their problems and to engage in a collaborative discussion of therapy goals as early in the therapy as possible. As clients are not always clear about their goals at the outset of therapy, this process may take several sessions. As the therapy progresses, these goals can be refined or adjusted according to the client's changing presentation or wishes.
- It is useful to be clear with clients about the tasks and process of therapy and to clarify how they want the therapy to proceed.
- Extratherapy 'homework' can be an effective adjunct to the therapy process. The therapist and client can engage in a collaborative discussion to choose or design homework tasks which best suit the therapy process at that time. These might include tasks which deepen the client's awareness, tasks which invite clients to change self-limiting or problematic behaviours or tasks which enhance a self-compassionate and self-nurturing stance.
- Wherever possible, the therapist should construct a clear case formulation which incorporates the client's goals and a conceptualisation of the client's core issues and use this as a guide to focus the therapy. This formulation can be revised and adjusted as the therapy progresses and as issues are resolved or new ones emerge.
- The creation of a collaborative safe space where the client can be open and vulnerable is an important part of the change process. Collaborative goal setting, demystifying the therapy process, ensuring that the client feels a sense of equality and mutuality in the relationship and appropriate self-disclosure can all strengthen the sense of safety in the relationship.
- The sense of safety is also enhanced when the therapist is open, genuine, contactful, warm, perceptive and non-judgemental and is emotionally robust and willing to challenge the client when necessary.
- The sense of safety and the client's change process are enhanced when the therapist actively seeks to create a permissive climate. This includes encouraging the client to take risks in the session, to explore difficult and painful material and to experiment with new ways of being and relating to others.
- The relationship is also strengthened by the therapist's validation and acceptance of the client. It is likely that this experience is internalised by the client and helps to overcome the client's negative self-judgement.
- Providing the client with pretherapy information about the nature, tasks and process of therapy and some accessible theoretical material can be useful to

help the client make an informed choice about starting therapy and to engage with the therapy process actively.
- Assessing and addressing the client's initial level of motivation for therapy and interventions which help the client to push through initial discomfort can help the client to engage with the therapy process.
- Exploring the client's past and present problematic relational experiences can be useful in assisting the client in changing negative self-beliefs and relational patterns which maintain his depression.
- Assisting the client in addressing experiences of isolation can be helpful in overcoming depression.
- Contingency planning and resourcing clients to manage future problems is likely to be helpful in preventing relapse.
- In identifying problems and constructing therapy goals, it is helpful if the therapist guides the client towards internal changes or towards goals which he can directly change, rather than goals based on events beyond the client's direct control.
- Attentiveness to repairing alliance ruptures and addressing interruptions in the therapy are likely to be beneficial.

Treatment planning

Clear, specific and individualised treatment plans support the therapy process and are an essential part of effective TA therapy (Clarkson, 1992; Stewart, 2014). A good treatment plan should help the therapist and client to remain focused and stay on track. This is particularly important when working short-term where there is not the luxury of being able to meander around issues. Even in longer-term therapy, focusing the therapy by using a well-thought-out treatment plan is good practice. Steps 1–7 below describe how to generate an individualised treatment plan for your client, and in step 8 you are invited to integrate this with the principles and key tasks described at the beginning of this chapter.

- Step 1: Identify the client's main symptoms and the main processes of his depression (you may find it helpful to review Chapters 2–4 in clarifying which processes seem to affect your client the most).
- Step 2: Identify factors and processes which maintain the client's depression (e.g. vicious cycles, contaminating process, perfectionism, self-critical internal dialogue).
- Step 3: Identify key changes that you believe would be most productive for your client (such as developing a self-nurturing internal dialogue, enhancing the ability to appraise oneself, others, situations and events positively or neutrally).
- Step 4: Work out how you can understand and conceptualise each problem and change using TA language (Chapters 2–4 may help with this).
- Step 5: Prioritise the key changes. Practising short-term therapy requires efficiency. It is worth considering which of the changes would have the biggest

impact for your client in terms of improving his overall functioning and well-being and reducing symptoms. A particularly efficient approach is to target the processes which maintain the client's depression before moving on to larger and more underlying script issues.

- Step 6: Integrate the changes you have identified with the client's therapy goals and phrase these as a series of tasks to be completed during the therapy. Check that the identified changes are consistent with the case formulation for the client and adjust accordingly.
- Step 7: Develop home practice tasks that the client can complete between sessions to enhance his progress in therapy (for example, taking regular exercise, doing daily mindfulness practice, completing self-awareness exercises).
- Step 8: Combine your treatment plan with the key therapeutic tasks and the principles for practice described above.

Addressing perfectionism

Perfectionism is a character trait which is highly correlated with increased risk of depression and anxiety and is strongly associated with increased levels of self-criticism (Enns & Cox, 1999). It has also been associated with a range of other problems, including low self-esteem, obsessive-compulsive tendencies, hopelessness, suicidal ideation and eating disorders (Egan, Wade & Shafran, 2011). It is important to draw a distinction between a healthy striving for excellence and an unhealthy sense of perfectionism. The key difference is if the individual bases her sense of self-worth on achievement, and whether or not she accepts 'good enough' as truly being 'good enough', the former representing perfectionism and the latter representing a healthier perspective.

Perfectionism can have a number of possible components, including:

- intolerance of mistakes (by self and others)
- unrealistic or excessively high personal standards
- unrealistic or excessively high expectations of others (this can include unrealistic expectations of the therapist)
- negative evaluation/comparison of self against others
- excessive reassurance seeking from others
- high parental expectations
- high parental criticism
- self-doubts about actions
- organising ability.

Maladaptive perfectionism is characterized by unrealistically high and inflexible standards for performance combined with overly critical and harsh self-evaluations, an inability to be satisfied with seemingly successful performance, compulsive tendencies, and chronic self-doubt. Adaptive perfectionism includes high but achievable or reasonable personal standards, a need for order and organization, self-evaluation that is independent of performance, an unwillingness to procrastinate, and strong motivation to better oneself and society.

(Aldea, Rice, Gormley & Rojas, 2010: 1195)

High levels of perfectionism are known to have a negative impact on the outcome of therapy and to have a strong relation to a poorer working alliance (Shahar, Blatt, Zuroff & Pilkonis, 2003; Zuroff *et al.*, 2000). There is also evidence that high levels of perfectionism are associated with poorer interpersonal relationships (Shahar *et al.*, 2003). It is possible that, due to the levels of shame and self-criticism which perfectionistic clients experience, they struggle to open up and 'be seen' in therapy. Also, it is possible that they are reluctant to enter the therapeutic relationship fully due to perceived expectation of criticism or rejection for their imperfections. It has also been suggested that, due to their unrealistic expectations of others, clients with high levels of perfectionism are less able to tolerate relationship ruptures and reluctant to engage in rupture repair (Zuroff *et al.*, 2000). Furthermore, clients who are highly perfectionistic may become easily disillusioned with their progress in therapy, which in turn increases the likelihood of poor alliance or drop-out. Despite this, there is evidence that clients who actively reduce their levels of perfectionism in therapy will do well and enjoy a favourable therapeutic outcome (Blatt & Ford, 1994). Therefore, it is of value to target perfectionism as a major strategy early in the therapy. Clients may not be fully aware of the extent of their perfectionism early in therapy, and there is some evidence that providing people with feedback about their degree of perfectionism may be helpful (Aldea *et al.*, 2010).

The goal of therapy is not to abandon personal standards or striving for excellence, but to re-evaluate and adjust standards and expectations and to remove the degree of experienced self-worth from achievement of perfection. This may involve letting go of unattainable goals which result in distress. Perfectionism has a particularly pernicious effect on goal achievement; often the individual sets unrealistic goals. If these goals are not met, then this provides source material for self-criticism. If the goals are met, then they are likely to be re-evaluated as having not been stringent enough, or achievement of them was a fluke or due to some external factor (and not due to the individual's efforts). With some people, their perfectionism (and associated fear of failure) results in procrastination and avoidance of activities which would expose them to the self-critical attack which they anticipate would follow from their failure to reach their unrealistic target. It is worth exploring with clients who have a tendency towards perfectionism if their goals are realistic, or just another manifestation of their perfectionism, and also to what extent their perfectionism impacts on their evaluation of their progress.

Conceptualising perfectionism using TA

Perfectionism can be conceptualised in TA as relating to strong Parental introjects around the need to 'be perfect', and an associated Child belief of not being good enough. This is likely to manifest in a broad 'be perfect' process, which influences the client's intrapsychic and interpersonal processes and is not just limited to what might be considered to be classic 'be perfect' driver behaviour. Invariably, the client will hold script beliefs around the need to be perfect, and will engage in discounting to maintain these. Contaminations relating to perfection are also likely to be present.

Addressing perfectionism

- Assess extent and nature of perfectionism in clients. Invite clients to explore the impact that their perfectionism has on different aspects of their lives.
- Encourage clients to monitor their perfectionism and identify when they are engaged in perfectionistic thinking.
- Encourage the client to allow for a degree of tolerance of mistakes, and an acknowledgement that excellence requires considerable practice, which will by necessity include some mistakes along the way.
- Promote engagement in self-compassion/self-nurturing internal dialogue in response to perceived failure.

Therapy of contaminating process

Rumination is a significant cognitive process in depression. Rumination is characterised by repetitive, negative and evaluative thinking. This tends to be focused on the self, past events, one's circumstances, concerns and depressive symptoms (Nolen-Hoeksema, Wisco & Lyubomirsky, 2008). Examples of thoughts an individual might experience when ruminating include: 'Why do I feel like this?', 'Why can't I feel better?', 'Why can't I change?', 'What kind of person does this make me?', 'Why do I always mess things up?', 'Why am I always so negative?' and 'Why couldn't I do that by myself?' Rumination usually starts with, or involves, a series of negatively biased questions, and will typically result in a series of negative internal responses which reinforce the depression and the individual's negative script beliefs. Also, when ruminating, the individual mistakenly tends to believe that rumination is helpful. Rumination can be conceptualised in TA theory as *contaminating process,* as it both generates and maintains specific contaminations.

It is beneficial for the therapy to target rumination/contaminating process specifically and to assist the client in finding more productive ways of thinking and reflecting. The presence of an underlying contaminating process can be inferred when the content of a specific 'live' contamination is challenged (either in the therapy session, or by the client outside sessions) and the client moves on to another negative thought in the style of a 'yes, but' rebuttal. In this instance, a series of discounting mechanisms are likely to be activated in order to maintain the negative script beliefs which the contaminating process reinforces.

Firstly, it is useful to consider what function and purpose the rumination/contaminating process has for the client. What does the client believe it will help him to do or not do (e.g. he believes it will motivate him to change, and will also prevent him from being lazy or selfish)? Once the intended purpose has been identified, the therapist can assist the client in finding alternative ways to achieve the intended outcome.

It can be useful for the therapist to be alert to the potential that occasionally clients get caught in a ruminative/contaminating process within a session, or may activate this process after a session (for example, by thinking 'Why couldn't I do that by myself?', 'What is wrong with me that my therapy is taking so long?' etc.). In this instance, it is helpful for the therapist to anticipate this, and possibly even raise this with the client and then help the client generate alternative and positive ways of thinking after the session.

Many clients who ruminate find it beneficial to use positive distraction or deliberately and actively to engage in activities in order to turn the direction of attention outwards and away from the excessively internal focus of contaminating process. Mindfulness meditation is also an appropriate strategy for counteracting contaminating process.

Decontamination

Decontamination is a largely cognitive process which results in a change in the Adult ego state and a 'clearing' or re-evaluation of a contaminated belief.

Identifying the belief

Contaminations are not always immediately obvious. The contamination/belief can be identified by:

- listening for the explicit content of what the client is saying;
- listening for the implicit content of what the client is saying;
- inferring its presence and then questioning to see if the client holds the underlying belief.

Exploring the contamination/contaminated belief

This includes understanding and honouring the origin of the contamination in light of the client's history. It is helpful to normalise this, to reduce the risk of the client feeling embarrassment or shame about contamination, and to minimise the potential for the client's self-critical ego state dialogue being activated.

Reframing

Reframing involves the reinterpretation of an event or situation from a different perspective, or changing the meaning that is inferred or attributed to the problem being discussed (Watzlawick, Weakland & Fisch, 1974). A simple example of reframing is how a problem under discussion which might be viewed as

114 Therapy protocol

'a disaster' could be reconsidered as 'an opportunity for growth and learning'. Reframing, therefore, does not change the essential facts of a situation, but rather changes the interpretation of the situation.

Re-evaluating a contamination by appealing to logic

The intention here is to stimulate critical thinking to evaluate the accuracy and appropriateness of the belief. This is best done through a process of systematic enquiry whereby the client comes to his own conclusions about the belief as opposed to lecturing or challenging. Contaminations can be challenged by inviting the client to explore the validity of the contaminated belief logically using a series of questions. For example, a client may believe that she is not deserving of happiness. In this instance, the therapist could ask the following questions:

> 'What sort of person deserves happiness and what sort of person doesn't?'
>
> 'What sort of criteria would be used to determine whether someone deserves happiness or not?'
>
> 'Do you meet those criteria?'
>
> 'So, should all people who do not meet those criteria be unhappy?'
>
> 'How long should this unhappiness last, or is this something which should last forever?'
>
> 'Do you feel all people are equal? Does that include you?'

Increasing cognitive dissonance

This series of questions will start to mobilise the client's Adult ego state, and will address the contamination from a series of perspectives. The intention is to raise some cognitive dissonance about the existing belief. In cognitive dissonance, the individual is presented with information which challenges her existing beliefs (Festinger, 1957). This induces some discomfort and needs to be handled sensitively to reduce the risk of the client feeling embarrassed or ashamed about her existing belief and to reduce the potential for the client becoming defensive. Information which generates cognitive dissonance can be discounted or distorted by the individual in order to maintain her script frame of reference. By sustaining gentle challenge, the therapist can help maintain sufficient pressure for the dissonance to be resolved by the client rejecting the old belief, accepting the compelling logic of the argument and developing a new belief.

Direct challenge

On some occasions, contaminations can be directly challenged or contradicted. This can be Parental and a high-risk strategy, as the client may feel hurt or angry

Key therapeutic processes 115

at the therapist's challenge, or may (on the surface) overadapt to the therapist but internally hold on to the belief. In this case, the client may believe that certain topics are then off limits and cannot be discussed with the therapist. Also, there is potential for alliance ruptures with such direct challenge. Furthermore, a direct challenge may activate a depressed person's negative self-critical dialogue. Nevertheless, direct challenge or contradiction can be a very useful intervention, if used with caution, and with a client who is amenable to such directness, and where the therapeutic relationship is strong. In such instances, it is worth exploring with the client how she feels about being challenged. If any alliance rupture is present, attend to this before proceeding with the session. When the client has been challenged, it can be helpful to acknowledge this and to invite the client to explore her reactions to the therapist's more challenging approach. This can be done by the use of statements such as: 'I realise I've been quite challenging at times today. I'm wondering what that's been like for you? I have a feeling you quite like directness, but I'm aware it can feel hard to be on the receiving end of it at times.'

Behavioural disconfirmation

Contaminations can be effectively challenged by inviting the client to engage in behaviours or activities (either in or out of the session) which may generate evidence which disconfirms the contamination. When disconfirming evidence has been found, it is helpful to note this in the session actively and explore this with the client. When this occurs, name the original contaminated belief and invite the client to re-evaluate this in the session. It is useful to ask the client what new belief he might have now in light of this new experience and information.

Case example

Michelle was having a hard time with her argumentative teenage son, which fed her belief that she was a bad mother (and therefore a bad person). Her therapist encouraged her to comment on this over lunch at work, and ask if anyone of her colleagues had experienced similar problems. The following lunchtime, Michelle joined a group of female colleagues in the staff room and during the conversation raised the subject of her arguments with her son. All of the women with children who were either teenagers or now grown up confirmed that their teenagers had indeed been sullen, argumentative and irritable and that this was just normal behaviour which would pass in time.

Provision of missing information

Sometimes people retain contaminated beliefs because of a lack of alternative information. In such instances, the therapist may choose to provide the client with the missing information. One example might be around emotions – a client who feels afraid of feeling pride in case it makes him arrogant and selfish can be advised that, as long as he continues to be caring and thoughtful towards others, he can feel a sense of pride in his own achievements without running the risk of becoming selfish.

Working with feelings

In this protocol, we begin working with the client's feelings right from the first session. As the therapist is getting to know the client, and is finding out more about her situation, the therapist remains empathic in his stance towards the client. Validation and permission are highly therapeutic and experienced as supportive and empathic. Begin by generally exploring the client's emotions. Attempt to enhance the client's awareness of these in the therapy process, by seeking to develop a fine-grained understanding of the nature, origins and contexts of her emotions. Where the client has particular emotional sensitivities, help her to identify what the developmental origins of these are.

Emotional literacy work

Emotional literacy work can be a very useful aspect of therapy for people with depression. This involves learning to identify, name and articulate different feelings (Steiner & Perry, 1999). Many people who are depressed struggle to make sense of and articulate their emotions, and when asked what they are feeling may reply that they don't know. This might mean that they are feeling overwhelmed by a confusing mixture of feelings, some of which may be conflicting. To complicate things further, their internal interpretation and symbolisation systems may be negatively biased, which makes expressing and understanding complex emotional states difficult (Gilbert, 2007). It can be helpful to explain to clients how feelings are often not straightforward or easy to understand, and to give them some idea of how you intend to work with these in therapy. One way of doing this might be in a statement such as:

> Most of the time, we feel a whole range of emotions. This is similar to a cocktail, or a pan of soup, or a cake, where different ingredients are blended together in different proportions. Once combined, it can be difficult to tease apart the separate ingredients. Similarly, emotions, once blended together, can be hard to disentangle. As I see it, part of our task here is to help you separate out all of your different feelings, make sense of them and maybe re-evaluate them.

It is particularly helpful to normalise the client's emotions and emotional reactions. All primary feelings are, at their roots, both useful and helpful. They motivate us and also trigger behaviours which are intended to obtain some kind of social advantage. Also, there is usually some kind of stimulus which has triggered the emotion. Help the client to identify what the stimulus is and if his emotional reaction is appropriate to the stimulus (see Blenkiron, 2010; Lee, 2006; Moiso, 1984). Identifying the stimulus and the associated emotion is one way of clarifying whether the client's emotional reaction is a primary or secondary emotion. Primary emotions are always linked to an appropriate stimulus, have a level of intensity and expression which is realistic according to the situation, have a natural duration, are often addressed with a specific interpersonal response and will be processed and resolved within an appropriate time span. Examples of typical stimuli which are associated with specific emotions include:

- sadness: linked to past or expected loss, hopelessness and helplessness, self-pity;
- fear: some (real or imagined) threat or danger;
- anger: some damage is occurring, or rules are broken or expectations unfulfilled, sense of injustice or unfairness;
- guilt: personal standards broken or not reached;
- shame: sense of being a bad person for having transgressed some social rule which will result in disapproval from others.

Find out if the feelings the client is wanting help with have ever been useful to him – if he can't think of anything, prompt him to see if instances can be identified. Emphasise that all feelings are normal – it is the strength of them and what we do with them that can sometimes be problematic. It can be useful to explain that one of the goals of the therapy is to help the client to regulate his feelings better. Where clients say that they would like to eradicate or 'get rid' of a particular emotion, explaining that it isn't good or healthy to get rid of entire emotions completely (for instance, fear can be highly appropriate in situations where there is a real danger and where it prompts the client to take appropriate action) can be helpful.

Many clients find it useful to identify, in sessions, what triggered their emotions and emotional responses. Most of the time there is something which has activated any given emotion. This trigger may be an external event, the client's interpretation of an external event or something internal, such as a thought or memory. Triggers do not need to be immediate – there can be a 'delayed reaction'. It can be helpful to assist clients to identify if there is some kind of delayed reaction to their emotional states.

It can also be helpful to identify the internal and behavioural responses that the individual has to his emotional states and to appraise these in terms of their helpfulness, i.e. could the feeling have been handled better? Normalise whatever reaction the client had, or at least approach it non-judgementally and rationally. For instance, avoidance can be a strategy used for short-term management of anxiety; however, in the long term it actually makes anxiety worse, and reinforces the avoidant behaviour and the message that there is indeed some kind of danger which needs to be avoided. Often, behaviours are intended to produce some kind of immediate, short-term relief, but actually can contribute to the problem in the long term. It is useful to think of both the short- and long-term consequences of emotional-coping behaviours.

Increased affect tolerance

It is productive to encourage clients to 'stay with the feeling' during sessions and to increase their affect tolerance. The therapist should aim to keep the emotional arousal level within a moderate range to promote optimal change and to increase the client's ability to tolerate stronger emotions.

Emotions and implicit learning

Strong emotions act as a powerful stimulus for learning. Whether we consciously recall it or not, we implicitly remember our emotional responses to situations and events. We tend to repeat things which produce good feelings and avoid things which will produce unpleasant feelings. This is the basis of implicit learning. Such emotional memories tend to operate at an unconscious level, probably via triggering of the amygdala. By learning to pause, identify feelings and reappraise them in the present moment, we learn to respond emotionally in new ways and gain control over what may have been automatic emotional responses. The reflection and reappraisal of emotional responses will help clients to engage their Adult ego state, which when done repeatedly will increase their ability to self-regulate their emotions.

Positive feelings in depression

For many people with depression, positive feelings are problematic. For example, they may repress positive feelings (especially, positive feelings about their self) due to believing at some level (implicit learning – script) that these feelings are forbidden, or will lead to negative consequences.

Sometimes people who are depressed stop themselves from feeling positive, enjoyable emotions and sensations by telling themselves that feeling pleasant emotions means:

1   they are 'tempting fate', and by feeling good this means something bad will inevitably happen
2   that they do not deserve to feel happiness
3   that they will somehow be punished for feeling joy or pleasant feelings
4   that the pleasant feelings mean that they have forgotten something
5   they are 'disobeying' and 'being bad'.

The irony of this, of course, is that in preventing the emergence of positive feelings or somehow squashing these enjoyable emotions or sensations they are actually stopped in their tracks and the negative consequence they may fear was

Key therapeutic processes 119

going to happen has in effect happened. Thus, the strategy which is intended to protect them actually acts against them, and contributes towards their depression and/or anxiety.

Negative events or bad feelings which emerge after enjoyable feelings are experienced are seen as evidence that the client's fears were right. This of course is irrational, as no one can maintain positive feelings in any kind of healthy way indefinitely, nor can all bad things be prevented. Furthermore, people with depression often use 'faulty attribution', whereby they interpret anything positive (such as good feelings or events) as being connected to or about other people and anything negative is about themselves.

Vicious cycles

As human beings, we are hard-wired to avoid (real or perceived) discomfort. Whilst the avoidance of discomfort is a natural urge, it can have negative consequences and can reinforce or maintain problems. Furthermore, when people feel distressed, they are more likely to engage in behaviours which provide some kind of immediate gratification or relief, even though these behaviours may be counterproductive or unhelpful. Frequently, these behaviours end up becoming persistent and self-perpetuating cycles which contribute to the maintenance of their problems. These patterns can be described as vicious cycles (see Widdowson, 2014b), and have links to concepts in cognitive-behavioural therapy (Garland, Fox & Williams, 2002; Veale, 2008) and cognitive analytic therapy (Ryle & Kerr, 2002). The behaviours or internal process associated with these vicious cycles tend to be associated with an individual's symptoms in some way. For instance, someone who is depressed would be likely to feel lacking in motivation to do anything and would also not anticipate experiencing much enjoyment from activities. Because of this, she would be less and less inclined to do anything, such as go out and see friends or engage in some kind of exercise. Because of this, she has a reduction in enjoyable activities and her energy levels may well decrease. The individual may well also feel annoyed at herself for not wanting to do anything, which may intensify her self-criticism. The increased internal self-criticism would make the depression worse and the person then is trapped in a vicious cycle of feeling worse and worse (Figure 8.1).

Assisting a client in identifying her own vicious cycles can be very productive. Once your client can recognise her own vicious cycles, you can engage her in a discussion about how she can interrupt these patterns. It is worthwhile explaining to the client that disrupting her vicious cycles may well lead to some temporary discomfort or require considerable effort to begin with, but that this discomfort or effort will be relatively short-lived and will pay off in terms of increased gains in therapy. Any therapeutic interventions which interrupt the maintaining factors of a client's problem(s) are likely to be effective, have a quick positive result and may also help to prevent relapse.

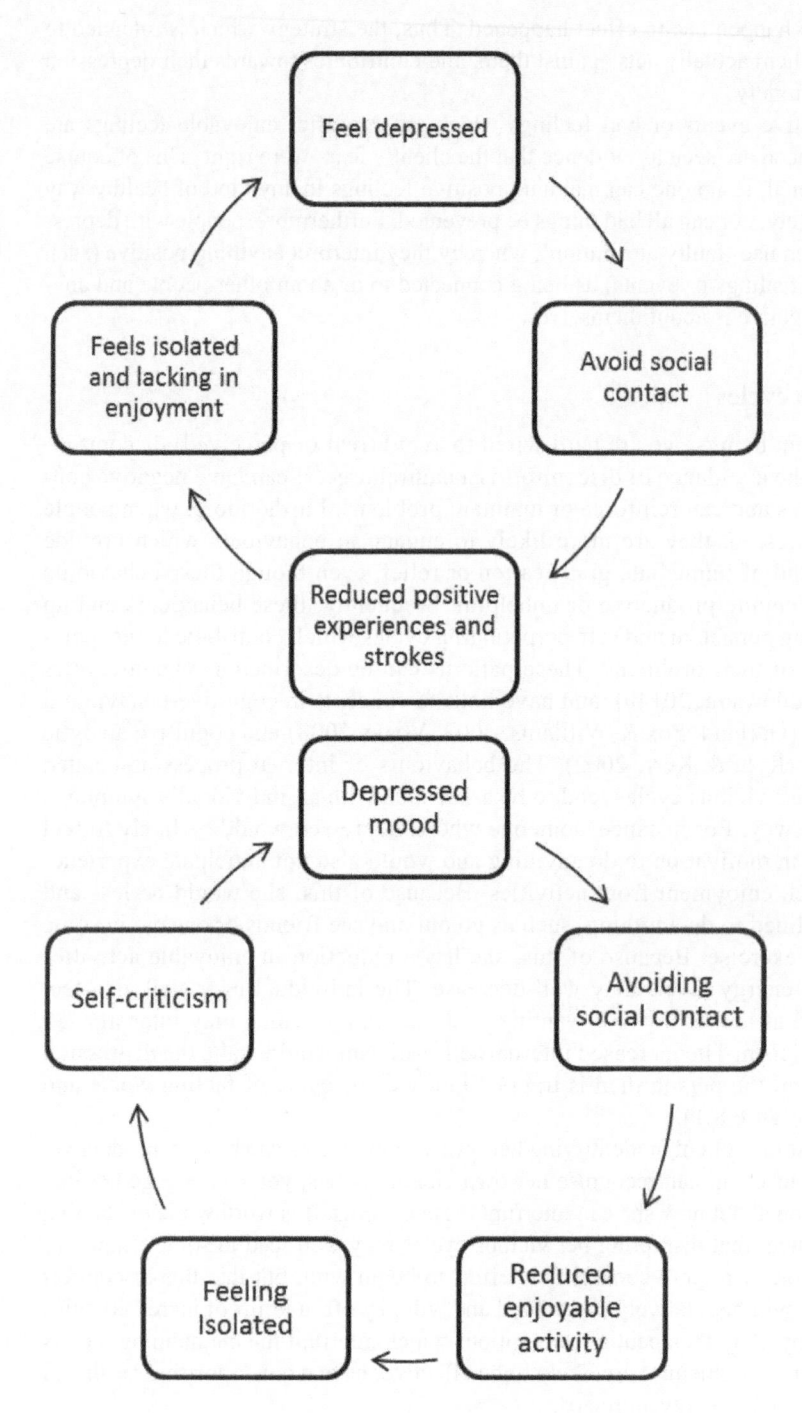

Figure 8.1 Examples of vicious cycles in depression.

Discussing suicidal ideation and suicide risk

Suicidal ideation of varying degrees is common, especially in people with depression. The guidelines below are intended as an introduction to thinking about and working with suicidal ideation and risk. They are not intended as a replacement for training and supervision about risk assessment and management. All therapists who work with clients are advised to seek out risk assessment training to develop their skills and knowledge in this area. There are several TA texts which are also useful in gaining underpinning knowledge about working with suicidal clients. These are: Stewart (2010b), which provides an excellent overview of the background and process of escape hatch closure, and also Widdowson (2010), which explores suicidal ideation using TA theory. Mothersole (1996) and Ayres (2006) both stress the importance of providing a space for the client to talk about suicidal ideation and existential issues freely and frankly without the therapist rushing to engage the client in escape hatch closure.

It is sensible to draw a distinction between suicidal ideation (thinking or fantasising about suicide) and suicidal intent (where there is an actual wish or desire to die). Suicidal ideation is not necessarily an indicator that a client is at risk, whereas suicidal intent is an indicator of high levels of risk and requires urgent intervention. Where the therapist identifies or suspects either suicidal ideation or suicidal intent, she is advised to engage the client in a frank and open discussion about his thoughts. The therapist is advised to make full and detailed records of such discussions in the client's notes. The therapist needs to make sure that she has taken reasonable steps to explore the issue fully with the client and has taken appropriate action. In all cases of both suicidal ideation and intent, the therapist should discuss the issue with her supervisor as a matter of urgency and develop an appropriate treatment plan to manage such risk. The therapist may use the following questions to guide her exploration of suicidal risk with her clients.

Ask about suicidal ideation

- Have you thought that life is not worth living?
- Have you thought about ending your life?
- Have you made plans or thought about ways you could kill yourself?
- How often do you have these thoughts?
- Do your reasons for living outweigh your reasons for dying?

Assess intent and plan

- How do you feel when you start thinking about killing yourself?
- Have you had specific thoughts or plans about taking your life? What are those plans?
- Have you done anything or taken any steps to prepare for taking your own life (suicide notes, making a will, arranging means to kill self)?
- Do you think that you could go through with it and kill yourself?

- Frequency, context (time, setting, planning, substance abuse, impulsivity), method, consequences, intent and feeling about discovery/survival/causing long-term damage to self or others are all important characteristics.
- Why now? (in cases where the client reports a sudden onset or increase in suicidal thoughts or wishes).

Taking account of known risk factors is one way of assessing for suicide risk; however, as an approach it is limited in that, although it can indicate when someone is at risk, it cannot accurately predict whether a person will or will not commit suicide. The client's level of risk needs to be considered at point of entry into therapy, whenever there is a change in the client's circumstances (job, relationship, medication, etc.), when the client has experienced a psychosocial stressor (loss/grief, humiliation), if a deterioration in the client's mental state occurs or when the client is experiencing prolonged distress which is not improving.

Indications of immediate risk involve: threatening to kill or harm self, looking for ways to harm self, attempting to procure means to attempt suicide (e.g. stockpiling pills) and talking about death or suicide.

Additional factors

- Any psychiatric disorder, past or current suicidal behaviours (this does not include previous suicidal thoughts), medical diagnosis/illnesses, functional or cognitive impairment (depressive symptoms, anxiety, panic, psychosis, hopelessness, worthlessness, severe self-criticism, anhedonia, agitation, anger, impulsivity).
- Psychosocial stressors, e.g. loss of independence, family history of suicide, family conflict, divorce/relationship difficulties, debt, legal problems, substance abuse, violence, physical/sexual abuse.
- Assess personality strengths/resources and weaknesses, coping strategies.

Therapeutic approaches to suicidal ideation and intent

Always seek to establish empathic rapport using a calm, non-judgemental approach. Start by asking general questions around the issue of suicide and let your questions become increasingly specific as the dialogue develops. It is vital that the therapist empathically explores with the client his thoughts and feelings about suicide and, in particular, helps the client to articulate the emotional pain that is driving his suicidal ideation.

As suicide is such an emotive subject, strong emotions are often stirred. Like all people, therapists have their own personal views about suicide, and also usually care deeply about their client's well-being and hold on to hope that life can be better for their client. Therapists also have strong fears about their career and professional reputation should one of their clients commit suicide. All of these combine to form powerful countertransference reactions to any indication that their client might be suicidal. Be aware that the client may well feel very scared and ashamed of his feelings and therefore be reluctant to tell the therapist about suicidal feelings. It is possible that the client may pick up on the therapist's anxieties and/or may feel deep shame about suicidal impulses and therefore may not disclose the existence or extent of such thoughts and wishes to the therapist. Suicidal ideation can be seen as a last resort of a client who feels unable to regulate his feelings. Therefore, it is important to discuss strategies for self-management of distress during sessions. For example, the client needs to have an 'action plan' in place for how he is going to deal with intense feelings and suicidal ideation at 2 a.m. In such instances, the therapist should ensure that the client understands that active and imminent intent to commit suicide is an emergency situation and that he should seek medical attention immediately. It is absolutely essential that you seek supervision at the earliest opportunity to discuss any concerns you may have about a client's suicidal ideation and level of risk. Furthermore, it is prudent to keep extensive notes about what you discussed with the client, the interventions and approach you used with him, your thoughts about his level of risk and the evidence you have drawn on to form your conclusions.

Do not let personal feelings get in the way, rush or ask leading questions, push the client into defending his views or actions, minimise his distress or discount the seriousness of his thoughts/actions.

Changing internal ego state dialogue: from self-criticism to self-nurturing

Conceptualising self-criticism

Self-criticism is a key feature of depression (Kannan & Levitt, 2013). Using the structural model of ego states, this can be conceptualised as a negative internal dialogue originating in the Parent ego state. If using the functional model of ego states, this could be viewed as a strong internal Critical Parent and a weak or poorly functioning internal Nurturing Parent. Explaining the functional model to clients and sketching out the self-critical internal dialogue can be profitable in giving them a framework to understand what they are experiencing and to explain the rationale behind the therapeutic goal of changing the internal ego state dialogue.

Using the third-order structural model of ego states (Figure 8.2), self-criticism can be considered as a negative Parent–Child dialogue; this can be either a P_2–C_2 dialogue (where a specific but identifiable introject is cathected) or a negative P_1–C_1 dialogue, or even both. Generally P_0 would not be considered as part of a self-critical process, but would be relevant in conceptualising that the individual did not internalise a sufficiently affectively soothing/responsive caregiver and therefore has a P_0 which is unable to provide self-soothing and respond to profoundly dysregulated affect in C_0.

For some people, activating self-nurturing causes a paradoxical painful reaction. It can generate intense feelings of grief, particularly if they did not receive adequate warmth and care in childhood. Also, people who have been abused in

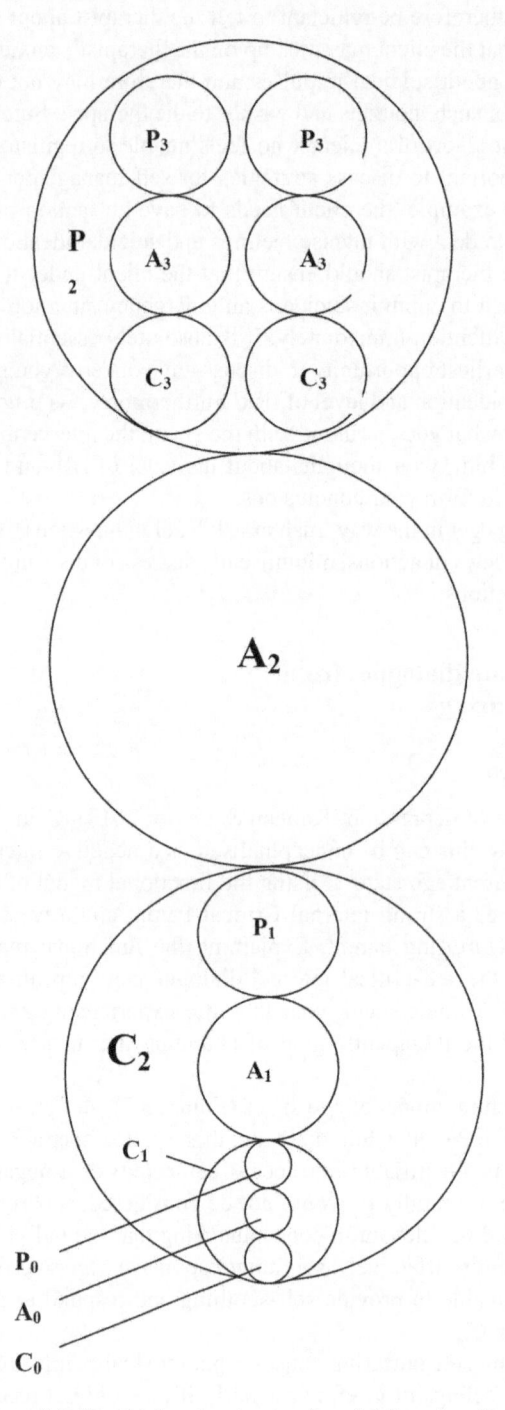

Figure 8.2 The third-order structural model (based on Berne, 1961).

some way by family members may associate soothing with emotional pain. In such cases, receiving nurturing may trigger painful implicit memories and self-protective warning signals which leave the person anxious (Gilbert, 2007).

Many depressed people struggle with feelings of being undeserving of care and nurturing. Their script beliefs which tell them they are a bad person are so intense that they effectively block any receiving of care and nurturing. In order for the client to accept the self-care and nurturing, the therapist will need to start to address these negative script beliefs. Depressed people tend to respond negatively to their own emotional distress and feeling angry with themselves for being upset is a common reaction. Unfortunately, at best this does nothing to reduce the level of distress and often increases it. It can be advantageous to explain this to clients to help them see the value of developing a self-nurturing internal dialogue.

There are several metaphors which can be used to help clients see the value of reducing self-criticism and increasing self-nurturing. The first is to ask the client to:

> Consider two children: one has been brought up being encouraged to explore and experiment in the world. When she was either physically or emotionally hurt she was cared for and offered love. When she made mistakes, she was understood and still accepted. The other child has grown up being laughed at, criticised and told he was stupid and pathetic, especially if he was hurt, vulnerable or had made a mistake. So, how would each of these two children grow up? What would they be like as grown-ups?

Or:

> Imagine there is a young boy who loves playing football and dreams of growing up to be a star player for his favourite team. In one of his training sessions, he misses a goal. Imagine the team coach then yelling at him and telling him how stupid and worthless he is. Can you imagine what will be happening for the boy? If you then imagine an alternative approach, where the coach says to him, 'That was bad luck, but never mind. I think next time you will improve if you. . .' and then the coach explains to him what would work better next time. Which out of these two is the better football coach?
>
> (Adapted from Blenkiron, 2010)

Therapeutic strategies to change internal dialogue: reducing the critical voice

Firstly, therapists are advised to remain conscious of their own need for self-care. In other words, work on developing your own self-nurturing internal dialogue! This aspect of self-care is particularly important: there is research evidence (Hayes, Gelso & Hummel, 2011) to show what many of us already know – that therapists who have a higher degree of self-criticism are less able to facilitate change in this area with their clients. Secondly, therapists are advised to be aware of the high potential for depressed clients to experience interventions as shaming,

126 *Therapy protocol*

or for them to use aspects of the therapy as material for their shaming and self-critical internal dialogue. Consider using language in ways which minimise potential for shame, frequently ask clients about their reactions to interventions and the therapy as a whole and normalise any setbacks. Phrasing interventions using principles such as those suggested by Allen and Allen (1997) can be of use in supporting the client's change process.

Developing the observing self

Much self-critical internal dialogue operates at the edge of awareness. Frequently, people do not even recognise that they are engaged in a self-critical process. The first step is drawing awareness to this. Explaining the Parent–Child model of internal dialogue can assist clients in developing their awareness of this aspect of their inner process. Another way is to encourage clients to pay attention to how they give themselves negative strokes.

Verbalising the critical voice

It is helpful to ask clients to verbalise their usual self-critical thoughts and to ask them what feelings accompany those thoughts (e.g. shame, disgust, anger, hopeless frustration).

Homework to express the critical voice

Clients can be invited to write down in a journal the self-critical thoughts they have. This does not tend to increase the intensity of the critical voice, but, instead, usually enables clients to become aware of the intensity and frequency of their critical thoughts, and also provides direct content which can be explored and re-evaluated in therapy sessions.

Identify the introject

Ask the client: 'Does this remind you of anyone? Did anyone speak to you like this?' Alternatively, you could ask clients to give their critical voice an image to represent it.

Perceived advantages to self-criticism

At its heart, there is often a positive intention behind the self-criticism. Ask your client what she believes is the advantage for her in her self-criticism. Many feel it keeps them alert and motivated and stops them from making mistakes (in reality, it doesn't, but while they believe this, any change work is unlikely to have any effect). Self-criticism may also be a defence against shame, or an attempt to control anticipated shaming: 'I will shame myself before you can' (Alison Ayres, personal communication, 15 October 2014).

Direct challenge is less effective

It is unusual for self-criticism to be changed by direct challenge, or by simply offering the client positive affirmations. Such challenges or positive statements are very likely to be internally countered by a series of 'yes, but' thoughts which discount the therapist's challenge.

What is the evidence?

Clients can be asked, 'What is the evidence?' for the accuracy of their self-criticism, and can be invited to ask themselves, 'What am I basing my criticism on?'

Alternative explanations

Ask the client: 'What other reasons might there be? Are there any other ways of looking at this?' This is particularly suitable when drawing conclusions about self, or interpretations of others' behaviour. Invite clients to let each explanation linger and explore their emotional reactions to each. This slows the process down a little, which can allow these new thoughts and feelings to settle and for their effect to sink in.

Counterarguments

Identify a negative thought and then come up with a series of counterarguments. Be aware that many people who are depressed can demolish the counterarguments with a series of 'yes, but' discounts – these also need to be tackled (sometimes repeatedly) and then the whole process can be re-evaluated.

Self-blame

This is a common feature of the thinking process of many depressed people. They will tend to blame themselves for problems in their life or in the life of others around them, or even for their depression. Gilbert (2007) recommends encouraging clients to start and consider events to be multifactorial; that is, they have many different contributing factors and the client's actions (or inactions) may be one of many. In relation to self-blame for their depression, clients can be encouraged to consider the implications of thinking through: (1) that their depression is their fault; (2) that their depression is not their fault; and (3) that they may have some part to play in the maintenance of their depression. In each of these scenarios, clients are invited to think through what they might be able to do in response to each possibility.

Self-criticism over unpleasant feelings

Emotional dysregulation and strong unpleasant emotions are key features of depression. Many depressed people have contaminations or script beliefs relating to feelings which cause them to feel angry or frustrated with their self for experiencing such feelings. For instance, they may say something like: 'I am a bad person because I feel so angry and resentful all the time'. In this instance, the therapist can conduct some emotional literacy work with the client, and also explain that such negative emotions are a feature of depression (and so will fade over time), and that it is normal to feel unpleasant feelings or have unpleasant thoughts from time to time.

Accepting conflicting feelings

It is very normal for people to experience a range of thoughts, feelings and wishes in relation to any given situation which may conflict with each other. This can be distressing for people who are depressed, who may get cross that they cannot decide what to do, or what is right. In this case, it is useful to accept that conflicting feelings are normal, and to work out which 'on balance is most right'. Sometimes, the client may need to accept that both positions are right, or that neither is wrong, or that there is no right or wrong but just 'good enough for now'. Some clients who are prone to 'black-and-white thinking' can particularly struggle with the need to resolve their conflicting feelings. In all of the above instances, supporting the client in learning to tolerate ambiguity may be beneficial.

Should, ought and must

These three words often indicate that the client is speaking from her Parent ego state. The absolute necessity of these messages can be questioned, and alternative rewordings can be explored with the client (such as 'it is desirable to', or 'I choose', 'I could', 'I might', or even 'I believe it is best to'). The intention here is to take the Parental moral imperative and judgement out of the statement.

Therapeutic strategies to change internal dialogue: developing the nurturing voice

There are several aspects to developing a self-compassionate, nurturing internal dialogue. Overall, the therapist is helping to support clients in taking a stance of understanding, acceptance and recognition of their basic humanity and kindness in relation to their shortcomings and flaws (Gilbert & Procter, 2006; McKay & Fanning, 1992; Neff, 2003). Acceptance is a key aspect of developing self-nurturing. Clients may struggle with the concept of 'acceptance' if they confuse it with hopelessness and powerlessness, or if they interpret it as meaning 'everything is great'. The word acceptance in this context is a more neutral process of simply accepting that this is the way things are. In this protocol, we are seeking to promote clients' self-acceptance, their ability to accept their feelings (including states of acute distress) and acceptance of the human condition and the (often unpredictable and chaotic) nature of the world. It is human nature to make mistakes and to be imperfect. We are not alone in this, and our imperfection and the experience of suffering are universal truths. We do not always live up to our own or others' expectations, and some people are very self-judgemental about this. Acceptance and understanding of one's own limitations and flaws are other core components of self-compassion.

Self-acknowledgement of feelings

Clients can be encouraged to adopt an accepting position in relation to their feelings, such as, 'Yes, I feel like this, and it is unpleasant.' This can be an effective approach to take when clients are struggling to accept that they are feeling in a particular way. A position of acceptance is a matter-of-fact approach which opens the door for more direct ways of addressing the problematic emotion. Trying to stop a feeling usually has the paradoxical effect of heightening or holding the emotion at its peak intensity (Ehring, Tuschen-Caffier, Schnulle, Fischer & Gross, 2010), whereas acceptance (which is not the same as actively liking an unpleasant feeling) often results in the painful emotion subsiding.

Developing self-understanding

In promoting self-understanding we are assisting the client to answer the question: 'How did I come to be like this?' The therapist can help clients to develop a sense of compassion for who they were in the past and the circumstances they were in. This involves letting go of the need to judge and label self and others. Instead, clients can be supported in offering understanding, and sometimes even forgiveness, to their 'past self'.

Internalising the therapeutic relationship

The therapist seeks at all times to maintain an empathic, understanding stance towards the client. This enables the client to internalise a compassionate, nurturing and affect-regulating other, possibly via introjective transference (Hargaden & Sills, 2002). Essentially, this means that the client will to some extent internalise or introject the therapist or, more specifically, his experience of his relationship with his therapist, which then becomes a growth-enhancing intrapsychic presence for the client.

Modelling self-acceptance

The therapist can act as a powerful role model of how to be self-accepting, self-compassionate and self-nurturing. This is best done with humility and (non-gallows) humour.

Index cards

The therapist can discuss and even suggest alternative self-nurturing, accepting and understanding internal dialogues in sessions. It is sensible to write these on index cards and give them to clients for them to take away and read between sessions, particularly if they encounter difficulties.

Be aware of subtle self-criticism

Sometimes clients change their internal dialogue to another form of self-criticism; for instance, 'I shouldn't be so upset about this' contains a self-critical judgement. Such statements tend to be slightly angry, critical and lacking in compassion and encouragement. The therapist is advised to help clients to identify these subtle self-criticisms (in session) and adjust the wording of their replacement internal dialogue accordingly.

Acknowledge any positive change efforts

Encourage your clients to give themselves positive strokes for any positive steps they take towards change, no matter how seemingly small or insignificant. This also includes self-praise for attempting to make changes, even when these have been unsuccessful. For instance, instead of thinking and/or saying 'It didn't work. I must be useless', the client would be invited to state, 'Although it didn't work, at least I tried'. A statement such as 'Look, I'm being self-critical again!' (which may in itself be another self-critical statement, or at least trigger more self-criticism) could be changed to: 'It's good that I've recognised that I was being self-critical again'.

Focusing on positive qualities

Balance self-criticism by taking an inventory of the client's positive qualities (he may struggle with this, so this may need to be an ongoing intervention).

Friend technique

'Would you say this to a friend? How would you react to a friend or family in the same situation? What would you say?'

Dealing with reluctance by proposing an experiment

If clients feel afraid or reluctant to develop self-nurturing internal dialogues and activities, they can be asked if they would be willing to do so as a 6-week experiment. If, at the end of this time, they feel that it is not working for them, then they can simply stop and revert to their usual ways.

Self-reparenting imagery

One option is to use guided visualisation and imagery techniques to offer compassion, care and nurturing to their Child ego state, or to their distressed grown-up self (James, 1974, 1981).

Two-chair work

Two-chair work (Goulding & Goulding, 1979) is particularly effective at addressing self-criticism and developing a self-nurturing internal dialogue. The client is invited to put the self-critical voice in one chair. The client is guided through the two-chair work and in both voicing the self-criticism and responding to it from an Adult state. It is particularly beneficial if the client responds to their self-critical voice from their Adult ego state in a manner which conveys empathy, understanding and assertiveness (as opposed to taking a combative stance). It can also be fruitful to help the client articulate what the self-critical voice's positive intention is and to respond to that from Adult ego state, finding healthier alternatives. Before engaging in two-chair work, developing a thorough understanding of the method and its contraindications is advised. In addition to undertaking specific training in using two-chair technique, the reader is advised to consult *Changing Lives Through Redecision Therapy* by Mary Goulding and Robert Goulding (1979), and also to read points 86 and 87 in *Transactional Analysis: 100 key points and techniques,* by Mark Widdowson (2010).

Parent interview

Using the parent interview method (McNeel, 1976) to address self-criticism is also effective when the self-critical voice can be clearly identified as originating from a parent figure. As the parent interview is another two-chair technique, the recommendations above also apply to this method.

Soothing imagery

This combines gentle relaxation with generating an image of a safe, relaxing and calming place, such as a beach, a walk through a forest, grandmother's kitchen or a friend's house. Some people find that including a safe, calm and protective person in the imagery (such as a grandmother, kind teacher or friend) can be especially soothing.

Sensory self-soothing

Use all five senses to create a pleasant environment (music, scents, food, touch, etc.). Encourage clients to engage their senses deliberately to create intentional awareness of the 'here and now' and to develop their capacity for mindfulness.

Compassionate letter writing

Invite clients to write a compassionate and self-nurturing letter from their Adult to their Child ego state (Retief & Conroy, 1981).

Loving-kindness meditation

Clients who are familiar with, and who like, mindfulness meditation can be encouraged to experiment with loving-kindness meditation.

Homework and behavioural contracting

In the case series from which this treatment guide is derived, the therapists often negotiated 'homework' or between-session activities with their clients which were intended to move the therapy along. On analysis of these cases, it would seem that homework was

> primarily intended to serve two purposes: firstly, development of self-awareness, and secondly to promote behavioural experimentation to challenge specific maladaptive patterns. TA therapists traditionally promote active change in their clients and will negotiate with the client to plan specific actions that they believe will help the client move towards their overall therapy goals (Stewart, 2007). Analysis of the case studies highlighted an implicit conceptualisation that drives this process – namely the challenging of avoidance.
> (Widdowson, 2013: 327)

The third purpose behind homework is to promote 'systematic experiential disconfirmation' of the client's script. The therapist helps the client to design and follow a series of behavioural experiments which will systematically challenge the client's existing maladaptive patterns.

The therapist is advised to be alert for opportunities in the session to identify between-session homework with the client. Homework strategies work best when they have been collaboratively designed by the therapist and client. Due to its associations with school, 'homework' can be an evocative and problematic word for many clients and may invite a regressive response. Alternative phrases include 'home practice' or 'between-session tasks'. Always write down suggested home practice assignments, and either ask the client to make a note of them in the session, or write the note yourself. When negotiating between-session tasks, it is useful to ask the client; 'Can you envisage any problems with doing this? Is anything likely to get in your way or stop you from doing this?' If the client can identify any potential problems, ask how he intends to address these.

When clients are depressed, between-session home practice can seem pointless and too much effort. When in remission, many clients underestimate the need to maintain home practice and recovery activities, and often let these slip. Such activities are invaluable and are likely to make a substantial difference to the overall outcome of the therapy. It is worth explaining to clients that it is a good idea to persist with these activities, even when they don't feel like it, and to continue with them for some time after they feel they have got better in order to prevent any relapse. It is useful to explain to clients that it is best to spend between 10 and 40 minutes per day on home practice or other activities which will promote their recovery. Explain that these can be woven into many of their daily activities without too much disruption, and that if they deliberately and systematically commit time to these activities they are likely to improve quicker and have a much stronger response to the therapy.

It is helpful to remind clients of the usefulness of engaging with any home practice generated in therapy sessions. One suggested wording is:

> The time you spend here, with me, in therapy, is about 1% of your waking hours. It is only 1 hour of the week. What you do with the remaining 167 hours of the week is absolutely crucial, and can make all the difference to how successful the therapy is.

Managing non-completion of between-session tasks

It is not unusual for clients to report that they did not complete their between-session tasks, or did not allocate enough time for good-quality home practice. Clients often find it difficult to fit the homework into their lives, or may struggle with prioritising, or may simply forget. In other cases, non-completion is part of the client's lack of self-care, despondency and hopelessness or possibly even due to a lack of assertiveness. Tackling non-completion of home practice is best done in a gentle and inquiring manner.

- Ask clients what got in the way of them completing their home practice, and explore with them strategies they might use to overcome these barriers.
- Check to see if the home practice task made sense to them and if they felt it was understandable and practical.
- Check that the client understood the relevance of the task and why it was suggested.
- Emphasise the importance of completion of home practice to promote change.

Managing ongoing repetitive resistance, avoidance and non-completion of between-session tasks

> I am in a bit of a quandary about how we can move forward. I believe that you want things to be different, and that you want to feel better, but I'm seeing that it has been difficult for you to put the changes we have discussed into practice. Do you have any thoughts on what we can do to make this easier for you, or maybe how we can look at what is stopping you from putting changes into place or how you are perhaps, out of awareness, stopping yourself?

Clients who have a tendency towards being reactive and oppositional (and for whom the non-completion of tasks becomes part of their struggle) can respond to paradoxical interventions. An example of a paradoxical intervention might be to raise the possibility of ending the therapy:

> It seems like it's really hard for you to engage with your therapy actively outside of sessions. For this to work, it is absolutely vital that you really push yourself to move forward. It seems like perhaps this is not the right time for you to be making changes, and I'm wondering if there is much sense in us continuing at this time and perhaps postponing therapy until you feel more able to engage. What are your thoughts and reactions about that possibility?

When the therapy feels like it is stuck

On occasions where the therapy feels stuck and unproductive or as if it is drifting aimlessly, it can be productive to do a brief review of the therapy. When doing so, review your treatment plan and adjust it accordingly. Check the overall therapy contract (in particular, the contract for the therapy goals) and recontract with the client where necessary. It can also be constructive to engage the client in a summary and review of the therapy so far. Where the therapy feels stuck, it is also wise to check that the client is happy with the therapeutic relationship and address any problems. This can be done simply by asking questions, such as: 'How are you feeling about how we are working together?' and 'Is there anything you want me to do differently?'

Sometimes, the therapy can become stuck in some way due to an unidentified countertransferential response, for example, when the therapy in some way evokes the therapist's own material. In order to rule out or address this possibility, it is wise to discuss the sense of stuckness in supervision.

TA problem-solving protocol

Problem-Solving Therapy (PST) is an evidence-based treatment which has been successfully used for a number of psychological problems, most notably including depression, for which it has strong evidence of efficacy (Cuijpers, Straten & van Warmerdam, 2007; Malouff, Thorsteinsson & Schutte, 2007). It has been used explicitly by cognitive-behavioural therapists since the 1960s, although TA also has a strong tradition of using PST interventions. Within PST, the emphasis is on assisting clients in identifying and analysing problems and on them creatively generating a range of solutions to their problems to move out of 'stuck points' and develop a sense of personal efficacy.

TA has traditionally been an active problem-solving approach which has invited clients proactively to identify problems, define goals and seek solutions to their problems. The basic PST protocol has been adapted, and is presented here for TA practitioners. It contains all the main features of PST, but relates to a number of TA concepts so it can easily be integrated or adapted for use by

TA practitioners. The primary TA concepts that guide this protocol are: ego states (in particular, strengthening the Adult ego state), hard behavioural contracting (Stewart, 1996, 2007), passivity and discounting (Schiff *et al.*, 1975). This model also links to the first three stages of Woollams and Brown's (1979) treatment plan by taking the client through the stages of motivation, awareness and contracting in relation to a specific problem.

This protocol may be useful with certain clients who are ready for and wanting a behavioural focus to solve specific problems. You are invited to experiment, play with and adapt this protocol to suit your own personal way of working and each individual client. If you do decide to use this with your clients, please be aware it is usually not possible to move through all the steps within one session. Pay close attention to and enquire how your client is experiencing this model and check whether she is finding it useful or not. If it is not proving to be helpful, stop using it immediately, and take some time to explore with your client what the experience was like, and how she was experiencing you in the process.

Although the steps are described below in a linear fashion, as though they are discrete stages, in reality they often overlap somewhat. As the conversation between you and your client unfolds, you can move backwards and forwards addressing different presenting aspects of the situation and move along in a relatively seamless manner.

Method

Preliminary step: consent contracting

Before you begin using the protocol, ask your client if she would be interested in using a structured problem solving method. It is perhaps a good idea to explain that you will be helping the client work through different stages of problem identification and generating solutions to help her move forward, and that hopefully she will develop her own problem-solving skills which she can use whenever she needs to. If the client agrees, then you have a consent contract to proceed with using the protocol.

Step 1: Defining the problem

In this first step, the therapist and client take time to identify and explore the client's problems. Each individual problem is worked with separately, although, frequently, our clients' problems are interlinked, so it can be valuable to have an overview of other problems to see if they cast light on some aspect of the situation or solution. In the discussion at this stage, the therapist helps the client to explore and clarify the problem and to break the problem down into its different components. It is important that the therapist does not try to convince or persuade the client at this stage, and confrontation is likely to set up client resistance and be counterproductive. The aim is to facilitate a deep Adult analysis and deconstruction of the problem. Occasionally, this is sufficient and the client can feel that she has processed the problem enough to move forward.

EXAMPLE QUESTIONS FOR STEP 1

'If we assume for a moment that you haven't spoken about this to me before, and that we're going to start right from scratch, what is the problem for you right now? How would you describe it in your own words?'

'Will you say some more about how this problem affects you and gets in the way in your life?'

'How does this leave you feeling?'

'Although this might seem like a strange question to ask, is this a problem that you want to solve?'

'I'm wondering if in the past you've tried to ignore this problem, in the hope that it would go away or that someone else would do something about it?'

'It seems like this is quite a complex problem, and I can see why you might have got stuck with this, as there are lots of different aspects to it. How about we take a few minutes and break it down into its different components? I have a feeling that trying to tackle this in one go is going to leave you feeling overwhelmed and it will just get unmanageable, so I'd suggest we look at each part and tackle it one step at a time'.

It is useful to summarise the conclusions of this stage before moving on to the next one, by restating the problem and adding in an empathic response which emphasises the client's experience, enables you to check that you have understood the client and enhances the client's motivation for change. For example:

'OK, so let me summarise: the problem is that you are [experience/problem/pattern]. Also you are feeling fed up and frustrated with doing this and see that this is causing conflict with you and your partner and you feel that your home life will be much more harmonious if this problem is sorted out. Is that right?'

It is also useful to ask clients about any action they might have already taken to deal with the problem:

'Is there anything you have already tried out to deal with this?'

If the client has already tried taking action, it can be worth exploring with him what action he has taken. Sometimes this in itself suggests various options for the client or the client may realise that he may need to persist with these actions in order to solve the problem.

Step 2: Assess motivation and address ambivalence

At this stage, the therapist is seeking to enhance the client's overall level of motivation. Some clients express a strong desire for things to be different but experience some reluctance to change or may feel ambivalent about making changes. The client's different ego states may have different views about the problem and the prospect of change, and this step can help the client to identify and articulate any ego state conflict. This step also starts to move the client through the discount matrix (Mellor & Schiff, 1975) towards taking responsibility for change and implementing problem-solving behaviours.

EXAMPLE QUESTIONS FOR STEP 2

'Can you say something about what your main reasons are for wanting this change?'
 'How are things going to be different for you when you have sorted this out?'
 'Can you think of any advantages and disadvantages to tackling this?'
 'It is natural for people to feel a little bit apprehensive about changing things. I'm wondering if you have any concerns about making changes?'
 'If I can play devil's advocate for a moment, I wonder what is the argument in favour of staying as you are, and what is the argument in favour of changing?'

Step 3: Establishing realistic contract goals

At this stage, the client is encouraged to articulate goals directly related to the identified problem(s). The SMART goals method (Doran, 1981) can be helpful in identifying a behavioural frame for the client's goals. This means helping the client work out goals which are *specific, measurable, attainable, relevant* and *time-bound* (see also Stewart, 2006).

Step 4: Explore alternatives

Here, the therapist helps the client to generate as many solutions to the problem as possible. Where possible, the therapist should encourage the client to come up with her own possible solutions – even wacky ideas. The intention here is to encourage some Adult in the Child (A_1) solutions (Little Professor) to the problem. The therapist is advised to withhold any judgement of the different solutions and, where possible, to avoid getting caught into a game of *'why don't you . . . – yes, but'* or unnecessarily advising the client about specific courses of action.

Once different solutions are identified, the therapist then helps the client to evaluate the pros and cons of each option. Another possibility is exploring the client's reactions to each of the potential solutions on the list from each of his ego states. For example, 'My Parent thinks. . .' Some clients might wish to rank ideas and solutions in terms of their desirability. It can be useful to highlight that in some situations there are no easy or straightforward answers, each solution may well have some drawbacks and that these have to be considered on balance against the problem. It can also be useful to ask the client how he thinks others will react to his changes. It is important to pay attention to whether the client's solution involves *someone else* doing something different, as change which relies on others changing is tenuous, to say the least. In such instances, the therapist should invite the client to focus on what *he* can do differently, regardless of how others behave.

138 *Therapy protocol*

Step 5: Action planning

Here, the therapist helps the client to plan what steps she might take to implement her chosen solution(s). Using the principles of behavioural contracting (Stewart, 2006), invite the client to make a series of agreements about what actions she is going to do between sessions. Ensure that any agreed actions are relevant, manageable and realistic. It is also important that they make sense to the client and that the client can see the rationale behind them. It may be worth checking if the client has the skills and resources to take the necessary action, and if not, how she can acquire these skills or what support is available to him. It is worth engaging in some pre-emptive troubleshooting and contingency planning such as identifying what might get in the way and how your client might handle that.

Step 6: Taking action

This stage tends to take place between sessions. It can be worth asking clients to make notes about their progress and their experience of taking action.

Step 7: Evaluating the outcome

At the next session, ask the client if he managed to implement the actions and what the outcome was. Ask the client what the experience was like and also what the experience of using this protocol has been like. When the client did not have a good outcome or has not managed to implement the actions, help to explore what the obstacles were. It is important to take a compassionate stance in the face of non-implementation or poor outcome, as the client may well feel bad about his 'failure'. In this instance, it is valuable if the therapist helps the client to take a stance that does not reinforce his negative script beliefs.

Promoting interpersonal change

Introduction

TA is rich with models to understand and change interpersonal relationships. Promoting interpersonal change is a central part of this protocol. The tasks of therapy include:

- helping the client to develop positive stroking patterns;
- facilitating the client's attachment to life, others and the world;
- supporting new ways of relating to others which enhance self-worth.

Actively supporting clients in taking steps to improve their relationships and increasing their levels of social support is a beneficial strategy in therapy for depression.

Interpersonal problem solving

The therapist is encouraged to engage the client in interpersonal problem solving at various stages throughout the therapy. The problem-solving protocol can be adapted to suit interpersonal problems. The therapist helps clients to explore the nature of the problems they are experiencing and find alternative solutions for these problems.

Use of direct interpersonal feedback

The therapist is also encouraged to offer the client feedback about how she is relating to the therapist and how the therapist experiences her, where appropriate. Feedback can also be provided on the client's reports of her interactions with others.

Behavioural contracting

The creative use of behavioural contracting to promote healthy interpersonal relationships is recommended. Existing research suggests that depressed people who maintain regular social activities have a better prognosis than those who do not. Therefore, it is worth contracting with clients for them to have at least one social engagement per week.

Multiple selves: exploring ego states in relationships

Help clients to explore how they present 'different selves' in different relationships and in different circumstances, and how they can be their 'best self' in any given situation.

Teach the functional model and transactional options

The therapist can easily teach clients the basics of the functional model of ego states and assist them in analysing their relationships and exploring new options for positive transactions.

Promote healthy dialogue

At various stages in the therapy, the client will likely discuss her relationships. It is recommended that the therapist encourages the client to explore unhelpful relationship and transactional patterns and find healthier and more productive alternatives. Where the client reports particular problems with her partner, it is permissible within this protocol for therapists who have had training and experience in working with couples to have one or two couple sessions with the client and her partner to work on improving their communication style. In such sessions, the therapist should engage the couple in a guided dialogue and be highly directive in supporting positive communication strategies. It should be noted that this way of working can be highly effective, but also has many potential pitfalls and requires additional supervision to manage carefully and ethically.

Assertiveness coaching

The therapist can do brief assertiveness coaching in sessions to help clients who struggle to be assertive. This can be general assertiveness skills coaching or related to specific events.

Stroking prescription

In the 'stroking prescription', the client is invited deliberately to offer a minimum of three positive strokes a day to people they encounter. If they can do more, that is even better. The person must mean the strokes, and may have to think to find something to provide strokes about. The intention here is to actively create an environment where strokes are plentiful.

Identifying stroke filters

The therapist can teach the client about how strokes can be filtered out, and assist clients in identifying how they discount positive strokes which are given to them.

The drama triangle

The drama triangle is easily taught to clients, who often like its simplicity and immediate relevance to many problematic situations. Clients can be assisted in identifying the different behaviours and internal dialogue they have in each drama triangle position, and what events and situations are particularly likely to encourage them into each role. Support the client in finding alternative, healthy behaviours and ways of relating which move out of the drama triangle. One example is the 'Winner's Triangle' (Choy, 1990), where Persecutor behaviours are replaced with assertiveness, Rescuer behaviours are replaced with caring and Victim behaviours are replaced by vulnerability.

In here – out there – back then

The therapist can help the client to explore links between current problems and patterns (including ones in the therapy room) and historical patterns and problems. Exploring the association, similarities and significance of these can be fruitful ('This seems similar to/This reminds me of when you . . . '). This process can highlight and change aspects of the client's script or protocol, and can also promote deconfusion.

Assorted interventions

'Trying on for size'

This experiential intervention can be used to heighten clients' awareness of their implicit script beliefs, to heighten the affective charge within the session and to invite clients to experiment with new beliefs. This can also be used to stimulate a healthy response to some kind of negative internal dialogue. The therapist starts by saying:

'I wonder if you'd be willing to try an experiment [wait for positive response]. I'm going to say something in a minute and I'd like you to try it on for size. . . .'

This can be followed by one of the following two statements:

1 'When I say it, I'd like you to really hear what I'm saying and at the same time notice your internal reaction. [Say whatever it is you want to say.]'
2 'OK, I'm going to say something that I'd like you to repeat. As you say it, notice your reaction and let me know if the statement feels true for you. [Say the statement.]'

After the client has repeated the statement, the therapist has several options for how to take the process further, such as:

'So, as you say it, does it feel true for you?'

'What reaction do you have as you say that?'

'Do you notice any resistance to that, or any sense that it's not true for you, or that you're not allowed to think like that?'

If the client answers that she does experience some resistance, ask:

'How come? What is it about it that you can't allow yourself to believe that?'

If the client starts to accept the statement as true, or as partially true, then the therapist can say:

'OK, so now what I want you to do is just stay with it for a few minutes. Just mentally repeat it a few times. Notice how you're feeling as you do so.'

Drawing on the client's experience to challenge script beliefs about others

It is useful to identify in the early phase of therapy the client's primary 'feared script outcomes'. In particular, it is helpful to explore the client's script beliefs relating to other people, and, where relevant, what he fears other people will do. For example, does the client fear that other people will dominate him, or be cruel or rejecting towards him? Consider what she feels he must not do, so as to prevent such an outcome (for example, he must never speak his mind or be assertive). Also, what are the client's script expectations about himself in relation to others, for instance, does he expect that he will have to forgo his own needs, or does he fear that he will end up alone? Check out any hypotheses you have regarding such feared script expectations with your client to verify their subjective validity.

Under the fantasies section of the client's script system diagram, add in the statement: **'if I ... then others will ... [feared outcome]'**.

Whenever the client does his feared action (such as speak his mind, or say no, for example), and does not get the feared response, draw this to the client's attention. This can also be done in the therapeutic relationship, where the client can be invited to notice the therapist's reaction and see if it matches his feared reaction. This provides an opportunity for systematic experiential disconfirmation of the client's script beliefs by bypassing the client's normal, script-based attentional biases.

Reinforcing and verifying perspective change

In therapy, we often get the sense that the client has gained a new awareness or experienced some kind of change in perspective. When this happens, it is worthwhile commenting on this, both to confirm that a change has taken place and to reinforce the change. At such times, the therapist might say:

> 'It looks like you're seeing things differently now. What are you seeing now that you weren't seeing before?'

> 'It seems like you have a new awareness right now. What is it that you're now aware of?'

> 'What is it like for you to hear yourself say that?'

Strategies for specific symptoms

Sleeping problems

When clients report sleeping problems (particularly insomnia), then the first-line intervention should be to recommend sleep hygiene methods (see 'self-help for depression' hand-out in Appendix 2).

Low energy

Exercise is probably the best method of increasing energy levels. Recommend that the client take some exercise. This can be as little as 5 minutes of exercise, gradually building up to 30–50 minutes of exercise at least three times per week. Encourage the client to work on the principle that 'some is better than none'. Many depressed people struggle with motivation and energy and so may find it difficult to start taking some exercise, in which case suggest that your client starts with something simple, such as walking to the local shop, or walking to the end of the street and back, taking the stairs instead of the lift at work, or walking to the next bus stop on the way to work in the morning.

Hopelessness

Inexperienced therapists sometimes attempt to 'cheerlead' the client out of hopelessness by being positive and encouraging the client to think positively. As a strategy, this is unlikely to work. It can be useful to let the client know that, in your experience, in the vast majority of situations, there is something which can be done to improve things. It can be helpful to encourage the client to engage in Adult re-evaluation of situations to consider the potential for change in different contexts. Depressed people tend to use mechanisms of discounting and view negative circumstances as stable, global and unchanging. The use of a problem-solving method may be useful for some clients who are feeling overwhelmed by problems.

Hopelessness about the outcome of therapy can be addressed within the first sessions. Firstly, let the client know from the outset that there is considerable evidence to indicate that therapy can be highly effective for depression. Any improvement on outcome measures within the first four sessions suggests that the client is likely to have a good response to therapy. Pointing this out can be beneficial and can promote a sense of hope in the client.

Indecision

Recent research has found that people who scored highly on a neuroticism scale actually made better decisions when they did so quickly, as opposed to taking their time (Bella, Mawn & Poynor, 2013). It is possible that people with depression may end up feeling indecisive by taking too long to make decisions over simple matters. When considering more complex issues, using a structured protocol such as the problem-solving method may help. It can be useful to highlight that, when we have complex or difficult decisions to make, very rarely do we find a solution or course of action which feels 100% right – if one such solution existed, then it could be considered that the situation would not be much of a problem, as that solution would be easily implemented. In reality, complex or difficult decisions are likely to require us to follow the choice which 'on balance is the better, or more desirable course of action'.

Fears

Many people with depression experience some degree of anxiety. This may be free-floating and generalised, or specific to situations. Inviting clients to explore their catastrophic fantasies can be useful, for example by asking 'So what is the worst thing that can happen here?' or 'What would be so bad about that?' The intention here is to engage the client's Adult ego state to reappraise the situation. This may also support clients to re-evaluate some of their script beliefs.

Shame

Often, clients will not openly reveal the aspects of themselves about which they are most ashamed. They fear that if you know these things about them, you will reject them or think less of them (Gilbert, 2007). When there is a pervasive sense of shame, strokes are easily rejected or discounted by the depressed person. At some level, they are likely to think: 'If you really knew me, you wouldn't think that' or 'You're only saying that to be nice. Inside, I am bad and you just don't know it yet'. When clients experience shame but do not feel able to express it, they often talk indirectly, making self-critical and often angry statements, such as 'I feel so stupid' or even 'You must think I am pathetic and that I am wasting your time'. It can be appropriate to raise the issue of shame with the client gently by saying something like:

> 'It seems like you feel very vulnerable and exposed.'
>
> 'I get the impression you feel ashamed of feeling/thinking this way.'
>
> 'I'm wondering if you are concerned that I might judge you or think less of you because of this?'
>
> 'No, I'm not judging you at all, but it seems like *you* are. I'm wondering if you feel that you are pathetic and like you're wasting my time. I'm guessing you feel a mixture of feelings, such as frustration with yourself and shame about sharing these personal things with me.'

If the client agrees and this is the first time she has acknowledged such feelings, it can be productive to say:

> 'I understand that. I know it feels very difficult and painful to acknowledge these feelings, but it will be really useful if you can let me know if you feel this sense of shame in our sessions. I know it will be hard, but would you be willing to tell me, or even to use the word "ashamed" in our discussions?'

Gilbert (2007) draws an interesting distinction between internal and external shame. Internal shame is connected to fears and beliefs individuals have about their self and what will happen to them; external shame is connected to the fears and expectations they have about how others see or will see them and the judgement and/or rejection that they expect will follow. It can be helpful to encourage clients to tease out these two aspects of their shame experience. It can be particularly productive to explore with clients how they think their external shame operates in relation to the therapist, for example by asking: 'And do you feel that I might react in that way towards you, too?'

The best approach for dealing with shame is to cultivate an intervention style which is empathic, patient, permissive, normalising and validating.

'Unfinished business'

Where clients have significant 'unfinished business' with a particular person or event from their past, they can be invited to do an empty-chair piece of therapy. Here, the client puts the person (or situation) where there is unfinished business into the empty chair and expresses her unexpressed feelings. This is different to two-chair work, where the client would switch seats, as in empty-chair work the client does not switch roles.

Obsessing and catastrophising

Catastrophising is a particular form of grandiosity (Schiff *et al.*, 1975), whereby the client magnifies the negative significance of an event. Usually, this is accompanied by discounting of her ability to cope with the situation. As such, interventions which challenge discounting and grandiosity can be suitable. Where the client engages in catastrophising, help her to engage her Adult ego state to re-evaluate the situation and gain a sense of perspective.

For example:

'It seems like you're telling yourself that this is so truly terrible that it's intolerable.'

'In the grand scheme of things, how important is this? Will it matter in 6 months' time? A year? 10 years?'

Black-and-white thinking

The client can be encouraged to think in 'shades of grey' or, as a colleague describes it, 'all the colours of the spectrum in between'. This can be done in a range of different ways, such as finding a range of words which describe a degree of subtlety, or drawing a scale from one polarity to the other, such as 'good–bad', 'success–failure' and asking the client to work out his stance in relation to the polarity and to explore how the shades of grey can be distinguished (for instance, is a murderer more or less 'bad' than he is?). This exercise is best done from a playful position which avoids a situation where the client feels attacked, shamed or defensive (Gilbert, 2007).

Excessive reassurance seeking

It is worth exploring with the client what is driving his excessive reassurance seeking, for example, is it based on his own self-worth which leads him to believe no one will like him but simultaneously creates a strong desire for approval? Invite the client to become aware of when he is excessively seeking reassurance and to identify his internal responses when reassurance is given.

Negative-feedback eliciting

Here, the client can be seen actively to seek out negative strokes which will confirm her negative script beliefs. This can be seen as largely a behavioural and transactional problem and the client can be encouraged to do this less often, whilst in therapy her underlying script beliefs about self-worth and her relational expectations can be explored.

Unassertiveness

Although problems with being assertive are shared by many people, those who have depression find that their lack of assertiveness can maintain depressogenic interpersonal patterns and lead them to feel resentful. Often, they will be afraid of being assertive due to fears that if they are, they will be rejected or attacked. Also, they often feel that they do not have the right to stand up for themselves and may even feel that they deserve to be treated badly. These fears, concerns and beliefs need to be addressed before the person can experiment with more assertive behaviour. Be alert to any displays or reports of assertive behaviour, and stroke the client for using them, and support the client's continued assertiveness.

Termination phase

The termination phase is a crucial part of the therapy and it is important that sufficient time is given to ensure this phase is managed effectively. In 16-session therapy, it is recommended that the last two sessions be focused on issues relating to ending therapy. This ending period can be shortened to one session in the case of very brief therapy or lengthened appropriately in the case of long-term therapy.

As this is a short-term therapy protocol, it is wise to consider the ending from early in the therapy and the therapist is advised to refer to the ending of therapy regularly throughout work with the client. This will assist with the maintenance of therapeutic movement, although do bear in mind that some clients may find such reminders distressing. This is particularly likely to be the case with clients who have histories of disrupted attachments or traumatic loss. In this instance, do not avoid raising the ending with the client, but be aware that the client may well feel distressed and explore her feelings about the ending. It can be useful to say to the client something such as: 'I know it may feel painful to discuss this, and that you may want to avoid this discussion, but it is important that we prepare adequately for the ending of the therapy.' This will facilitate an open and frank discussion. When the client is distressed, empathise with this, and use affect regulation strategies. It can be helpful to ask the client to reflect on her experiences of endings and ask how she can ensure that the ending process is as therapeutic as possible for her.

Review of progress

Help the client to review her progress over the course of the therapy. It is recommended that the notes from the initial session are checked to see what progress the client feels she has made in relation to her presenting problem.

It is also recommended that data from outcome measures are used to highlight the extent of the client's symptomatic improvement. It is practical to use these to assess if there are residual symptoms or areas which are unaddressed which the client may need to work on after termination. Ensure that the client has an action plan for continuing with her progress and, where significant residual symptoms are still present, consider extending the therapy or the use of maintenance therapy.

It is appropriate to review the client's therapy goals to see how much progress has been made in relation to each contract goal. Frequently, clients achieve changes during therapy that were unexpected or surprising. Inviting the client to reflect on and describe these surprising changes can be a useful strategy.

Stroking the client for these changes and celebrating them is an important part of the termination process and models for the client how to account for and self-stroke change.

The therapist may need to prompt clients to recognise the changes they have made and to ensure that the process remains upbeat and positive.

It is important that lack of progress be adequately understood and conceptualised. It is not uncommon for clients with depression to see any lack of progress as being related to their own shortcomings and to discount the impact of extratherapy factors which have impeded progress.

Planning future action

It is worth asking clients to come up with an action plan about how they will continue to make changes and make further progress after the therapy has ended. Commonly, clients notice that they continue to improve after therapy has finished and they may find it encouraging for the therapist to pass on this information.

Contingency planning

It is inevitable that life will be difficult at times – this is just part of the human condition. Even though we cannot always predict what will happen, we can predict that misfortune, bereavements, sickness and problems will occur at some time, regardless of how well we plan for things. Also, along with the ups and downs of life, moods naturally fluctuate.

It is important that clients feel adequately resourced to deal with future problems in order to prevent relapse. It can be useful to ask clients what problems they anticipate happening in the future, and how they expect they will manage these problems. Inquiring about what resources the client has for managing their feelings, or for getting support, is also a useful strategy. At this point, it can be reassuring to clients to know that they can return to therapy in future, should the need arise.

Identifying prodromal symptoms

Part of the contingency planning process includes discussing with clients what prodromal symptoms or 'early-warning signs' of potential relapse they might look out for, and how they might manage these. As fluctuations in mood are quite normal, it is important to normalise this and perhaps suggest a certain time limit whereby, if symptoms persist, the client would be advised to seek help. Generally, it is probably worth seeking help for depressive symptoms which have lasted for 2 weeks. If these early-warning symptoms are caught early, full relapse may be prevented, and it is possible that only a few sessions of therapy may be needed for the client to return to normal functioning.

Maintenance therapy and relapse prevention

There is convincing evidence that 'maintenance therapy' sessions are effective at maintaining progress and preventing relapse (Frank, 1991; Frank *et al.*, 2007). It is worth discussing with the client towards the end of therapy the option of continuing therapy using maintenance sessions. Maintenance sessions can be negotiated and scheduled at intervals of between 1 and 3 months.

Identifying key interventions/significant sessions

Ask clients what they feel were the most helpful interventions or the most significant sessions, or what the most important aspect of therapy was for them. One strategy is to ask the client in the penultimate session to think about what were the most helpful aspects of therapy and to discuss this with you in the final session.

Exploring feelings about ending therapy and goodbyes

Clients sometimes express apprehension about ending therapy and may be concerned about how they will manage without the therapist. It is important to empathise with these concerns, but to keep in sight the changes and progress that the client has made.

Summarise the therapy

It can be useful to spend a little time engaging the client in a collaborative discussion which reviews the entire therapy, for example, by identifying what the major themes and changes have been throughout the process.

Uneventful endings

It is worth remembering that many endings are fairly straightforward, and do not need any great fuss to be made. Berne (1966: 314) remarked that at the end of a successful therapy the client would ask: 'Is that all?'.

Part III
Neuroscience of depression and medical treatments

9 A primer on the brain and the neuroscience of depression

Introduction

The adult human brain weighs about 1.5 kg and, as such, is around 2% of body weight. Despite this, it consumes 20% of all oxygen within the body and 25% of blood glucose. It has the texture of tofu, and the main building blocks for brain cells are essential fatty acids.

Neurons and glial cells

The basic building blocks of the human brain are neurons and glial cells. The adult human brain contains vast numbers of neurons – around 100 billion of them. Each neuron has on average 1,000–7,000 synaptic connections with other neurons (and can have tens of thousands of synaptic connections), meaning that an adult brain has between 100 and 500 trillion synapses (greater than the number of stars in our galaxy). If that is not impressive enough, neurons actually only comprise around 10% of the cells in our brains. The other 90% of brain cells are glial cells (although they only make up around half of the weight of the brain). There are three types of glial cells, one which makes the fatty myelin sheath which protects the long axons of the neurons and helps electrical impulses to flow smoothly, one which acts like an immune cell for the brain and the third, astrocytes, which wrap themselves around thousands of synapses and act like 'housekeepers'. Astrocytes assist by feeding the neurons, enhancing chemical signalling, cleaning up debris and adjusting blood flow, as well as having a crucial role in the formation of synapse connections and then protecting and preserving them. Also, astrocytes are centrally involved in the synaptic pruning process by marking out 'old' or 'unused' synapses which can be destroyed.

Although the signals which pass along the length of a neuron are electrical in nature, when the signal reaches the cell's terminal, it changes to a chemical one. Neurotransmitter chemicals are released which pass across the gap between cells (the synapse) and pass the signal on to the adjoining neuron.

Neurotransmitters

Neurotransmitters are brain chemicals which are used to signal between neurons across the synapse. These chemicals are synthesised in the brain from amino acids (protein) and several vitamins, including vitamins B_6 and C. There are many different neurotransmitters used within the brain and they can be classified into several main categories. The categories of most interest to psychotherapists are: amino acids (including glutamate and gamma-aminobutyric acid (GABA)), monoamines (including dopamine, noradrenaline and serotonin), peptides (including endorphin, enkephalins and opioids) and hormones (such as oxytocin and prolactin). The vast majority of neurotransmitters have one of two primary effects – excitatory or inhibitory – although some have dual effect, depending on where they are released and which neuron receptors are activated by them. The brain is generally very efficient at using neurotransmitters and will often recycle them in a process called reuptake. A basic understanding of some neurotransmitters can be useful to therapists in making sense of how the brain functions and in understanding depression and other disorders and how various medications work.

Glutamate is the brain's main excitatory chemical and is a key component of formation of memory systems and is involved in modifying systems within the brain, so it is thought to be central to learning and brain plasticity. *GABA* is the brain's main inhibitory chemical and many sedatives and tranquillising drugs work by activating the GABA system. Low GABA levels are also associated with anxiety, hence why tranquillisers have their effect on anxiety. *Noradrenaline* (US spelling: norepinephrine) is involved in producing states of alertness and memory formation, but also affects the body by stimulating the autonomic nervous system (for example, physical fight-or-flight reactions). *Dopamine* is involved in reward systems and in generating positive feelings. Many addictive drugs work by stimulating massive release of dopamine and preventing its reuptake, which creates their effect and stimulates cravings and urges to take the drug repeatedly in order to re-experience the reward. *Serotonin* is well known as the 'feel-good' neurotransmitter and, although a large proportion of the body's serotonin is located in and around the intestines, the serotonin in the brain is centrally involved in mood, sleep, appetite, memory and the regulation of a number of body systems. *Acetylcholine* is involved in memory formation, and in particular is released into the hippocampus to help form memories, and it is also involved in rapid-eye-movement sleep. In extreme or traumatic situations, excessive amounts of acetylcholine are released which effectively 'jam' the hippocampus, and this has the effect of interfering with the process of memory formation. Several hormones act as neurotransmitters. *Oxytocin* is a hormone which is involved in sexual arousal, bonding and attachment, promotes trust and empathy and has an antianxiety effect. *Prolactin* is also associated with bonding and attachment and in generating feelings of well-being. Psychiatric medications tend to work by their effect on one or two neurotransmitters. However, mental states are complex and likely to be influenced by a wide array of neurotransmitters, thus interventions which target just one or two neurotransmitters are somewhat limited.

Another brain chemical which is of interest is *brain-derived neurotrophic factor* (BDNF). This is involved in the survival of vital neurons and neural connections as well as stimulating the creation of new brain cells (neurogenesis). BDNF appears to have an important role in the long-term potentiation of memory, and in learning and memory in general. There is some evidence to suggest that people with depression have lowered levels of BDNF (Krishnan & Nestler, 2010). It is believed this is due to increases in cortisol in the brain. Lower levels of BDNF appear to be most noticeable in the hippocampus, which may have a role in the negative biasing of memory seen in depression. Intellectual stimulation, exercise, calorie restriction and several depression treatments (including antidepressants) are known to increase levels of BDNF in the brain.

The hypothalamic–pituitary–adrenal (HPA) axis is believed to be disrupted in depression. This system is centrally involved in a large number of bodily hormone systems, and so can have a profound effect on all aspects of one's physical and emotional well-being. Levels of the stress hormone cortisol tend to be chronically elevated in people with depression, which can negatively affect certain regions of the brain, in particular the amygdala (in effect, sending a continuous stress stimulus), the hippocampus (which impairs neurogenesis and memory function) and the prefrontal cortex (PFC: which impairs affect regulation, rational thinking and executive function). In non-depressed people, cortisol levels tend to spike just prior to and shortly after waking in the morning. This creates some energy and motivation to get out of bed. Curiously, waking cortisol levels in depressed people are generally low, which may go some way to explaining the difficulty in waking up and getting motivated that many depressed people experience in the morning (Krishnan & Nestler, 2010). It is possible that disruptions in the HPA axis play a part in the problems depressed people have with self-activation, energy levels, their body clock and appetite (Sharpley, 2010).

Hemispheres of the brain

The brain is divided into two hemispheres: the left hemisphere and the right hemisphere. Whilst the vast majority of brain functions are diffused across both sides of the brain, there is some evidence to suggest that each hemisphere is more dominant in particular functions (note: dominance is not the same as 'exclusively functioning'). In particular, the right hemisphere appears to have greater *influence* over emotions and, in particular, negative emotions, whereas the left hemisphere appears to have greater *influence* over rational, logical thought and language. Despite the limitations of models of hemispheric dominance, there is some evidence to suggest that people with depression may have a hyperactive right hemisphere and a hypoactive left hemisphere, which may have a role in the negative thinking style and negative affectivity in depression (Hecht, 2010).

Lobes of the brain

The brain is divided into four lobes and the cerebellum (which is associated with motor control and coordination). The lobes are: the frontal lobe, parietal lobe, temporal lobe and occipital lobe. The occipital lobe processes visual stimuli.

The parietal lobe has a strong role in sensory processing and bodily sensation. The temporal lobe plays a part in memory, language and meaning making. The frontal lobe is particularly associated with advanced cognitive, rational and social processes and emotional regulation.

Brain structures

There is considerable connectivity between centres of the brain. Neurons do not operate in isolation but connect to many other neurons in diffuse networks which exist throughout the brain. Nevertheless, certain centres within the brain have particular influence over certain functions. Some of these brain structures are of particular interest to psychotherapy.

The limbic system

The limbic system is a very old part of the brain which is centrally involved in emotion. The *amygdalae* (singular: amygdala) are two small almond-shaped structures which process all sensory data and, where necessary, activate a fight-or-flight response. They are also believed to be involved in other negative emotional states to be overactive in depression (Auerbach, Webb, Gardiner & Pechtel, 2013; Sacher et al., 2011; Sharpley, 2010).

The *thalamus* is the brain's relay centre. It is believed to be involved in the regulation of homeostasis, the body clock and wakefulness.

The *hypothalamus* has a particular role in the synthesis and release of various neurotransmitters associated with mood and reward.

The *hippocampus* has a major role in memory. In particular, it is associated with generating new memories and memory retrieval. Several studies have found reduced hippocampal volume in people with depression (Harrison, 2002; Sharpley, 2010).

The *anterior cingulate gyrus* is associated with attention, concentration, motivation and emotional awareness, and disrupted activity in this area has been associated with depression (Harrison, 2002; Sacher et al., 2011).

The *ventral striatum* and *nucleus accumbens* are two brain regions known to be connected to the experience of reward anticipation and pleasure (Sacher et al., 2011). It is possible that these areas are underactive in depressed people, hence the experience of anhedonia and loss of interest or excitement in positive activities.

Other brain structures associated with emotion

The *PFC* and, in particular, the *orbitofrontal cortex* have a major role to play in affect regulation, motivation, social and interpersonal functioning and rational thought. The PFC is, broadly speaking, less activated in depressed people, meaning that they need to develop strategies to activate this region of the brain in order to regulate their emotions effectively and process information rationally. Disrupted activity in the PFC has been observed in people with depression

(Harrison, 2002; Sacher *et al.,* 2011; Sharpley, 2010). Specifically, problematic activity in the dorsolateral PFC has been reported in depressed persons (Auerbach *et al.,* 2013). This part of the PFC is associated with attentional focus, and it is possible that some disruption in this region accounts for some of the problems depressed people have with prolonged and excessive focus on negative stimuli. Overall, reduced PFC functioning has been observed in depressed people, which would negatively impact on the person's ability to regulate emotions and think clearly, which in turn would set up a self-reinforcing loop of increased stress and amygdalar activation and heightened cortisol levels, which would further dampen PFC activity (Sharpley, 2010).

The *insula* is associated with bodily experiencing of emotion and emotional awareness. A recent small-scale study found that an underactive anterior insula was associated with good response to cognitive-behavioural therapy and poor response to a selective serotonin reuptake inhibitor drug and, conversely, an overactive anterior insula was associated with good response to the selective serotonin reuptake inhibitor and poor response to cognitive-behavioural therapy (McGrath *et al.*, 2013).

> A role for the anterior insula in major depression is well established. The insula is crucial in mediating the translation of visceral experiences to subjective feeling states. Additionally, anterior insula activity is linked to behaviors relevant to depression including interoception, emotional self-awareness, decision making, and cognitive control. The anterior insula is extensively connected to various frontal, limbic, and brainstem regions, including the anterior cingulate cortex, amygdala, and hypothalamus. Volume reductions of the anterior but not posterior insula have been described in currently ill patients with MDD [major depressive disorder] as well as patients with remitted MDD compared with healthy controls. Changes in insula activity occur with a variety of treatments for MDD, including medication, vagus nerve stimulation, deep brain stimulation, and mindfulness training, suggesting a role for this region in mediating antidepressant response and remission more generally.
>
> (McGrath *et al.*, 2013)

This study is somewhat limited, firstly by its relatively small sample size and secondly that this does not account for people who respond best to combined treatment approaches or people who respond to neither. Nevertheless, it is an interesting and potentially promising line of inquiry.

Theories relating to depression

One current theory speculates that stress and inflammatory responses within the brain result in decreased production of BDNF, which in turn limits neural plasticity. The inflammatory response (linked to cortisol, etc.) causes some neural degeneration, which in turn results in further inflammation, causing a cyclical and ever-worsening response. There is some evidence that the reduction in BDNF production is greatest in the hippocampus, limbic system and cortex, which suggests that this plays a part in the experience of a negatively locked cognitive-affective cycle, which is part of depression. There is certainly some evidence that exercise, weight loss (for people who are obese), intellectual stimulation and physical and pharmacological treatments (such as antidepressants) all increase BDNF production (and thus increase neurogenesis), and therefore are all useful aspects of an integrated treatment approach for depression. There is also some evidence that exercise increases the production of GABA, which has a soothing effect.

The neurogenic hypothesis proposes that 'new neurons in the adult brain are needed for proper mood control and for antidepressant efficacy' (Eisch & Petrik, 2012: 338). In several studies, the hippocampus, which is involved in mood regulation and memory functioning, has been observed to be smaller in volume in depressed, untreated subjects (e.g. Sheline, Gado & Kraemer, 2003). Other studies have suggested that reduced production of new cells in the hippocampus may be related to depression (healthy adult humans produce around 700 new cells in the hippocampus every day). As the hippocampus is closely associated with memory functions, it is possible that neurogenesis in this brain structure increases overall neural plasticity, and thus positively influences pattern differentiation and adaptive memory. In depression, the memory tends to be negatively biased and to focus overly on negative stimuli, thus reinforcing a series of depressive memories which appear to the individual to support their negative perceptions. Unfortunately, this generates stress, which is evidenced by an increase in cortisol and other stress-related hormones which also suppress neurogenesis, thus making the depression more entrenched (Spalding *et al.*, 2013).

Prolonged stress leads to a chronic state of elevated cortisol. In addition to causing immune suppression, this can negatively affect memory, reduce levels of neurotransmitters associated with positive mood (such as serotonin, dopamine and endogenous opiates) and generate a sense of constant threat, which in turn triggers further cortisol release (Gilbert, 2007).

These theories are controversial, and not without their critics, although it would appear likely that people with untreated depression not only experience a reduction in neurogenesis of cells in several regions of the brain, but that depression involves a complex series of interacting endocrine and neurotransmitter signalling cascades.

Genetic influences on depression

There is some evidence that a short form of the 5-HTTLPR gene (one of the serotonin transporter genes) creates some kind of genetic predisposition towards depression and is associated with increased anxiety and neuroticism. It must be noted that the presence of such a gene does not mean that a person will inevitably become depressed, as there is substantial gene–environment interaction which takes place; that is, the environmental influences of the individual can modify the influence of this gene and in effect can switch the gene 'on' or 'off' (Gottlib & Joorman, 2010).

Effects of psychotherapy

Psychotherapy has demonstrated an ability to help bring cortisol levels to within normal range, increase serotonin levels, reduce amygdalar activity, increase amygdalar-PFC connectivity and restore normal activity levels within the hippocampus (see Sharpley, 2010, for a review of this research). Although the field of neuroscience and psychotherapy is still in its infancy, it would appear that psychotherapy promotes greater neural integration, up-regulates areas of sluggish activity and down-regulates areas of excessive activity, helps to promote optimal secretion of neurotransmitters associated with well-being and assists with the creation of new synaptic connections as old memories are retranscribed and new ones are created. Psychotherapy can be viewed as the provision of a relational environment that promotes optimal neural plasticity. 'Psychotherapists are applied neuroscientists who create individually tailored enriched learning environments designed to enhance brain functioning and mental health' (Cozolino, 2010: 341).

10 Medical treatment for depression

Note: this chapter is for guidance purposes only. Medication can only be prescribed by a medical doctor or licensed prescriber. It is essential that any proposed changes in medication be discussed with a medical doctor, prescriber or pharmacist and only take place under medical supervision. It is also important to note that, whilst the information here is accurate at time of writing, medical science is constantly changing. This document has been based on protocols in use in the USA and the UK. Other countries may have different treatment protocols.

The figures for antidepressant use are truly staggering. In 2011, 46.7 million prescriptions for antidepressants were issued in England alone. In 2012 the figure was 50.1 million prescriptions and by 2013 this had risen to 53.3 million. The cost to the UK's National Health Service in 2013 for these drugs was £282.1 million. Despite many public debates and much controversy surrounding the rates of antidepressant prescribing, antidepressant use remains high. Psychotherapists will regularly encounter clients in their practice who are taking antidepressant medication. It is useful for therapists to have an understanding of the major drug treatments for depression in order to support their clients.

Whilst the National Institute for Health and Care Excellence (NICE) guidelines recognise that psychotherapy is the treatment of choice for mild and moderate forms of depression, severe depression usually requires combined psychotherapy and pharmacological treatment. Studies have shown that the use of antidepressants for mild depression has little benefit and may be no better than a placebo. However, the benefits of antidepressant medication in severe depression are considerable (Fournier, De Rubeis, Hollon *et al.*, 2010) (Table 10.1). Drug treatment is particularly useful where there is significant sleep, appetite and concentration disturbance, and with suicidal ideation.

Although medication alone may be effective for treatment of depression, it does not address any underlying vulnerabilities or the psychological and interpersonal difficulties which contribute to the depression and, therefore, there is a high likelihood of relapse once medication is ceased (Evans *et al.*, 1992; Feldman & Feldman, 1997).

Despite its relatively poor performance for subclinical and mild forms of depression (Baumeister, 2012) and the preference for psychotherapy for such

Table 10.1 Depression severity and preferred treatment options

	Psychotherapy	Medication	Combined psychotherapy and medication
Mild	Yes (singly)	No	No
Moderate	Yes (singly or in combination)	Possibly (singly or in combination)	Possibly
Severe	Yes (with medication)	Yes (singly or in combination)	Yes (recommended)

cases, antidepressants are commonly prescribed for people at this milder end of the depressive spectrum. It is not hard to understand why this may be: general practitioners experience massive demand for their services, which they are expected to deliver to ever-larger populations in increasingly shorter consultations. Psychotherapy provision within the health services is also overstretched and underresourced, and patients referred for talking therapy may have to wait for many months before an assessment appointment becomes available. During this time, the person with depression may experience considerable worsening of symptoms, which would have a consequent effect on demand for health services. Given this situation, prescribing antidepressants which are (generally) safe, effective, easily tolerated and likely to have a quick action makes logical sense for patients who are unable to afford private psychotherapy.

Combined psychotherapy and medication is the treatment of choice for severe depression. Repeated studies have demonstrated significant benefit of combined psychotherapy and drug treatment approaches for severe depression. Where symptoms are severe, or are causing significant physical impairment (such as sleep or appetite disturbance), in cases of suicidal ideation or where there is insufficient response to psychotherapy, then referral for medication is advised (see below). Sleep deprivation in particular can be very distressing and can impair the ability to concentrate and, as such, can negatively affect a person's ability to engage fully with therapy. A profound sense of despair, where the client feels nothing will make any difference, is also an indicator for combined drug treatment and psychotherapy. In this instance, it is possible that the client will struggle to form an alliance or invest emotional energy in therapy without some kind of mood improvement.

How to suggest medication to clients

Where the client is experiencing severe or treatment-refractory depression, medication may be indicated. It is important to bear in mind that any suggestion that a client consult her doctor to explore drug treatment is likely to have relational and transferential significance for the client. Whilst some clients feel very supported and cared for by their therapist by suggestions to consider medication, others may have negative reactions, and may feel that this means that their therapist thinks that they are 'too much' for them to manage, or they may interpret this as meaning that their therapist thinks that they are weak. It is helpful to ask the client: 'How do you feel about me raising this?'

Other clients have concerns about dependence or addiction. It is worthwhile exploring if the client has any such concerns. Medication can be suggested using the following:

> Medication can provide some biochemical support to what we are doing so you can make full use of the therapy. Also, it can significantly speed this process up. We can certainly do this without medication, but you may find it easier and quicker if you combine therapy with medication. It's really up to you. Also, for some people, medication can give a little 'buoyancy' which can help with day-to-day living. It won't solve your problems, but it might make them a little easier to manage. In the meantime, we'll concentrate on dealing with your situation and in addressing any underlying susceptibility to depression that you might have. How about you take this discussion away with you and give it some thought and let me know next session what you have decided.

Communicating with medical practitioners

It is often useful to write brief letters to clients' general practitioner (GP) regarding your work together and if a medical consultation is needed regarding starting or stopping medication. It is good practice to send an initial courtesy letter to the patient's GP to inform him that you have started therapy with his patient. This is particularly the case with clients who are on medication. Some clients who are not on medication have reservations about the therapist letting their GP know that they have depression or are in therapy due to concerns that this will be written in their medical records. Where the client is experiencing mild to moderate depression, and does not want the GP to know, the therapist can exercise her own clinical judgement and discretion about whether to pursue the matter. Where the client is experiencing severe depression or is on medication, it is worth explaining to the client that this is not only a professional courtesy, but to ensure the client gets the right treatment. Reassure the client that the content of therapy sessions will be kept confidential, and the letter will focus primarily on the client's depression and general progress. Where the client has concerns about the letter, it can be useful to give the client the letter and suggest that he books an appointment with his GP and takes it along with him to hand to the GP in the consultation.

Suggested wording for a referral letter

Dear Dr [name]

Re: [client's name and date of birth]

I have recently seen your patient [name] for a consultation. I am of the opinion that [she or he] is currently depressed, and is experiencing [list main symptoms]. I have screened [him or her] using [name of measures], and the results suggest [indicate level of severity]. I would be grateful if you would have a consultation with this patient and consider the possibility of antidepressant medication.

We have agreed to work together for [x] number of sessions. I will contact you again when we have concluded the therapy, or in the case of any deterioration to [name of client]'s condition.

Yours,

[your name]

Suggested wording for a courtesy letter for clients on medication

Dear Dr [name]

Re: [client's name and date of birth]

Your patient [name] has recently started working with me for treatment of [his or her] depression. I understand [she or her] is currently being prescribed [name of medication, dosage and frequency]. Screening using [name of outcome measures] indicates that [she or he] is currently experiencing [severity of depression]. I will be continuing to monitor [his or her] progress, and will advise you of any improvement or deterioration.

Yours,

[your name]

Suggested wording for a letter for discontinuation of medication

Dear Dr [name]

Re: [client's name and date of birth]

As you are perhaps aware, I have been working with [name of client] for treatment of [his or her] depression for a period of [time]. I am aware that [she or he] has been prescribed [name of medication and dose] by you. I am pleased to report that [she or he] has made substantial progress. At the time of starting therapy [she or he] was screened using [name of outcome measures]. [His or her] starting scores indicated [severity level]. [His or her] current scores indicate [severity level]. Consequently, I would be grateful if you would consider reviewing [his or her] medication. [Name of client] has indicated that [she or he] would be interested in exploring options for discontinuation of medication with you. We have agreed to continue working together for a period of [number of sessions or weeks], during which I will be willing to help [him or her] manage any withdrawal syndrome and monitor [his or her] situation for any indicators of relapse. In the case of any deterioration, I will of course contact you again.

Yours,

[your name].

Recent findings from the Sequenced Treatment Alternatives to Relieve Depression (STAR*D) study suggest that it is beneficial to switch medication when the depressed individual does not respond to drug treatment after 6 weeks. The process of switching medication can be continued until a reasonable response has been achieved. The STAR*D study recommended switching medication to another medication class.

Antidepressants[1]

Antidepressants are, as one would expect, primarily used in the treatment of depression and mood disorders. They are also often prescribed for anxiety disorders, obsessive-compulsive disorder, pain disorders and eating disorders. After 3 months of treatment, the proportions of people with depression who will be much improved are 50–65% if given an antidepressant, compared with 25–30% if given an inactive 'dummy' pill, or placebo. An antidepressant is considered to have a 'sufficient response' if there is a 50% reduction in symptoms, with a 'partial response' being where there is a 25% reduction in symptoms. Remission is where there is an almost complete reduction in symptoms. Recovery is indicated when full remission from all symptoms has been maintained and there is a return to full, normal functioning.

Between 30% and 50% of people treated with any given antidepressant do not show a response to that particular drug. Where there has been insufficient response to the medication after a period of 4–6 weeks, it may be necessary to increase the dose or switch medications in order to find the right drug for the individual. Usually, a selective serotonin reuptake inhibitor (SSRI) is selected as the first antidepressant. In the case of insufficient response, dosage may be increased. If the drug is still not having the desired effect, commonly the patient is switched to a different SSRI. If the patient still has little or no response then s/he may be switched to a serotonin–noradrenaline reuptake inhibitor or mirtazapine. If there still no beneficial effect then the prescriber may consider the use of a tricyclic antidepressant.

SSRI drugs are designed to raise levels of serotonin in the brain. The response to an SSRI can be noticed within 1 week, although the full effect may not be felt for a period of 3 weeks. As SSRIs have a relatively low toxicity, they are safer for people at risk of suicide attempts.

A reasonable time to wait for a response to treatment is 4 weeks. If no response has occurred after 6 weeks, refer the client back to her physician to consider adjusting the dose or switching medication. It is important that medication is continued, even after remission, for a period of 6 months to prevent relapse. Gradual withdrawal is recommended (see below).

Most antidepressants are believed to work by preventing the reuptake of certain neurotransmitters, such as serotonin and noradrenaline (US: norepinephrine), although these theories are incomplete, and all the mechanisms are not properly understood at present.

Selective serotonin reuptake inhibitors

SSRIs act on the serotonin receptor system and are the usual first-line drug treatment of choice, as they are generally well tolerated, although, like all medications, they do have some side-effects. The low side-effect profile is a major advantage of these medications over other drug treatments. They are also relatively non-toxic (Von Wolff, Holzel, Westphal, Harter & Kriston, 2013). Low toxicity is an important consideration when managing clients with suicide risk.

The main antidepressant effect of SSRIs can be experienced by the end of the first week of treatment. Effects continue to build during the first 4 weeks of treatment (Taylor, Freemantle, Geddes *et al.*, 2006).

Currently, citalopram is the most commonly prescribed SSRI (Table 10.2). SSRIs are also often prescribed for anxiety disorders (anecdotal reports suggest sertraline is particularly good for anxiety). As paroxetine has the shortest half-life of all SSRIs, it is reported to have the worst withdrawal syndrome of the SSRI drugs.

Serotonin and noradrenaline reuptake inhibitors

The main mode of action of SNRIs is at the serotonin and noradrenaline receptor systems in the brain. In addition to being used as an antidepressant, they are sometimes used for anxiety, fibromyalgia and neuropathic pain. Anecdotal reports suggest that the withdrawal syndrome from SNRIs can be particularly unpleasant.

Table 10.2 Common antidepressants and usual dosage

Common medications	Drug class	Usual start dose	Usual therapeutic range
Citalopram	SSRI	20 mg	20–60 mg
Escitalopram	SSRI	10 mg	10–20 mg
Fluoxetine	SSRI	20 mg	20–60 mg
Paroxetine	SSRI	20 mg	20–60 mg
Sertraline	SSRI	50 mg	50–200 mg
Duloxetine	SNRI	60 mg	60–120 mg
Venlafaxine	SNRI	37.5 mg	75–375 mg
Mirtazapine	NaSSA	15 mg	15–45 mg
Nefazodone	SARI	50 mg	150–300 mg
Trazodone	SARI	150 mg	150–600 mg
Amitriptyline	Tricyclic	25–50 mg	100–300 mg
Doxepin	Tricyclic	25–50 mg	100–300 mg
Imipramine	Tricyclie	25–50 mg	100–300 mg

SSRI, selective serotonin reuptake inhibitor; SNRI, serotonin–noradrenaline reuptake inhibitor; NaSSA, noradrenergic and specific serotonergic antidepressant; SARI, serotonin antagonist and reuptake inhibitor.

Noradrenergic and specific serotonergic antagonists (NaSSAs)

Mirtazapine is the main medication in this class of drugs. It tends to be prescribed when SSRIs have not worked, or for people with severe depression who also have problems sleeping. Because it causes drowsiness, it is usually recommended that it is taken at bedtime. Anecdotal reports suggest that mirtazapine causes substantially increased appetite, particularly for carbohydrate foods.

Serotonin antagonist and reuptake inhibitors (SARI)

This class of drugs is rarely prescribed any more, although it may still be used by people with chronic depression; therefore, therapists may occasionally encounter clients taking these medications. SARIs are known to be particularly liver-toxic, which makes them unsuitable for people with suicidal ideation. Trazodone causes drowsiness, so tends to be used for depression with sleeping problems.

Tricyclic antidepressants

Tricyclics are an older type of antidepressant and tend to be prescribed either for people who have been on these drugs for many years, or for people who have not responded to any of the newer drugs, such as SSRIs. They affect noradrenaline and serotonin in the brain. They are quick-acting, and so useful when a speedy effect is needed; however they are highly toxic, so not suitable for people at risk of suicide attempts. Also, they tend to have a higher side-effect profile than the newer medications, such as SSRIs. As drowsiness is one of the more common side-effects, they are useful in treatment of agitated depression. Low-dose amitriptyline is often prescribed for neuralgia and neuropathic pain (for example, post-shingles pain).

Bupropion is a newer antidepressant and is sometimes used for treatment-resistant depression. It is a dopamine noradrenaline reuptake inhibitor. It is most commonly prescribed under the name Zyban as a smoking cessation aid. As it is a fairly new drug, there is not as much information available regarding its use compared to many other antidepressants.

There is insufficient evidence to support the use of treatment augmentation with a second antidepressant for non-responders. However, some drugs (notably, mirtazapine) have a sedative and appetite-stimulating effect, which may be useful. Nevertheless, the addition of a second antidepressant is not supported by the current literature (Rocha, Fuzikawa, Riera, Guarieiro-Ramo & Hara, 2013).

Side effects of antidepressant medications

Like most medications, antidepressants also have some side-effects. These tend to be fairly mild, and will usually improve over the first few weeks. SSRIs and SNRIs have similar side-effects, which include: dry mouth, drowsiness, headaches, sexual dysfunction (men generally report problems ejaculating), nervousness (sometimes even anxiety), gastrointestinal disturbance (diarrhoea or constipation, nausea), insomnia and appetite changes such as increased or decreased appetite. Side-effects from these drugs are usually mild.

Common side-effects of tricyclics include: increased heart rate, drowsiness, dry mouth, constipation, headaches, urinary retention, blurred vision, dizziness, confusion and sexual dysfunction.

Weight gain and appetite increase are common side-effects of all psychoactive medication, although, with good diet and regular exercise, this effect is moderated. Some medications, such as mirtazapine or trazodone, cause drowsiness, which makes this particularly useful for people who have problems sleeping.

Withdrawal

There are two main reasons medication is stopped. The first is in order to switch medications where there has been insufficient response to the first drug; the second is when a person has recovered and is no longer experiencing symptoms. Usually, it is recommended that antidepressant use is continued for a period of 6 months after recovery. This is to prevent the risk of relapse in this sensitive time period. Withdrawal from antidepressants needs to take place gradually, with dosage being reduced in small increments 1 week at a time. Risk of relapse is greatest in the first 2 months after cessation of medication.

Withdrawal symptoms are common in cessation of all antidepressants, and withdrawal needs to be approached carefully, and ideally should take place over an extended period of time (particularly with SSRIs). Common withdrawal symptoms include gastrointestinal disturbance (such as diarrhoea), sleep disturbance (including weird and vivid dreams) and depressive or anxiety symptoms, which can at times be very severe. Many people report odd periodic physical sensations, such as 'an electric shock through their brain', which can be distressing. Some medications are reported to have a worse withdrawal syndrome than others. For example, anecdotal reports suggest that withdrawal symptoms from SNRIs such as venlafaxine, duloxetine and paroxetine are particularly hard.

Supporting clients who are stopping medication

It is important to stress to clients that sudden withdrawal is not recommended and that any withdrawal *must* only be done with medical supervision and with the agreement of the prescriber. It is worth explaining that withdrawal symptoms tend to appear after a few days, peaking around 5–10 days after cessation, and tend to ease at around 14 days after last dose.

Other medical treatments

Complementary medicine treatments

S-adenosyl methionine (SAMe) or St John's wort may be considered as complementary medicine treatments for depression. Both have shown promise in several trials and are generally well tolerated. Please be aware that St John's wort has many drug interactions and must *not* be taken without consulting a physician or pharmacist if the client is taking *any* other medication. SAMe has also been successfully trialled as an adjunct treatment for people with treatment-resistant depression who are also taking SSRI drugs (Papakostas *et al.*, 2010). SAMe is safe and is not known to have any adverse drug interactions.

Light-box therapy can be useful for seasonal affective disorder. Some people with non-seasonal depression also find the use of a light box to be helpful. A recent study confirmed the usefulness of light-box therapy with antidepressants for non-seasonal depression (Dallaspezia *et al.*, 2012).

One safe nutritional strategy which has some empirical support is the use of zinc supplements to boost the effect of antidepressants (Jacka, Maes, Pasco, Williams & Berk, 2012; Lai *et al.*, 2012). As standard-dose zinc supplements are safe, relatively inexpensive and available in many pharmacies and supermarkets, clients who are interested in nutritional and complementary treatments may find them to be of use. Other nutrients which have shown promise are vitamin D, folate and magnesium. These dietary supplements are also easily available and safe to use (Humble, 2010; Jacka *et al.*, 2012).

Antipsychotics

Whilst primarily used in the treatment of psychotic states, low-dose antipsychotics are also sometimes prescribed by psychiatrists in addition to antidepressants for the treatment of severe depression (particularly depression with psychotic features such as delusions).

Antipsychotics are sometimes referred to as *neuroleptic* drugs. Quetiapine is a newer, second-generation antipsychotic and can be used in low doses as an adjunct treatment for depression (with antidepressants). It is useful for severe depression, agitation, deep emotional dysregulation and insomnia. Some people are prescribed quetiapine to take on an 'as and when needed' basis to help them calm down or sleep.

Commonly used antipsychotic drugs include: haloperidol, chlorpromazine, mellaril, stelazine, depixol, clopixol, clozapine, risperidone and olanzapine. Olanzapine (one of the newer antipsychotics) is often used over some of the older drugs as it is better tolerated. It is sometimes prescribed together with an antidepressant for severe depression, psychosis or bipolar disorder. Another second-generation antipsychotic, risperidone, is sometimes prescribed for treatment-resistant depression or for depression where there is comorbid severe anxiety (Mahmoud, Pandina, Turkoz *et al.*, 2007). Because of their action on dopamine receptors in the brain, some of the older antipsychotics can have strong Parkinson's disease-like side-effects, which are known as tardive dyskinesia. Antipsychotics frequently cause weight gain, which can be very distressing to patients who are prescribed these drugs. They can also negatively impact motivation and cause sluggishness and memory impairment. Dryness of the mouth is a commonly reported side-effect. Dizziness, drowsiness, nausea and constipation are other common side-effects. Generally, antipsychotics are prescribed by a psychiatrist and anyone on these medications would need their use and withdrawal carefully medically supervised.

Benzodiazepines

Although benzodiazepines are not used in the treatment of depression, they are included here as therapists may encounter clients who are taking them for other problems. Benzodiazepine drugs (such as diazepam, lorazepam, temazepam and nitrazepam) are tranquillisers which have hypnotic, sedative, anxiolytic, anticonvulsant and muscle-relaxing properties. They are primarily used in the short-term treatment of acute anxiety. As benzodiazepines can actually increase depressive symptoms, they are rarely used in depression, although they may be prescribed for short-term management of comorbid anxiety. They are often used as a quick-acting drug in an acute psychiatric emergency, such as psychotic or manic episodes. Interestingly, they are contraindicated for use in obsessional disorders. Usually, people who are terrified of flying can easily get a prescription for a small number of diazepam from their GP to manage the anxiety of flights, particularly long-haul flights. Benzodiazepines are quick-acting and stay in the system for a long time, which can be useful where a prolonged effect is needed, but can be problematic as the individual can experience a 'hangover' from their usage. They are safe for short-term use; however they must not be used with alcohol. Because they cause respiratory repression, overdose results in high fatality rates.

Diazepam is the most commonly prescribed benzodiazepine in psychoactive usage. It comes in 2, 5 and 10 mg tablets. Benzodiazepines are highly addictive, with dependency occurring in as little as 3 weeks of daily use; therefore they are not suitable for anything other than short-term use. Sudden cessation can be very dangerous, and withdrawal needs to be managed carefully with medical supervision and needs to take place over a long period of time, with medication reduced in small increments. Withdrawal will take several weeks and maybe even as much as several years in long-term dependency. Withdrawal symptoms include anxiety symptoms, irritability, sleep problems and feelings of depersonalisation, all of which can be very intense. Because of this, many patients panic and feel their original symptoms are returning, and so resume their previous dose, thus maintaining the dependency. Patients need to be advised that withdrawal symptoms are common and unpleasant and that the symptoms need to be worked through; they can be reassured that the symptoms will lessen in a few weeks.

Beta-blockers

Beta-blockers are drugs primarily designed for use in some heart conditions, such as angina and arrhythmias. Their primary action is on the sympathetic nervous system, and so they are often used in the short-term treatment of anxiety and panic symptoms. They lower heart rate and stop palpitations (propranolol reduces tremor, so is popular in treatment of anxiety) associated with anxiety, and so interrupt the feedback loop that occurs in anxiety (the person feels the heart racing, which in turn exacerbates the anxiety symptoms). As anxiety is often comorbid with depression, therapists may occasionally encounter clients who have been prescribed these drugs for management of anxiety symptoms. Propranolol and atenolol are commonly prescribed beta-blockers. Side-effects can include nausea, headaches, dizziness and problems getting to sleep. Beta-blockers are quick-acting, and so can be used for situational anxiety, such as before giving a public speech. They are not recommended for long-term use, and are not suitable for patients with asthma and similar conditions.

Mood-stabilising drugs

Mood-stabilising drugs are a core component of treatment of bipolar disorder, and they are occasionally prescribed by psychiatrists as an adjunct treatment for people with severe, chronic depression where standard drug treatment has not been effective. Mood-stabilising drugs include lithium and some anticonvulsants such as carbamazepine and sodium valproate, which are sometimes also used for this purpose. Mood stabilisers are often combined with an antidepressant, although antidepressants (particularly SSRIs) can trigger mania or hypomania in those who are prone to these states. Lithium dosage needs to be monitored carefully, with patients generally being admitted to hospital while the correct dose is established in order to avoid kidney damage.

Electroconvulsive therapy

Electroconvulsive therapy (ECT) is rarely used in modern psychiatry, and tends to be reserved for people with severe, treatment-resistant depression. It is also used in severe postpartum depression and psychosis, and is sometimes the only effective treatment for severe catatonic depression. ECT is known to be effective and has a high response rate to treatment. It is usually administered in an inpatient setting, with 6–12 treatments carried out over a number of weeks. It is, however, an extreme treatment, and is a frightening prospect for most people. Recently, transcranial magnetic stimulation has been examined as a safer, less 'invasive' alternative to ECT, and has shown promise for use in severe, treatment-resistant depression.

Physical and experimental treatments

There are a range of physical and experimental treatments which have been explored as potential treatments of depression. For example, light-boxes have been trialled with people with depression and have shown to be a potentially useful adjunct to treatment (see above). Several studies have also found that a sleep deprivation and light therapy protocol can be useful in inpatient treatment of severe depression (Echizenya, Suda, Takeshima & Inomata, 2013). Hormone treatments may also be of use, particularly where there is some underlying hormonal problem. One study found that treatment using testosterone gel was effective for men with low testosterone levels and treatment-resistant depression (Pope, Cohane, Kanayama, Siegel & Hudson, 2003). Other experimental treatments are currently being investigated. For instance, several studies have found that ketamine (an anaesthetic drug which is also used recreationally as a 'club drug') may have some antidepressant effect.

Physical exercise

There is evidence to support the use of physical exercise for the treatment of depression (Cooney et al., 2013). It would appear that exercise alone has only a mild antidepressant effect. The UK's NICE guidelines for treatment of depression recommend exercising for 45–60 minutes three times a week. There is certainly a strong argument in favour of encouraging clients with depression who do not have any physical health problems (or, in the case of people with health problems, those who have their physician's agreement) to engage in regular exercise as part of their treatment programme.

Note

[1] Medication dosage data taken from the American Psychiatric Association (2010) *Practice Guideline for the Treatment of Patients with Major Depressive Disorder*.

Conclusion

It is my hope that this book has provided you with a solid grounding in the theory and practice of transactional analysis (TA) psychotherapy for depression. I also hope that you will feel more confident in working with clients with depression and that you will be able to take the knowledge and suggestions described in this book and apply these creatively in your own practice. Although the main focus of this book has been depression, it is likely that you will be able to use many of the strategies described (such as the role induction process) advantageously with a wide range of clients. Please do not use the material in this book rigidly; rather, use it with a spirit of enquiry and curiosity. Try out the suggestions and keep the ones that work.

Although there is an enormous body of research literature on both depression and psychotherapy, there is still much to be learnt about the process and mechanisms of change. There is considerable variance amongst TA practitioners in terms of how they work with their clients. On the surface, these approaches can appear incompatible with each other. It is my view that experiential change mechanisms unify these, and that the underlying change processes are more similar than they are different. Time will tell, and further research will provide greater detail about the nature of therapeutic change and how we can maximise our effectiveness in practice.

I will be continuing to develop resources for therapists, training workshops and further research into the process and outcome of TA psychotherapy at the University of Salford. Please feel free to contact me or check out what the latest developments are via the University or any of the TA organisations worldwide. You can also keep abreast of current TA research by signing up for the free, open-access *International Journal of Transactional Analysis Research* at www.ijtar.org.

I welcome your feedback about this book, and I am particularly interested in hearing about your innovations and discoveries connected to the material I have presented here. TA psychotherapy is a growing and developing approach, and its vitality comes from the energy of people who use TA to promote change. This book has been based on and developed directly from research. I hope that it has gone some way to demonstrating that psychotherapy research findings can be practical, easy to implement in practice and can enhance the therapeutic process. I invite you to participate in the evolution of TA, in whatever way you can.

The work of a therapist is tough and demanding and can require considerable emotional energy. It is also immensely rewarding, intellectually stimulating and deeply engaging, and there is often much laughter in with the tears and pain. I hope that this book will help to sustain and guide you in those difficult times and support you in co-creating more of the satisfying times.

Appendices

Appendices

Appendix 1
Getting the most out of therapy

Therapy involves establishing a therapeutic relationship between the client and the therapist which differs in nature and structure to any other relationship. The bulk of the work of therapy is conversational in nature, and yet the conversation and relationship differ from the normal patterns of relationships and conversations that you might have in your day-to-day life. As such, psychotherapy can seem rather strange at the outset, and it is helpful to have some idea about how it works, what you can expect and how you can get the most benefit out of it.

One of the ways in which the therapeutic relationship is different to other relationships is that, in therapy, both people are focused on the client. Your therapist's job is to help you increase your understanding of yourself and your situation, and to help you gain the resources you need to make changes in your life. The therapeutic relationship is designed to be both a supportive and a challenging environment that promotes optimal growth.

Firstly, it can be very helpful if you and your therapist have a discussion about your expectations of the therapy and the therapist. Lack of clarity on this at such an early stage can get in the way later on, and it is useful for you both to have a clear and realistic sense of what you expect from each other, and from the whole process.

We know from lots of previous research that clients who are actively involved in their therapy achieve better outcomes from therapy. In transactional analysis (TA) therapy, the client is expected to be an active participant at every stage in the therapy process. Therapy is not something 'done to' you – it is something you actively engage with.

You will be invited to set your own goals and objectives for your therapy. In this respect, the client very much sets the agenda. It is helpful if you come to therapy with some idea of what it is that you want to get out of therapy. It is fine if you are not clear to begin with, and a lot of people begin therapy in exactly that situation. In such situations, the early part of therapy is focused on exploration and on helping you develop some clarity around what you want and to set your goals. Your goals will provide the focus for the therapy. It is important that you and your therapist are clear about your goals for therapy. When you are both clear about where you are and where you want to get to, this can be likened to getting in a car with a destination in mind and a map and a clear idea of where you are now. Working out the route is far easier when you have a clear idea of where you want to get to!

Sometimes clients set very large and ambitious goals. It is fine to have ambitious goals, although, sometimes if the therapy is relatively short-term, then these goals might need to be reworked to make them realistic and achievable for the time available. Your therapist will help you generate realistic and achievable goals.

As part of being an active participant in your therapy, and to facilitate the process of change, your therapist and you are likely to come up with 'homework' for you to do in between sessions. This can include things like using relaxation techniques, writing down your thoughts or feelings about something or practising new behaviours. Any 'homework' that you come up with together, or that your therapist suggests, will be specifically designed to help you with some aspect of your problem and to help you achieve your goals, or to take what you have learnt in therapy into your everyday life. Previous psychotherapy research shows that engagement with and completion of such homework contributes significantly towards positive outcomes in therapy. Regardless of whether your therapist recommends 'homework' or not, it is helpful if you spend time between sessions thinking about your therapy and, in particular, if you take forward the insights you gain in therapy into your day-to-day life and experiment with new ways of thinking, feeling, behaving and interacting with others as a result of the conversations you have with your therapist.

When you come to sessions, it is fine for you to have a clear agenda for the session, and it is fine for you to come without an agenda – there is no one right way of working, and it may be that you and your therapist try different things at different times to work out what is right for you at that particular time.

Therapy requires you to be fully present and experiencing in the moment, but also to have a part of you that is simultaneously observing yourself and how you are reacting and responding to what is happening in the session. Full engagement in therapy requires a high degree of honesty and transparency of thoughts and emotions and a willingness to speak about things that you wouldn't ordinarily speak about. In doing so, you may be aware that you are not discussing everything that is coming to mind and that you are concealing some of your thoughts. It might be that they are painful, or embarrassing, or you might feel afraid of the potential implications of what you are about to say, or you think your thoughts are too trivial, or maybe you are concerned about what your therapist will think of you. Something like this happens to most people at some point in therapy. When you encounter reluctance like this, it is best dealt with by telling the therapist that you are hesitating, or feeling embarrassed or worried, or whatever the difficulty is, as your feelings and thoughts will be important. It can be very hard discussing issues that are so private and things that you may never have spoken about before. Often, the things we are most reluctant to discuss end up being some of the most important things to discuss in therapy. It is important to remember that it is not your therapist's job to judge you and your therapist is not likely to be shocked by what you might say. You can talk about whatever you want to talk about, and you will not need to dredge up the past if you do not want to. Your therapist will be particularly interested in how things are for *you* and your unique way of thinking, feeling and experiencing yourself, others and the world.

In sessions, your therapist will ask lots of questions and find out as much as s/he can about your thoughts, feelings, sensations, reactions, hopes and fears about many things, including experiences in your day-to-day life, the problems and situations that brought you to therapy, your experiences within sessions, and also experiences from your past. Your therapist will do his or her best to understand how things are from your point of view, and to understand how you feel and what you think. These questions will give the therapist information but, most importantly, they will help you gain greater insight and understanding into the nature of your problems and increase your self-awareness. In therapy, the emphasis is very much on the client engaging in a process of self-discovery.

As part of this, you will look at what you can do to improve things for yourself, how problems come about and what you can do about them, and also how you came to be the person you are and how you got to be in the situation you are in. Your therapist will also provide a degree of challenge and invite you to look at things in new ways.

Generally, therapists do not give advice and will not tell you what to do or what choices you should make in important decisions in your life. Your therapist will, however, help you to work out your options, work out specific courses of action, examine the pros and cons of each course of action and examine your thoughts and feelings regarding your options.

Sometimes your therapist might be able to provide you with some explanation to help you understand what is going on for you, or how you came to be in the situation you are in. It is fine for you to ask for explanation, although this cannot be rushed, and sometimes it can take a long time to work out the different pieces of the puzzle. As part of this, your therapist may share ideas or bits of theory which you might find useful.

If you have a tendency to overanalyse things or 'think too much', your therapist might suggest a more experiential approach instead. On the other hand, explanation and theory can help you make sense of situations which are confusing or distressing and can help you work out different options and ways of responding in different situations. The best approach is the one that is right for you, at that particular time, and your therapist will do what s/he can to ensure that s/he is working with you optimally at each stage of the therapy.

Your therapist will probably place a great deal of emphasis on the here and now and what is going on for you in the session. Therapists generally believe that understanding the here and now is the key to figuring out what is going on for you and working out a way forward. This can include discussing how you are relating to each other in the sessions. It is difficult to explain this, but it is something you will experience in sessions quite quickly and, although it might feel a little strange at first, you will soon become used to such frank, open discussions.

Therapy can at times be painful or feel embarrassing. It is important that, if you feel that, you are honest about it with your therapist. The feelings people have about therapy and their therapist are often of vital importance. By paying attention to these feelings, and exploring them together, you and your therapist can learn a great deal about your problems, your ways of viewing things, your thinking patterns and, of course, how you relate to people. Therapy provides a unique environment to do precisely this. For example, sometimes people feel a little anxious, or inexplicably ashamed, or sometimes they even start worrying that their therapist might be judging them. All of these feelings are important. Even though it will feel a little strange at first, you will be encouraged to share whatever is on your mind, particularly relating to coming to therapy or your therapist, no matter how strange or irrational it might seem.

As the therapy progresses and the work gets deeper, your feelings will also very likely intensify. This can feel very strange, and sometimes even a little frightening. What is important is that whatever you are feeling about your therapist and the therapy relationship is important, and it is important to be honest about those feelings and bring them out into the open where you can look at them and understand them. As part of this, you might find that, on occasion, you feel very angry with, or even in some way hurt by, your therapist. These feelings are very important, and although you might not feel like it, it will be important that you find a way to express them to your therapist. Your feelings will be taken seriously and your therapist will help you to find a way forward. It is absolutely fine to say what you think your therapist is thinking, and to ask your therapist what s/he is thinking. Generally, your therapist will be clear and direct with you, although s/he might respond indirectly. If s/he responds indirectly, there will be a reason for this, and s/he will be clear with you about this.

It is absolutely fine to talk about subjects that may seem to be unrelated and to 'jump around' in sessions. Your therapist will be able to manage this, and will stop you and get clarification if necessary. Generally, there is some kind of link between topics, and your therapist will be listening out for emerging patterns, themes and links between the things you discuss. Also, in listening carefully to you, your therapist will be finding out more about *how* you think, not just listening to the content, so even jumping around can be useful from the therapist's point of view. Sometimes things don't make much sense during sessions, and it is often in the time between sessions when you have had time to process what was discussed and for your thinking to 'settle into place' that things will start to make more sense. Some sessions will feel very intense, whereas other will leave you feeling unsure about what was discussed or whether there is any point continuing. It is important that you mention your feelings about this to your therapist. Also, sometimes, sessions which you might have felt were frustrating end up being the ones where the underlying issues were beginning to be discovered and eventually you and your therapist can figure out where your frustration was coming from.

Timing is important, and the process of therapy cannot be rushed. It is something which unfolds over time. One way of thinking about it is to imagine the construction of a new building – it might take a long time for the foundations to be laid, and the ground work to be done, but these are crucial in determining the strength of the new structure.

Appendix 2
Self-help for depression[1]

Depression is an extremely common problem and it is estimated that one in ten adults will experience depression at some point during their life. It is a complex problem which has many differing symptoms, which can include: a sense of loss of pleasure and interest in life and activities, feelings of worthlessness, guilt, inferiority, inadequacy, helplessness and weakness, together with an overwhelming sense of sadness, despair, loss of hope and self-hatred. Depression can also cause impaired concentration and memory, indecisiveness and intense self-criticism. Suicidal ideation of varying intensities is extremely common in depressed individuals. Also, there are a number of physical symptoms associated with depression which can include fatigue, lethargy, sleep disruption, restlessness and agitation, headache, muscular pain, back pain, weight loss or gain or appetite changes and loss of sexual desire.

Fortunately, there are a number of things you can do which can help you to feel better. The problem, however, is often motivation and feeling that any attempts to help yourself will be hopeless. That is part of how depression works – it leaves people feeling hopeless and drains any motivation from them. The difficulty is that feeling like things are hopeless and feeling tired and lacking in motivation to do anything put people who are depressed on a downward spiral that leads them to feel worse.

When people are depressed, they begin to do less because they don't feel up to doing their usual things. The problem is that this tends to make the problem worse, as, eventually, people who are depressed do less and less and then feel bad about themselves because of the reduction in their activity levels. Doing less also means that people who are depressed do not have enough positive and enjoyable activities in their life to help generate or sustain good feelings.

Although you might feel tired, hopeless and lacking in motivation, it is essential to your recovery that you take active steps to help yourself recover from your depression. There is considerable research which shows that people who have depression who put time and energy into activities which will help them recover have a substantially higher rate of recovery, will get better quicker and are less likely to relapse than those who hope and wait for their depression to change by chance. Similarly, research has demonstrated that people in therapy who consistently complete any between-session 'homework' also have better outcomes to their therapy.

All of the things listed here are known to help improve mood and feelings of well-being. These recommendations work best when you consistently put them into practice over a period of time – none of them will work like a 'magic cure' and change everything immediately but, when used regularly and in combination, they can help you to feel better. Be patient when using them as the effect of using them gradually builds up and increases over time.

It is important that you are realistic with yourself – everyone's mood fluctuates to some extent, so, even when you put these things into practice, you will still have bad days. That doesn't mean that things aren't working; it just means that, today, they might not be so effective. Persist with them and, over time, they may help you to feel much better.

Also, remember, you will get things wrong, forget to do things and make a mess of things from time to time – this is normal, and part of being a person. We all mess up, get things wrong and forget things from time to time. Don't give yourself a hard time for making mistakes.

It can be hard to find time to do things to make yourself feel better. Most people lead very busy lives and have a lot of demands on their time. The purpose of these recommendations is to help you feel better about yourself – if you feel better about yourself you may well find that other things in your life improve. It is important to prioritise *you* and to really commit to feeling better. Making big changes in how you feel will require time and effort on your part – it is recommended that you put in at least 20 minutes per day into activities that will contribute to your recovery.

If you have a lot of housework or studying to do, it is very easy to see the whole lot and become disheartened and feel overwhelmed by it all, and then lose any motivation to do anything about it. Breaking things down into small chunks can help with this. For instance, spending 15 minutes on something you are finding hard to face (such as the housework or studying, or even taking some exercise) starts making a difference – it might not be much at first, but doing something is better than doing nothing. Following the guidance outlined here will help you with your therapy and to feel better much more quickly.

Physical exercise

There is some evidence to suggest that exercising three times per week has a mild antidepressant effect and can improve mood and general feelings of well-being. It is best to choose a type of exercise you enjoy (walking, swimming, exercise classes or weight training) and to stick to it.

Feeling in the mood to exercise is difficult for many people who feel depressed, but it is worth pushing yourself. You can start with a 10-minute walk and build up gradually if you feel very low in energy. If you build up your exercise levels to 45 minutes of exercise three times per week, you will find over a number of weeks that your energy levels increase and you feel better generally.

Diet

Some people find that their mood is improved by paying attention to their diet. Some nutritionists recommend the following advice, which you might find helpful:

- Increase your levels of omega-3 fats, either by eating oily fish regularly or by taking a supplement.
- Ensure you are getting enough vitamins and minerals – eat plenty of fresh fruit and vegetables and perhaps take a supplement.
- Eat two sources of protein each day to help your body build serotonin and other brain chemicals which affect your mood.
- Cut down on sugar and refined products (for example, switch to wholemeal rather than white bread).

These recommendations are all quite straightforward and in line with government healthy-eating guidelines. It can be hard to feel motivated to eat properly if you feel down, but it is important that you give yourself the best chance you can to help yourself feel better. Feeling healthier will help you to feel better about yourself.

Managing difficult thoughts and feelings

Trying to avoid or suppress certain thoughts or feelings is not very effective as a strategy. In order to feel better, we might need to examine and change how we think and feel about things. Bad feelings are inevitable – everybody feels upset or anxious or angry sometimes; it's just a natural part of life. It's just how we are made, and is part of being human. While we can't avoid feeling upset from time to time, we can learn skills to help us manage our difficult or painful feelings and to carry on with our lives even when we do feel upset.

It can help to remember that feelings are just feelings – even though they might feel terrible, they will pass, no matter how bad they feel. It is important to remember that, while we can't always control how we feel, we do have choices about how we act on our feelings and on what we do about our feelings.

It is unrealistic to think that you have to feel good all the time and to think that you can only do important things when you feel good. Feeling bad does not necessarily stop anyone from doing anything – you can still get on with your life even though you feel upset.

If you struggle with particular emotions, speak to your therapist about them and get some help in finding ways of managing them.

Self-care and self-nurturing

When people feel down, they often neglect themselves. It is important to take good care of yourself, and to do activities which you enjoy or that leave you feeling good. Sometimes, we can adjust how we approach some of the things we do every day to help how we feel. For example, we can turn some of our daily activities into opportunities to nurture or care for ourselves, such as deciding 'I am doing this to relax' when reading the newspaper or by making an effort over our appearance, even when we don't really feel like it. Things like this don't need to take up much time or effort or even cost anything but can help us to feel better.

Social contact

There is some evidence to suggest that regular social contact can improve mood and feelings of well-being. It can be hard to maintain social contact with people when you feel down, but it is important that you maintain regular contact with people. Humans are social creatures and interactions with other people give us 'emotional vitamins' which help us to be more emotionally healthy. Of course, some relationships are damaging or leave us feeling bad about ourselves – in such cases it can be best to reduce or even stop contact with someone who leaves us feeling bad.

In general, it is recommended that you have some sort of social contact at least once a week. It is worth speaking to your therapist about how you can improve your relationships and how you communicate with people to enable you to give and get the most out of your relationships and to make them more satisfying for you and others.

Improving your sleep and your body clock

Getting a good night's sleep is very important when you feel down. Unfortunately, many people who are depressed find that their sleeping patterns become very disrupted and they find it hard to get to sleep and to stay asleep long enough. These recommendations can help with getting back into a good sleep pattern and in improving the quality of sleep that you have. You will need to persist with these recommendations though, because they can take a few weeks before they start to take full effect. This is because changing your body clock is best done gradually, and over a number of weeks. Getting into a good routine is important in improving your sleeping patterns.

- Go to bed at the same time every day.
- Get up from bed at the same time every day.
- Get some exercise every day – even as little as 10 minutes can help. Some people find going outdoors and getting some fresh air and light is helpful. Avoid exercising late in the evening as this can keep you awake.
- Keep the temperature in your bedroom a little cooler than the rest of the house – if you are too hot this can interfere with your sleep.
- Try to shut out as much noise as possible and also keep your bedroom quiet when trying to sleep.
- Keep your bedroom dark to help your sleep. Light interferes with the release of sleep hormones, so you might want to get some heavier curtains or blinds or use an eye mask.

- Use your bed only for sleep and sex – don't watch television in bed.
- Avoid anything too stimulating before bed, such as playing computer games or watching anything exciting on TV or reading anything exciting or engaging.
- Avoid anything with caffeine in it during the evening. This includes tea, coffee, cola drinks and chocolate.
- Avoid using alcohol to help you sleep – alcohol reduces the quality of your sleep.
- If you are too hungry or too full this can disrupt your sleep. If you are hungry before bed, a small, light snack may help but avoid anything which will leave you feeling full or bloated.
- Avoid having daytime naps – this can be difficult if you are very tired and sleep-deprived, but naps during the day can affect the quality of your sleep.
- Try to avoid getting angry or annoyed if you are struggling to get to sleep. If you have been in bed awake for more than 30 minutes, get up and do something quiet and relaxing and then go back to bed when you feel sleepy.

Mindfulness

Mindfulness is a practice which was developed from meditation, and a lot of recent research has demonstrated it to be effective in helping people with depression and anxiety feel better. There is also research that strongly suggests that ongoing mindfulness practice helps people stay well once they are recovered.

Mindfulness basically involves training the mind to focus and pay attention in a particular way to the present moment and to do so non-judgementally. It can take quite a lot of practice to retrain the mind into good habits, but there is good evidence to show that regular mindfulness practice pays off, and people can experience good benefit from as little as 8 weeks of daily mindfulness practice.

There are two types of mindfulness practice – formal mindfulness meditation and applied mindfulness. Formal mindfulness meditation will need you to set some time (about 5–15 minutes) aside each day, whereas you can easily fit applied mindfulness into your daily life. You will benefit most from a combination of both methods, and from spending about 20 minutes a day on mindfulness practice.

Mindful breathing

The aim of mindful breathing is to develop a calm and non-judging awareness and to allow your thoughts and feelings to come and go without getting caught up in them.

- Sit comfortably, with your spine reasonably straight. It helps to close your eyes.
- Bring your attention to your breathing.
- Notice the sensations in your abdomen as you breathe in and breathe out. Your abdomen rises with the in-breath and falls with the out-breath.
- Thoughts and feelings will come into your mind: that's OK, because that's just how the human mind normally works. When thoughts and feelings pop

into your mind, you simply notice them, and then bring your attention back to your breathing.
- Likewise, you will probably become aware of sounds, smells, sensations, and so on. Once again, when this happens, just notice them and then bring your attention back to your breathing. In mindfulness, rather than following these thoughts or feelings, you allow yourself to let them go. You don't need to judge or criticise yourself for having them, and the purpose is not for you to start analysing your thoughts or feelings – the purpose is simply to recognise that they are OK and just to let them be. When you notice your thoughts and feelings, you just let them drift on by and then bring your attention back to your breathing.

Whenever you notice that your attention has drifted off, simply note that your attention has wandered, and then gently bring it back to your breathing. It is natural for various thoughts and feelings to enter into your awareness and for your mind to start to follow them while you are doing your mindfulness practice. No matter how many times this happens, just keep bringing your attention back to your breathing. Remember, the purpose of mindfulness is gradual retraining of your mind and switching off many of the day-to-day ways of thinking and being we use all the time.

Mindfulness with emotions

It can be very beneficial to use mindfulness skills to help manage your emotions. By focusing your attention on your breath, your body and the experience of the emotion, you can learn to take a step back from the emotion and to understand it. The purpose of using mindfulness to manage your feelings is to learn to accept the experience, rather than lessen the distress, although most people find that, in learning not to fear it or struggle against their emotions, this can help reduce the distress they feel. The process of using mindfulness with feeling involves noticing, naming, accepting and exploring your emotions.

To do this mindfulness practice, set aside a few minutes when you can be quiet and won't be disturbed. Start by bringing your attention to your breath. Notice your breathing and the sensations in your abdomen as you breathe in and out. Spend a few moments just noticing your breathing.

- First, notice what you are feeling and what that feels like.
- Next, name the emotion: what is it? What word best describes what you are feeling (for example, angry, sad, anxious, irritated, scared, frustrated...)?
- Then accept the emotion. It's normal to have lots of feelings, both pleasant and unpleasant. It can be helpful to understand what triggered the feeling and the set of circumstances that contributed to you feeling this way. Don't condone or judge the emotion. Simply let it move through you without resisting it, struggling against it or encouraging it.
- Finally, explore the emotion. How intensely do you feel it? How are you breathing as you feel the emotion? What are you feeling in your body? Where

do you feel it? What is happening to your posture when you feel this emotion? Where do you notice muscle tension? What expression do you have on your face when you feel this? As you pay attention to your feeling, does it change in any way (sometimes it will, sometimes it won't)? If you find that your feeling changes, notice how it changes. Does it change in intensity or where in your body you feel it, or does it change to a different feeling?

- What thoughts or judgements do you notice? Just notice those thoughts. Allow them to come into your mind, and allow them to pass. Any time you find that you're engaging with the thoughts – judging them or yourself for having them, believing them, struggling against them – just notice that process and bring your attention back to your breathing, and to the sensations you are experiencing in your body. If any other emotions come up, if anything changes, simply notice and repeat the steps above. At first, it can be difficult to do this if you feel upset but, as you become more practised, you can use this mindfulness technique when you feel more intense emotion.

Applied mindfulness – incorporating mindfulness practice into your day-to-day life

The principle of applied mindfulness is very simple – it is about deepening your engagement with the world, on really focusing on what you are doing and on being 'in the moment'. When you are using mindfulness, you will find that your mind keeps wandering – this is normal and nothing to worry about. If you notice that your mind has wandered, or you've started thinking about something else, just notice what it is that distracted you, and then gently bring your attention back to the exercise. Repeatedly letting go of distractions and bringing your attention back when it has wandered are key parts of mindfulness practice.

With applied mindfulness, your aim is to practise for just a few minutes at a time, but at frequent intervals throughout the day.

- Take an extra minute in the shower.
- Listen to sounds in the environment.
- Pay attention to the different sensations you are aware of all through your body.
- Pay attention to your posture at any given moment.
- 'Slow walking': slow down your walking speed and become aware of the flow of movement through your body.
- 'Slow eating': eat silently and more slowly than usual and become aware of all the colours, flavours and textures of your food.
- 'Mindful housework': you can even use mindfulness when you are doing the housework and turn your chores into an opportunity to be in the moment.

Note

1 Originally published in *The Transactional Analyst*, volume 1, issue 4, autumn, 2011. Reprinted with permission.

Appendix 3
Basic transactional analysis (TA) theory[1]

Ego states: understanding what goes on 'in the inside'

During the late 1950s, the psychiatrist Eric Berne developed his theory of ego states. Berne's ego state model is a simple but effective way to make sense of 'what goes on in the inside' for ourselves and others. As a theory, it has been incredibly useful and has stood the test of time. Knowing about and understanding ego states is useful because it gives us a way to explain and make sense of a number of phenomena, including:

- those fluctuations in mood, ways of thinking, behaviour and ways of relating which we all experience throughout the course of each day of our lives;
- why we react in certain ways in different situations;
- why we hold on to certain ways of being which deep down we know are completely irrational;
- the nature of our internal dialogue.

As with most TA theory, in order to help make it understandable and accessible, the terminology we use is simple, everyday language. The theory of ego states is one of the methods used in TA to understand the inner world. It categorises internal experience into three classes or different states. These are called Parent, Adult and Child (Figure A1).

The Parent ego state

The Parent ego state is made up of all the messages we have picked up from outside, external sources all through our lives. This includes our parents, parent figures such as grandparents and other relatives, older siblings, teachers and other authority figures, and even from society as a whole. It is like a recording of all the thoughts, attitudes, behaviours, ways of relating and responding that we have experienced others using.

The Adult ego state

The Adult ego state is the part of our personality which is adapted to the 'here-and-now' reality. It is age-appropriate.

PARENT EGO STATE
Behaviours, thoughts and feelings copied from parents or parent figures

ADULT EGO STATE
Behaviours, thoughts and feelings which are direct responses to the here and now

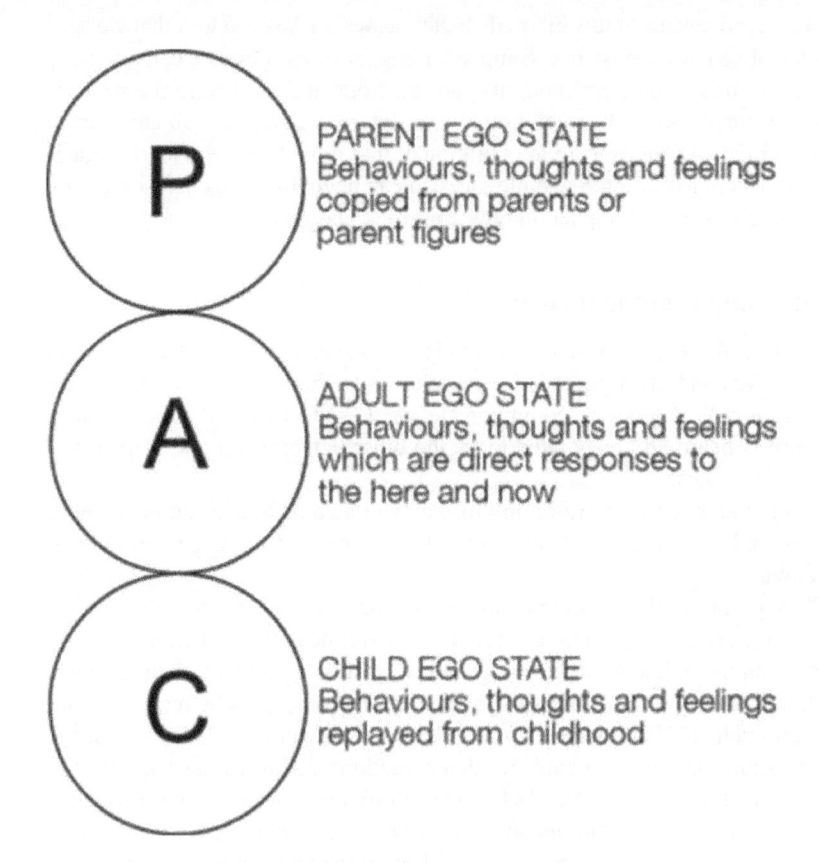

CHILD EGO STATE
Behaviours, thoughts and feelings replayed from childhood

Figure A1 The ego state model (Berne, 1961; Stewart & Joines, 1987).

The Child ego state

The Child ego state is made up of all our own personal history. It is the 'me who I was, back then'. This part of our personality experiences the internal and external world in exactly the same way that we did as a child, which includes the ways of thinking, feeling, behaving and relating to others that we used when we were younger.

Each ego state is continuously activated, although at any given time one will tend to predominate in our inner world. Our ego states are highly reactive to the environment and external stimuli, as well as to our own thoughts, feelings, wishes, desires, hopes, fears and fantasies, and also are responsive to our own behaviour and the behaviour of others.

Understanding internal dialogue

We all have an internal dialogue – our thoughts are often constructed almost as if they were some kind of conversation or running commentary on things.

188 *Appendix 3*

Often, we are not aware of this internal chatter, as we are so used to it that we tend to be desensitised to its existence. Simply 'tuning in to' its presence can be a very useful way to understand our thoughts and reactions and to change the way we feel and our behaviour. When you notice your internal dialogue, you can start to reflect on which ego states were in operation at that time. Once you start to identify and understand your internal dialogue, you can begin to change it – something that will have a profound impact on how you think and feel.

Understanding communication

Not only does the theory of ego states help us to understand what is going on inside ourselves and other people, it also helps us to think about and understand communication. Whenever we communicate, we do so from one of our ego states. This in turn is heard and responded to by the other person from one of that person's own ego states.

Thinking about communication in this way can help us to communicate more effectively and also to address situations whre communication goes wrong or breaks down.

If all is going well, communication runs smoothly. In the top drawing in Figure A2, we see a person asking someone 'What time is it?' If the other person responds from his or her Adult ego state and says, 'It is 3 o'clock', then the communication has been smooth and straightforward. However, if s/he responds with a comment such as, 'Why haven't you got your own watch?', as we see in the second diagram, then we can consider that something awkward has happened in the communication process. This helps us to think about how sometimes things can go wrong when we communicate with others – either we have, or the other person has, communicated in a way that is different to what one might expect, and this has left a feeling of things not being so smooth.

Sometimes communication takes place in a more indirect way, in that people can imply certain things without actually saying what they mean. Perhaps the best-known example of this is someone asking another person if s/he would like to come back for coffee. On the surface of it, this is a very simple and straightforward invitation; however, we all know that when a person asks someone to come back for coffee at the end of a night, there is often more than coffee on the person's mind!

Strokes

The word 'stroke' was derived from the need of an infant to receive physical touch. As grown-ups, Eric Berne suggested we substitute some of the need for physical touch with other modes of recognition. These demonstrate to us that our existence has been recognised (recognition hunger), and that we have been acknowledged in some way.

Strokes can be:

Basic TA theory 189

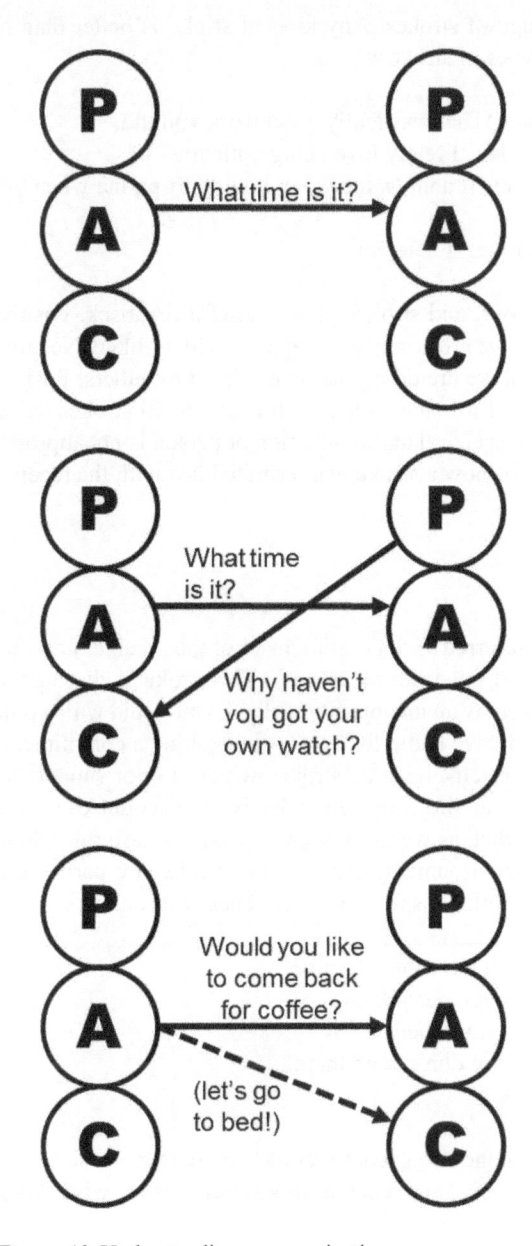

Figure A2 Understanding communication.

- verbal or non-verbal
- positive or negative
- conditional or unconditional.

Any transaction is an exchange of strokes. Any kind of stroke is better than no stroke at all. There are four types of strokes:

1 positive conditional stroke: 'That was really good work you did.'
2 positive unconditional stroke: 'I really love being with you.'
3 negative conditional stroke: 'It annoys me when you don't phone when you say you will.'
4 negative unconditional stroke: 'I hate you!'

Stroking can reinforce behaviour, and strokes give us useful feedback. Positive conditional strokes tell us what we are doing that is appreciated, or liked. Negative conditional strokes tell us what we are doing that is not liked by others. Positive unconditional strokes affirm us for being. Negative unconditional strokes tell us that we need to go somewhere else, or that this situation or person is not appropriate for us. The responsibility for how a stroke is interpreted lies with the receiver of the stroke.

Stroke filter

Strokes which do not fit the preferred variety or intensity of the receiver are often likely to be ignored, or filtered out from awareness. The stroke is discounted. Sometimes, this can be observed by an incongruity: 'Thank you' (said whilst pulling a face) or 'This old thing? I have had it for ages' (diminishing a compliment). Our stroke filter maintains our self-image as strokes which do not support the view we have of ourselves in our life script are selectively discounted. Claude Steiner came up with the idea that, as we grow up, we 'learn' certain rules about strokes from our culture and environment. Some of these rules are particularly strong in their influence on our relationship to strokes. These rules are:

- Don't give strokes when you have them to give.
- Don't ask for strokes when you need them.
- Don't accept strokes if you want them.
- Don't reject strokes when you don't want them.
- Don't give yourself strokes.

The transactional analyst, Adrienne Lee encourages us to counteract these restrictive rules and take permission to give and receive strokes freely as we wish. These permissions are:

- Do give strokes when you have them to give.
- Do ask for the strokes you want.
- Do accept the strokes you want.
- Do reject the strokes that you don't want.
- Do give yourself strokes.

Discounting

Discounting is a mechanism whereby we somehow 'distort' reality or see things in a way that reinforces our script. Jacqui Schiff and her colleagues defined discounting as 'minimising or ignoring some aspect of [one's self], others or the reality situation'. Discounting can be hard to spot, but it can have a profound effect on how we perceive ourselves, others and the world around us. Discounting also tends to be accompanied by grandiosity. This doesn't mean that someone thinks s/he is better than anyone else or has 'grand ideas', but instead means that some aspect of reality gets magnified, exaggerated or blown out of proportion. Grandiosity can be thought of as 'making a mountain out of a molehill', whereas discounting can be seen as 'making a molehill out of a mountain'.

In many problematic situations, people are both discounting and engaging in grandiosity. For example, the statement, 'I was so scared I couldn't think' involves a magnification of the feeling, as well as a minimisation of the person's abilities to think when scared. When people are anxious, they often overestimate the degree of threat connected to what they are feeling anxious about, and also discount their ability to cope. Not only do discounting and grandiosity reinforce life script, they limit options for problem solving, and they also inadvertently contribute to the maintenance of a problem.

Life script

As humans, we have an inherent need to make meaning of the world around us. In order to make sense of the world, we start to develop a narrative, or life script. In essence, this life script enables us to ask three basic questions we have in order to make our way through the world:

1 What kind of person am I? How do I see myself?
2 What are all these other people like? How do I see others?
3 What kind of world is this? What is life like? What can I expect?

The process of forming a script starts from the very earliest days of life, as infants start to experience how others relate to them, what happens when they relate to others, and as they try to make sense of the world around them and how they experience the world.

Our life script tends to operate outside our awareness, and is a form of implicit learning. We implicitly form conclusions about who we are, what we can expect from others and how the world is, based on our early experiences and how others react towards us.

Life script filters our experiences and influences how we interpret situations. Some aspects of our life script may be positive. Other aspects of our script are more problematic and can limit our options in life (or at least give us the sense that our options are limited). As such, they inhibit spontaneity and flexibility.

Script decisions are often made at times of stress and where choices are limited. These decisions can be made consciously or unconsciously. The bulk of scripting is done in early childhood; however, we may add to or amend script in adult life when under pressure or at times of extreme stress. At different times in our life we have to make choices and draw conclusions about ourselves, others and the nature of life. Script decisions are choices which impact upon our behaviour and way of interpreting the world, including how we evaluate ourselves and others.

Stan Woollams and Michael Brown suggested that children are particularly likely to draw negative conclusions from situations because of their relative lack of power and options, their inability to handle stress and their immature thinking capacity. Because of this, script decisions often seem irrational or extreme when viewed from a grown-up perspective. When we consider the situation and circumstances in which the individual developed script decisions, then they start to make sense. Ultimately, script decisions were made as a means of solving an immediate problem and in response to the information and resources the individual had at the time. For example, a child who is repeatedly in need of affection which is not forthcoming may make sense of this situation by coming to conclusions which, if we were to put them into adult language, would go something like: 'Something is wrong with me' or 'I will never get my needs met' or even 'It is dangerous to feel my feelings'. These conclusions are effectively 'learnt' and become script decisions.

Delivery of script messages

Script messages are delivered in a number of ways. These methods may be used singly or in combination. They may be delivered directly or indirectly, verbally or non-verbally. The way the message is sent and the content of the message is not necessarily the way it is received or understood by the child.

Don't messages (injunctions)

Bob and Mary Goulding observed that many of their clients came to therapy experiencing a sense that they shouldn't do certain things. They noticed that the 'don't' messages that their clients appeared to be following could be grouped into 12 themes, and that these usually related to early negative life experiences. The Gouldings referred to these 'don't' messages as injunctions. As you read this list, notice your reaction to each injunction. Many people find that they experience a strong intuitive sense of which messages resonate for them and find that they too may carry such messages at a subconscious level.

Don't be/don't exist	Don't belong	Don't be you
Don't be close/trust/love	Don't be a child	Don't be well/sane
Don't grow up	Don't feel	Don't succeed
Don't think	Don't be important	Don't . . .

Basic TA theory   193

Adrienne Lee developed a diagram which highlights the powerful 'sinking' effect these injunctions can have on us (Figure A3). Here, she shows them balanced with 'drivers', which people use to counterbalance the effects of the injunctions in order to feel that they are acceptable.

As you look at Figure A3, are there any of the messages which you can personally identify with?

Counterinjunctions (the main ones are call drivers). These are given in later childhood and tell you that you are OK if you do certain things, i.e., they give you conditional Okness. They come from the Parent ego-state of your parents.

Injunctions are given in early childhood, usually non-verbally. They come from your parents' Child ego-states. i.e., their unresolved childhood issues. Often both the giving and receiving of these messages occur out of awareness.

Drivers (in balloons): Try Hard, Hurruy Up, Please Others, Be Perfect, Be Strong

Injunctions: Don't Feel, Don't, Don't Be You, Don't Exist, Don't Belong, Don't Think, Don't Be Close, Don't Make It, Don't Be Well, Don't Grow Up, Don't Be Important, Don't Be a Child

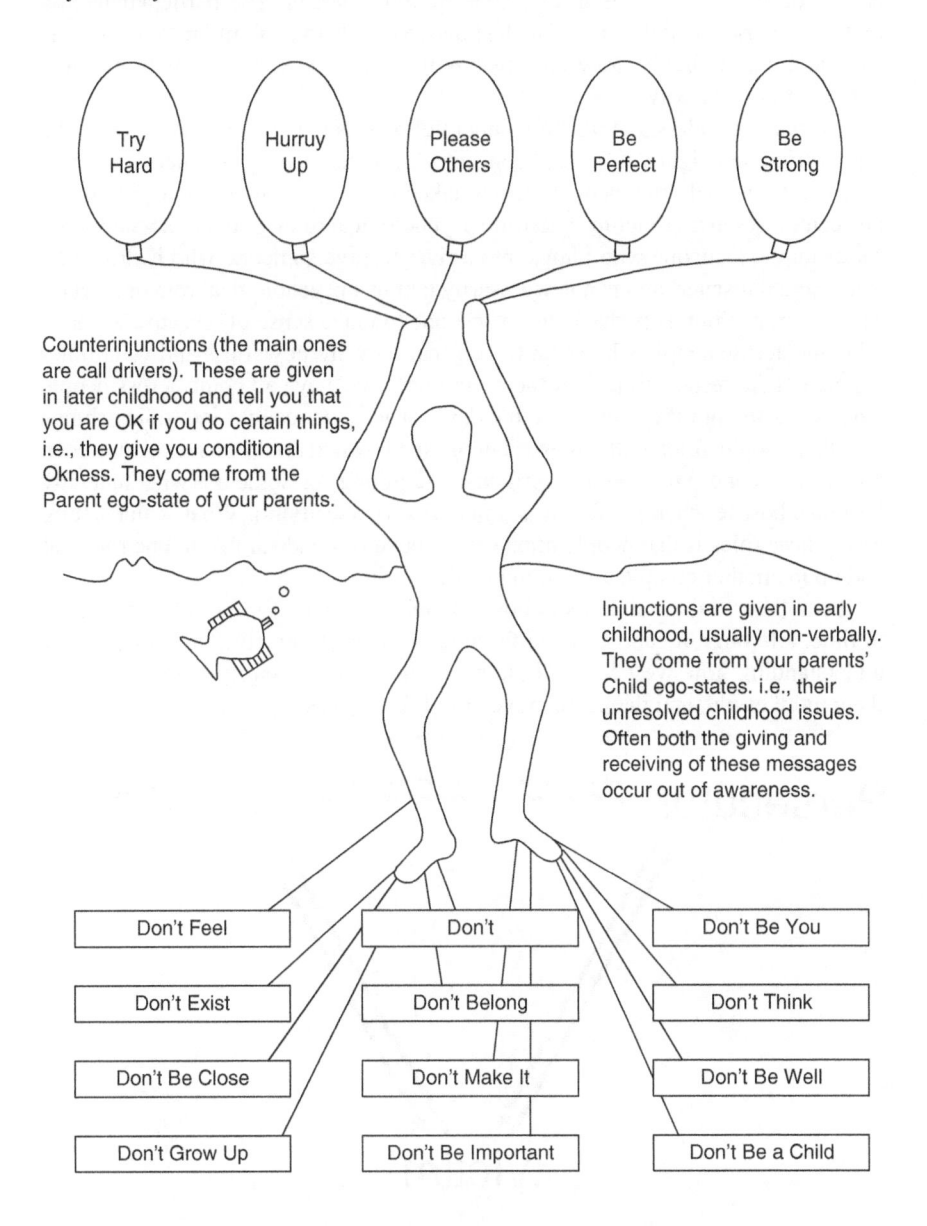

Figure A3 The drowning man, by Adrienne Lee, reprinted with permission.

Unhelpful relationship patterns

From time to time, all people get caught up in some kind of unhelpful relationship dynamic. Often, these have a repetitive feel to them and can be understood as following certain patterns. When we are caught up in these processes, we are usually not aware of what is happening, and they tend to end up with everyone feeling confused, or hurt, or wanting to blame the other person. The particular feeling that we experience at the end of such situations tends to be familiar to us in some way, and we implicitly draw conclusions from these situations which reinforce our script in some way.

One way of understanding these unhelpful relationship patterns is by using the drama triangle (Figure A4). This concept was developed by Stephen Karpman, who identified that often people seem to take up one of three psychological roles: persecutor, rescuer or victim. These are psychological roles, and not 'actual roles'; for example, someone who jumps into a river to save someone who is drowning is an 'actual rescuer' and is not necessarily taking a psychological role of rescuer. The victim position is perhaps the easiest one to make sense of, because we have all come across people who seem to feel that they are powerless and want other people to take responsibility for them. Similarly, we have all come across people who act as though they can 'save the day', or who get caught into doing things for other people, often without even being asked (rescuers). We have all also been around someone who seems to criticise everything, or someone who suddenly becomes hostile when we feel it is unjustified (persecutors). What is interesting about these roles is that people often switch positions and start from one role, but end up in another completely different role.

It can be useful to think about how you take up each of these roles from time to time. Although it can be uncomfortable to think of ourselves in each role, by understanding how we occupy these positions we can identify when we are in them more easily, and therefore move out of these roles.

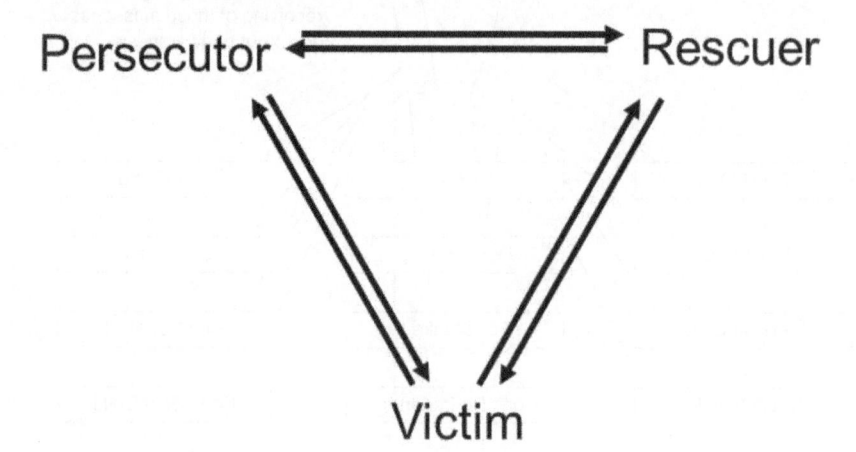

Figure A4 The drama triangle, by Stephen Karpman, reprinted with permission.

Primary and secondary emotions

Whether they be pleasant or unpleasant, we all experience emotions of different types and intensities. Feelings can come and go, and we often experience them as coming in 'waves'. At any one time our emotional state can be like soup, in that there can be lots of different 'ingredients' and it can be hard to identify what the separate emotions are.

There are different kinds of emotions, and making sense of them can be helpful when we are feeling bad in some way. Primary emotions are feelings which are a direct response to the here-and-now situation and are appropriate to the circumstances, and also the intensity of them is proportionate to what is going on. If we allow ourselves to feel our primary feelings and respond to them accordingly, they tend to resolve themselves. If we are sad, this is due to experiencing a loss of some kind. If we allow ourselves to be sad and perhaps seek comfort from others, the feeling will eventually subside (although this may take quite some time, depending on the situation). If there is some kind of danger, we experience fear, and we either want to run away or seek help and safety from others. If we feel that someone has behaved in a way that we feel is unacceptable, we feel angry. If we express this and the other person apologises, then, if we let it, our anger will subside (although there can be a brief time lag with this, whilst we allow ourself to calm down). If we are happy, we want to share this with others. If we get a positive response, our joy increases and we feel a sense of satisfaction.

Sometimes we feel things which are not appropriate to the situation (e.g. feeling fear when there is no actual danger, or convincing ourselves that there is a danger when in actual fact there is not), or we overreact with feelings that are out of proportion to the event. We might also have feelings which feel 'stuck' in some way, and which we never seem to resolve. Also, it is not unusual for people to feel one emotion as a substitute for another feeling. This is often the case for feelings which we somehow 'learnt' were unacceptable to others. For example, it is common for men to grow up believing that it is not OK for them to feel afraid. Consequently, some men will very quickly shut down their fear and instead respond with anger. Another type of secondary feeling is when we have a 'feeling about a feeling'. For example we might feel apprehensive about a forthcoming event, but then feel embarrassed about feeling some anxiety, or we might feel angry towards someone, but then feel guilty for feeling angry. It is not unusual for people effectively to 'block' certain feelings that they do not feel are acceptable, or which they feel ashamed about. All of these are examples of secondary emotions.

Secondary feelings are those feelings which have become stuck, and are difficult to resolve. By identifying the secondary feeling and the underlying primary feeling, we can start to untangle our emotions and go some way towards changing them.

There is a phenomenon known as state-dependent memory, which refers to how, when we are in a particular mood, it is fairly easy to access memories which have the same emotion attached to them. For example, if you are sat with an old friend, reminiscing about funny stories and events, it becomes easier to remember more and more such memories. Similarly, if we are upset or angry with someone, we can find it easy to recall other times we have felt the same way around that person. Both of these are examples of state-dependent memory.

Emotions can trigger thoughts and memories. Usually, this happens at a subconscious level, or at least out of our awareness. Even something which might be small and possibly even imperceptible can trigger any part of our associative network and the rest becomes activated automatically. Each new activation reinforces the network and makes it stronger.

Associative networks tend to have a negative flavour to them, and are comprised of negative internal dialogue, unpleasant emotions, sensations, fantasies, expectations and memories. Each time the network gets triggered, a new memory is added to the memory bank. With persistence, we can change our associative networks and develop more productive ways of handling our emotions.

Drivers

The drivers are named by the fact that they lend a 'driven' quality to our behaviour and our internal experience. It is as if we hold the driver as an unspoken motto about how we should behave at all times, and at some level believe that if we don't follow the driver we are somehow not OK. Drivers have their origins in the aspects of our development where we were being socialised by our parents and parent figures and learning what we needed to do or be in order to be acceptable, approved of and liked. In turn, we internalise these messages and live by them as implicit rules which tell us what we need to do both to be accepted and to prevent rejection.

Each driver has a positive, helpful and desirable aspect to it as well as a problematic, negative and limiting aspect to it. Unfortunately, the negative aspects of each driver tend to predominate and lead us into ways of being which are unhelpful and cause stress and problems in our lives. The five driver patterns are: *Be perfect! Be strong! Try hard! Please others!* and *Hurry up!* As you read this list, do you immediately identify with any of the driver patterns? Do you have any immediate sense of the presence of one or more of these drivers in you?

One of the tricky things about drivers is the fact that they are all socially desirable in some ways, and so our drivers can be encouraged and reinforced by others around us. The key is not necessarily to eradicate the driver completely, but to keep the desirable aspects of it and loosen the grip of the driver so we have more flexibility about how we respond to situations and don't feel an automatic compulsion to follow the driver message. I'll now explain each driver in more detail. As you read these descriptions, you will notice a sense of resonance with the descriptions which are most applicable to you. These drivers are only drivers when they 'drive' someone's behaviour and when the person feels not OK when not following the driver. Of course, these must not be identified on the basis of one clue only, but are indicative of a general process.

Be perfect!

People driven by *Be perfect!* are always striving for perfection or expecting others to be perfect, believing if they (or others) are less than perfect, then they are not OK. Their language is often precise and contains many sub-clauses. They are usually very neatly presented in appearance. They tend to be industrious and logical and have high standards. These high standards can, however, cause problems when they are unrealistic and perfectionistic. Failure to reach goals is distressing for people with a strong *Be perfect!* process. When they are under stress they can become very rigid in their thinking, and sometimes controlling in their behaviour.

Be strong!

Individuals who are caught in the *Be strong!* process valiantly attempt to keep their feelings under tight control, believing that any sign of feelings is a sign of weakness and something that would make them not OK. Their language may be 'distancing', such as 'That makes me sad', rather than 'I feel sad'. They can be relatively expressionless and still in their posture. They tend to be very reliable and independent. They often do not mind tasks which are repetitive and often like working on their own. They are good to have around in a crisis as they tend not to get too emotional.

Try hard!

People driven by *Try hard!* always appear to be in a struggle, believing that such struggling and repeated attempts are imperative to remain OK. By getting caught in the struggle, they can stop themselves from achieving what they want and instead stay stuck or, if they do progress, it tends to be a torturous and slow process. The driver is named because often these people 'try' to do something instead of actually doing it. For example, 'I'll try and get it finished' or 'I'm trying my best'. They often appear to be quite tense and will agree to take on a lot of tasks (even when it is not realistic to do so) but not complete them, despite working hard. People with a *Try hard!* process can be very creative and are often full of new ideas. A common problem for many people with a *Try hard!* pattern is a strong tendency to procrastinate or find obstacles.

Please others!

People whose behaviour is determined by the *Please others!* process believe that they must pacify and put other people first at all times and must be liked at all times in order to be OK. Their desire to please will often be indicated in their language, which will often be placating. They tend to make an effort to look nice. People with a strong *Please others!* process are usually very skilled at dealing with other people and taking care of them. They are often helpful and pleasant and concerned about doing the right thing. They hate the thought that someone might not like them or be upset about what they have done. When they are stressed, they can become very emotional and irrational. They often want to 'rescue' other people (and in doing so, do not let people do things for themselves)

Hurry up!

Hurry up! driven individuals are always rushing, and rushing others, believing that they (or others) are not OK if they do not hurry up. They may speak rapidly, and will usually be doing more than one thing at a time. They will often fidget and move a lot. People with a lot of *Hurry up!* tend to be quite lively, enthusiastic and adventurous. They are often quite efficient and good at multitasking.

A few words on balancing your drivers

- The problem with drivers is that they are essentially doomed to failure – no one can be perfect/be strong/try hard/please others/hurry up all the time.
- Drivers need to be balanced with their positive aspects, such as: speed, experimentation, agreeableness, endurance and excellence, which are all positive qualities (Clarkson, 1992).
- Be kind to yourself and accepting of the positive intention behind your driver-type behaviour, and forgive yourself when you are not (perfect, etc.) and do not determine your OK-ness as a person by it.
- Address the implicit fear of rejection and also the fear of being acceptable to others which fuel your driver. This will reduce the need to engage in the driver and give you greater flexibility in how you engage with the world.

Note

1 Modified from Lee (1997).

References

Abramson, L.Y., Metalsky, G.I. & Alloy, L.B. (1989). Hopelessness depression: a theory based subtype of depression. *Psychological Review*, 96: 358–372.

Addis, M.E. & Krasnow, A.D. (2000). A national survey of practicing psychologists' attitudes toward psychotherapy treatment manuals. *Journal of Consulting and Clinical Psychology*, 68(2): 331–339.

Ainsworth, M. & Bowlby, J. (1965). *Child Care and the Growth of Love*. London: Penguin Books.

Aldao, A., Nolen-Hoeksema, S. & Schweizer, S. (2010). Emotion-regulation strategies across psychopathology: a meta-analytic review. *Clinical Psychology Review*, 30: 217–237.

Aldea, M.A., Rice, K.G., Gormley, B. & Rojas, A. (2010). Telling perfectionists about their perfectionism: effects of providing feedback on emotional reactivity and psychological symptoms. *Behaviour Research and Therapy*, 48: 1194–1203.

Alfano, M.S., Joiner, T.E. Jr., Perry, M. & Metalsky, G.I. (1994). Attributional style: a mediator of the shyness–depression relationship? *Journal of Research in Personality*, 28: 287–300.

Allen, J. (2010). Discussion paper for International Association of Relational TA colloquium, October 30–November 7.

Allen, J.R. & Allen, B.A. (1997). A new type of transactional analysis and one version of script work with a constructionist sensibility. *Transactional Analysis Journal*, 27(2): 89–98.

Alloy, L.B., Abramson, L. Y.B., Whitehouse, W.G., Hogan, M.E., Tashman, N.A., Steinberg, D.L., Rosee, D.T. & Donovan, P. (1999). Depressogenic cognitive styles: predictive validity, information processing and personality characteristics, and developmental origins. *Behaviour Research and Therapy*, 37: 503–531.

Alloy, L.B., Abramson, L.Y., Tashman, N.A., Berrebbi, D.S., Hogan, M.E., Whitehouse, W.G., Crossfield, A.G. & Morocco, A. (2001). Developmental origins of cognitive vulnerability to depression: parenting, cognitive, and inferential feedback styles of the parents of individuals at high and low cognitive risk for depression. *Cognitive Therapy and Research*, 25(4): 397–423.

American Psychiatric Association. (1994). *Diagnostic and Statistical Manual of Mental Disorder*, 4th edition (DSM-IV). Washington, DC: American Psychiatric Association.

American Psychiatric Association. (2010). *Practice Guideline for the Treatment of Patients with Major Depressive Disorder* (3rd edin). Arlington, VA: American Psychiatric Association.

References

Ansbacher, H.L. & Ansbacher, R.R. (Eds.) (1956). *The Individual Psychology of Alfred Adler*. New York: Harper Torch Books.

Auerbach, R.P., Webb, C.A., Gardiner, C.K. & Pechtel, P. (2013). Behavioral and neural mechanisms underlying cognitive vulnerability models of depression. *Journal of Psychotherapy Integration*, 23(3): 222–235.

Ayres, A. (2006). The only way out: a consideration of suicide. *Transactions*, 4: 4–13.

Bagby, R.M., Cox, B.J., Schuller, D.R., Levitt, A.J., Swinson, R.P. & Joffe, R.T. (1992). Diagnostic specificity of the dependent and self-critical personality dimensions in major depression. *Journal of Affective Disorders*, 26: 59–64.

Barkham, M., Rees, A., Shapiro, D.A., Stiles, W.B., Agnew, R.A., Halstead, J., Culverwell, A. & Harringston, V.M.G. (1996). Outcomes of time-limited psychotherapy in applied settings: replicating the second Sheffield psychotherapy project. *Journal of Consulting and Clinical Psychology*, 64: 1079–1085.

Barrett, M.S. & Barber, J.P. (2007). Interpersonal profiles in major depressive disorder. *Journal of Clinical Psychology*, 63: 247–266.

Baumeister, H. (2012). Inappropriate prescriptions of antidepressant drugs in patients with sub-threshold to mild depression: time for the evidence to become practice. *Journal of Affective Disorders*, 139: 240–243.

Beblo, T., Fernando, S., Klocke, S., Griepenstroh, J., Aschenbrenner, S. & Driessen, M. (2012). Increased suppression of negative and positive emotions in major depression. *Journal of Affective Disorders*, 141(2): 474–479.

Beck, A. T. (1975). *Cognitive Therapy and the Emotional Disorders*. Madison, CT: International Universities Press.

Beck, A.T. & Beck, J.S. (1995). *Cognitive Therapy: Basics and Beyond*. New York: Guilford.

Beck, A.T., Ward, C.H., Mendelssohn, M.J. & Erbaugh, J. (1961). An inventory for measuring depression. *Archives of General Psychiatry*, 4: 561–571.

Beck, A.T., Rush, A.J., Emery, G. & Shaw, B. (1979). *Cognitive Therapy of Depression*. New York: Guilford Press.

Bella, J.J., Mawn, L. & Poynor, R. (2013). Haste makes waste, but not for all: the speed-accuracy trade-off does not apply to neurotics. *Psychology of Sport and Exercise*, 14(6): 860–864.

Berne, E. (1961). *Transactional Analysis in Psychotherapy*. New York: Grove Press.

Berne, E. (1964). *Games People Play*. New York: Grove Press.

Berne, E. (1966). *Principles of Group Treatment*. Menlo Park, CA: Shea Books.

Berne, E. (1970). *Sex in Human Loving*. New York: Penguin.

Berne, E. (1972). *What Do You Say After You Say Hello?* London: Corgi.

Binder, J.L. & Betan, E.J. (2013). Essential activities in a session of brief dynamic/interpersonal psychotherapy. *Psychotherapy*, 50(3): 428–432.

Blatt, S.J. (1974). Levels of object representation in anaclitic and introjective depression. *Psychoanalytic Study of Childhood*, 29: 107–157.

Blatt, S.J. (1991). A cognitive morphology of psychopathology. *Journal of Nervous and Mental Diseases*, 179: 449–458.

Blatt, S.J. & Ford, R.Q. (1994). *Therapeutic Change: An object relations perspective*. New York: Plenum.

Blenkiron, P. (2010). *Stories and Analogies in Cognitive Behaviour Therapy*. Chichester: John Wiley.

Bohart, A., O'Hara, M. & Leitner, L. (1998). Empirically violated treatments: disenfranchisement of humanistic and other psychotherapies. *Psychotherapy Research*, 8(2): 141–157.

Bower, G.H. (1981). Mood and memory. *American Psychologist*, 36: 129–148.
Bowlby, J. (1979). *The Making and Breaking of Affectional Bonds*. London: Tavistock Publications.
Bowlby, J. (1988). *A Secure Base: Clinical applications of attachment theory*. London: Routledge.
Brown, G.W., Harris, T.O. & Hepworth, C. (1995). Loss, humiliation and entrapment among women developing depression: a patient and non-patient comparison. *Psychological Medicine*, 25: 7–21.
Bureau, J., Easterbrooks, M.A. & Lyons-Ruth, K. (2009). Maternal depressive symptoms in infancy: unique contribution to children's depressive symptoms in childhood and adolescence? *Development and Psychopathology*, 21: 519–537.
Burns, D.D. (1980). *The Feeling Good Handbook*. New York: New American Library.
Burt, D.B., Zembar, M.J. & Niederehe, G. (1995). Depression and memory impairment: a meta-analysis of the association, its pattern, and specificity. *Psychological Bulletin*, 117: 285–305.
Cacioppo, J.T., Hughes, M.E., Waite, L.J., Hawkley, L.C. & Thisted R.A. (2006). Loneliness as a specific risk factor for depressive symptoms: cross-sectional and longitudinal analyses. *Psychology and Aging*, 21(1): 140–151.
Campbell-Sills, L., Barlow, D.H., Brown, T.A. & Hofmann, S.G. (2006). Acceptability and suppression of negative emotion in anxiety and mood disorders. *Emotion*, 6: 587–595.
Carl, J.R., Soskin, D.P., Kerns, C. & Barlow, D.H. (2013). Positive emotion regulation in emotional disorders: a theoretical review. *Clinical Psychology Review*, 33: 343–360.
Carroll, K.M. & Nuro, K.F. (2002). One size cannot fit all: a stage model for psychotherapy manual development. *Clinical Psychology: Science and Practice*, 9(4): 396–406.
Carroll, K.M. & Rounsaville, B.J. (2008). Efficacy and effectiveness in developing treatment manuals. In A.M. Nezu & C.M. Nezu (Eds.) *Evidence-based Outcome Research: A practical guide to conducting randomized controlled trials for psychosocial interventions*. Cary, NC: Oxford University Press.
Chambless, D.L. & Steketee, G. (1999). Expressed emotion and behavior therapy outcome: a prospective study with obsessive-compulsive and agoraphobic outpatients. *Journal of Consulting and Clinical Psychology*, 67(5): 658–665.
Choy, A. (1990). The winner's triangle. *Transactional Analysis Journal*, 20(1): 40–46.
Clarkson, P. (1992). *Transactional Analysis Psychotherapy: An integrated approach*. London: Routledge.
Cooney, G.M., Dwan, K., Greig, C.A., Lawlor, D.A., Rimer, J., Waugh, F.R., McMurdo, M. & Mead, G.E. (2013). Exercise for depression. *Cochrane Database of Systematic Reviews 2013*, 9: CD004366.
Constantino, M.J., Manber, R., DeGeorge, J., McBride, C., Ravitz, P., Zuroff, D.C., Klein, D.N., ... Arnow, B.A. (2008). Interpersonal styles of chronically depressed outpatients: profiles and therapeutic change. *Psychotherapy Theory, Research, Practice, Training*, 45(4): 491–506.
Constantino, M.J., Glass, C.R., Arnkoff, D.B., Ametrano, R.M. & Smith, J.Z. (2011). Expectations. In J.C. Norcross (Ed.) *Psychotherapy Relationships that Work: Evidence-based responsiveness* (2nd edn, pp. 354–376). New York: Oxford University Press.
Constantino, M.J., Ametrano, R.M. & Greenberg, R.P. (2012). Clinician interventions and participant characteristics that foster adaptive patient expectations for psychotherapy and psychotherapeutic change. *Psychotherapy*, 49(4): 557–569.
Cornell, W. & Landaiche, M. (2006). Impasse and intimacy: applying Berne's concept of protocol. *Transactional Analysis Journal*, 36(3): 196–213.

Cote, S.M., Boivin, M., Liu, X., Nagin, D.S., Zoccolillo, M. & Tremblay, R.E. (2009). Depression and anxiety symptoms: onset, developmental course and risk factors during early childhood. *Journal of Child Psychology and Psychiatry*, 50(10): 1201–1208.

Cox, B.J., Rector, N.A., Bagby, R.M., Swinson, R.P., Levitt, A.J. & Joffe, R.T. (2000). Is self-criticism unique for depression? A comparison with social phobia. *Journal of Affective Disorders*, 57: 223–228.

Cox, B.J., Fleet, C. & Stein, M.B. (2004). Self-criticism and social phobia in the US national comorbidity survey. *Journal of Affective Disorders*, 82: 227–234.

Cozolino, L. (2010). *The Neuroscience of Psychotherapy: Healing the social brain* (2nd edn). New York: W.W. Norton.

Crossman, P. (1966). Protection and permission. *Transactional Analysis Bulletin*, 5(19): 152–154.

Cuijpers, P., Straten, A. & van Warmerdam, E.H. (2007). Problem solving therapies for depression: a meta-analysis. *European Psychiatry*, 22(1): 9–15.

Cuijpers, P., van Straten, A., Schuurmans, J., van Oppen, P., Hollon, S.D. & Andersson, G. (2010). Psychotherapy for chronic major depression and dysthymia: a meta-analysis. *Clinical Psychology Review*, 30: 51–62.

Dallaspezia, S., Benedetti, F., Colombo, C., Barbini, B., Cigala Fulgosi, M., Gavinelli, C. & Smeraldi, E. (2012). Optimized light therapy for non-seasonal major depressive disorder: effects of timing and season. *Journal of Affective Disorders*, 138: 337–342.

Derogatis, L.R. (1983). *SCL-90-R: Administration, scoring and procedural manual-II*. Baltimore, MD: Clinical Psychometric Research.

Doran, G.T. (1981). There's a S.M.A.R.T. way to write management's goals and objectives. *Management Review*, 70(11): 35–36.

Duncan, E.A.S., Nicol, M.M. & Ager, A. (2004). Factors that constitute a good cognitive-behavioural treatment manual: a Delphi study. *Behavioural and Cognitive Psychotherapy*, 32: 199–213.

Dunkley, D.M., Zuroff, D.C. & Blankstein, K.R. (2003). Self-critical perfectionism and daily affect: dispositional and situational influences on stress and coping. *Journal of Personality and Social Psychology*, 84(1): 234–252.

Eberhart, N.K. & Hammen, C.L. (2006). Interpersonal predictors of onset of depression during the transition to adulthood. *Personal Relationships*, 13: 195–206.

Echizenya, M., Suda, H., Takeshima, M. & Inomata, Y. (2013). Total sleep deprivation followed by sleep phase advance and bright light therapy in drug-resistant mood disorders. *Journal of Affective Disorders*, 144: 28–33.

Ecker, B. & Toomey, B. (2008). Depotentiation of symptom-producing implicit memory in coherence therapy. *Journal of Constructivist Psychology*, 21: 87–150.

Ecker, B., Ticic, R. & Hulley, L. (2012). *Unlocking the Emotional Brain*. New York: Routledge.

Egan, S.J., Wade, T.B. & Shafran, R. (2011). Perfectionism as a transdiagnostic process: a clinical review. *Clinical Psychology Review*, 31: 203–212.

Ehring, T., Fischer, S., Schnulle, J., Bosterling, A. & Tuschen-Caffier, B. (2008). Characteristics of emotion regulation in recovered depressed versus never depressed individuals. *Personality and Individual Differences*, 44: 1574–1584.

Ehring, T., Tuschen-Caffier, B., Schnulle, J., Fischer, S. & Gross, J.J. (2010). Emotion regulation and vulnerability to depression: spontaneous versus instructed use of emotion suppression and reappraisal. *Emotion*, 10(4): 563–572.

Eisch, A.J. & Petrik, D. (2012). Depression and hippocampal neurogenesis: a road to remission? *Science*, 338: 72–75.

Ekman, P. (2003). *Emotions Revealed*. New York: Holt Paperbacks.
English, F. (1971). The substitution factor: rackets and real feelings. *Transactional Analysis Journal*, 1(4): 225–230.
English, F. (2010). It takes a lifetime to play out a script. In R.G. Erskine (Ed.) *Life Scripts: A transactional analysis of unconscious relational patterns* (pp. 217–238). London: Karnac.
Enns, M.W. & Cox, B.J. (1999). Perfectionism and depression symptom severity in major depressive disorder. *Behaviour Research and Therapy*, 37: 783–794.
Erikson, E.H. (1950). *Childhood and Society*. New York: W.W.Norton.
Erikson, E.H. (1959). *Identity and the Life Cycle*. New York: International Universities Press.
Ernst, F. (1971). The OK corral: the grid for get-on-with. *Transactional Analysis Journal*, 1(4): 231–240.
Erskine, R.G. (1980). Script cure: behavioural, intrapsychic and physiological. *Transactional Analysis Journal*, 10: 102–106.
Erskine, R.G. (1991). Transference and transactions: critique from an intrapsychic and integrative perspective. *Transactional Analysis Journal*, 21(2): 63–76.
Erskine, R.G. (1998). The therapeutic relationship: integrating motivation and personality theories. *Transactional Analysis Journal*, 28(2): 132–141.
Erskine, R.G. (2010). *Life Scripts: A transactional analysis of unconscious relational patterns*. London: Karnac.
Erskine, R. & Zalcman, M. (1979). The racket system: a model for racket analysis. *Transactional Analysis Journal*, 9(1): 51–59.
Evans, M., Hollon, S., DeRubeis, R., Piasecki, J., Grove, W., Garvey, M. & Tuason, V. (1992). Differential relapse following cognitive therapy and pharmacotherapy for depression. *Archives of General Psychiatry*, 49: 802–807.
Everaert, J., Koster, E.H.W. & Derakshan, N. (2012). The combined cognitive bias hypothesis in depression. *Clinical Psychology Review*, 32: 413–424.
Fairbairn, R. (1952). *Psychoanalytic Studies of the Personality*. London: Tavistock Publications.
Federn, P. (1952). *Ego Psychology and the Psychoses*. New York: Basic Books.
Fehlinger, T., Stumpenhorst, M., Stenzel, N. & Rief, W. (2012). Emotion regulation is the essential skill for improving depressive symptoms. *Journal of Affective Disorders*, 144: 116–122.
Feldman, L.B. & Feldman, S.L. (1997). Integrating psychotherapy and pharmacotherapy in the treatment of depression. *In Session: Psychotherapy in Practice*, 3(2): 23–38.
Feldman, G.C., Joorman, J. & Johnson, S.L. (2008). Responses to positive affect: a self-report measure of rumination and dampening. *Cognitive Therapy and Research*, 32(4): 507–525.
Festinger, L. (1957). *A Theory of Cognitive Dissonance*. Stanford, CA: Stanford University Press.
Fosha, D. (2000). *The Transforming Power of Affect: A model of accelerated change*. New York: Basic Books.
Fournier, J.C., DeRubeis, R.J., Hollon S.D. *et al.* (2010). Antidepressant drug effects and depression severity: a patient-level meta-analysis. *Journal of the American Medical Association*, 303: 47–53.
Frank, E. (1991). Interpersonal psychotherapy as a maintenance treatment for patients with recurrent depression. *Psychotherapy*, 28: 259–266.
Frank, E., Kupfer, D.J., Buysse, D.J., Swartz, H.A., Pilkonis, P.A., Houck, P.R., Rucci, P., Novick, D.M., Grochocinski, V.J. & Stapf, D.M. (2007). Randomized trial of weekly,

twice-monthly, and monthly interpersonal psychotherapy as maintenance treatment for women with recurrent depression. *American Journal of Psychiatry*, 164: 761–767.

Freud, S. (1914). Remembering, repeating, and working-through (further recommendations on the technique of psycho-analysis II). Reprinted (1953–1974) in *The Standard Edition of the complete psychological works of Sigmund Freud* (trans. and ed. J. Strachey), vol. 12, (pp. 145–156). London: Hogarth Press.

Freud, S. (1917–1958). Mourning and melancholia. *The Standard Edition of the Complete Psychological Works of Sigmund Freud* (trans. and ed. J. Strachey), vol. 12 (pp. 157–173). London: Hogarth Press.

Garland, A., Fox, R. & Williams, C.J. (2002). Overcoming reduced activity and avoidance: a five areas approach. *Advances in Psychiatric Treatment*, 8(6): 453–462.

Garland, E.L., Fredrickson, B., Kring, A.M., Johnson, D.P., Meyer, P.S. & Penn, D.L. (2010). Upward spirals of positive emotions counter downward spirals of negativity: insights from the broaden-and-build theory and affective neuroscience on the treatment of emotion dysfunctions and deficits in psychopathology. *Clinical Psychology Review*, 30(7): 849–864.

Gentes, E.L. & Ruscio, A.M. (2011). A meta-analysis of the relation of intolerance of uncertainty to symptoms of generalized anxiety disorder, major depressive disorder, and obsessive–compulsive disorder. *Clinical Psychology Review*, 31: 923–933.

Gilbert, P. (2007). *Psychotherapy and Counselling for Depression*. London: Sage.

Gilbert, M. & Orlans, V. (2011). *Integrative Therapy: 100 key points and techniques*. Hove: Routledge.

Gilbert, P. & Procter, S. (2006). Compassionate mind training for people with high shame and self-criticism: overview and pilot study of a group therapy approach. *Clinical Psychology and Psychotherapy*, 13: 353–379.

Gilbert, P., Clarke, M., Kempel, S., Miles, J.N.V. & Irons, C. (2004). Criticizing and reassuring oneself: an exploration of forms, styles and reasons in female students. *British Journal of Clinical Psychology*, 43: 31–50.

Gilliom, M. & Shaw, D.S. (2004). Codevelopment of externalizing and internalizing problems in early childhood. *Development and Psychopathology*, 16: 313–333.

Goodman, S.H. & Gotlib, I.H. (1999). Risk for psychopathology in the children of depressed mothers: a developmental model for understanding mechanisms of transmission. *Psychological Review*, 106(3): 458–490.

Gottlib, I.H. & Joorman, J. (2010). Cognition and depression: current status and future directions. *Annual Review of Clinical Psychology*, 6: 285–312.

Goulding, M.M. & Goulding, R.L (1979). *Changing Lives Through Redecision Therapy*. New York: Grove Press.

Greenberg, L.S. & Watson, J.C. (2006). *Emotion Focused Therapy for Depression*. Washington, DC: American Psychological Association Press.

Gross, J.J. (1998). Antecedent- and response-focused emotion regulation: divergent consequences for experience, expression and physiology. *Journal of Personality and Social Psychology*, 74(1): 224–237.

Gross, J.J. & Thompson, R.A. (2007). Emotion regulation: conceptual foundations. In J.J. Gross (Ed.) *Handbook of Emotion Regulation* (pp. 3–24). New York: Guilford Press.

Hames, J.L., Hagan, C.R. & Joiner, T.E. (2013). Interpersonal processes in depression. *Annual Review of Clinical Psychology*, 9: 355–377.

Hammen, C. (1992). Cognitive, life stress, and interpersonal approaches to a developmental psychopathology model of depression. *Development and Psychopathology*, 4: 189–206.

Hankin, B.L., Kassel, J.D. & Abela, J.R.Z. (2005). Adult attachment dimensions and specificity of emotional distress symptoms: prospective investigations of cognitive risk and interpersonal stress generation as mediating mechanisms. *Journal of Personality and Social Psychology*, B31:136–151.

Harford, D. & Widdowson, M. (2014). Quantitative and qualitative outcomes of transactional analysis psychotherapy with male armed forces veterans in the UK presenting with post-traumatic stress disorder. *International Journal of Transactional Analysis Research*, 5(2): 35–65.

Hargaden, H. & Sills, C. (2002). *Transactional Analysis: A relational perspective*. Hove: Routledge.

Harrison, P.J. (2002). The neuropathology of primary mood disorder. *Brain*, 125: 1428–1449.

Hayes, J.A. Gelso, C.J. & Hummel, A.M. (2011). Managing countertransference. *Psychotherapy*, 48(1): 88–97.

Hecht, D. (2010). Depression and the hyperactive right-hemisphere. *Neuroscience Research*, 68(2): 77–87.

Hertel, P.T. (2004). Memory for emotional and non-emotional events in depression: a question of habit? In: D. Reisberg & P. Herte (Eds.) *Memory and Emotion* (pp. 186–216). New York: Oxford University Press.

Hicks, B.M., DiRago, A.C., Iacono, W.G. & McGue, M. (2009). Gene–environment interplay in internalizing disorders: consistent findings across six environmental risk factors. *Journal of Child Psychology and Psychiatry*, 50(10): 1309–1317.

Hobbes, R. (1996). Attachment theory and transactional analysis part one – understanding security. *ITA News*, issue 46, autumn.

Hobbes, R. (1997). Attachment theory and transactional analysis part two – developing security. *ITA News*, issue 47, spring.

Hoffman, I.Z. (1983). The patient as interpreter of the analyst's experience. *Contemporary Psychoanalysis*, 19: 389–422.

Holmes, J. (2001). *The Search for the Secure Base: Attachment theory and psychotherapy*. Hove: Routledge.

Hooley, J.M. & Teasdale, J.D. (1989). Predictors of relapse in unipolar depressives: expressed emotion, marital distress, and perceived criticism. *Journal of Abnormal Psychology*, 98: 229–235.

Horowitz, L.M., Rosenberg, S.E., Baer, B.A., Ureño, G. & Villaseñor, V.S. (1988). Inventory of interpersonal problems: psychometric properties and clinical applications. *Journal of Consulting and Clinical Psychology*, 56: 885–892.

Horvath, A.O., Del Re, A., Flückiger, C. & Symonds, D. (2011). Alliance in individual psychotherapy. In: J.C. Norcross (Ed.), *Psychotherapy Relationships that Work* (2nd edn). New York: Oxford University Press.

Howland, R.H. (2008). Sequenced Treatment Alternatives to Relieve Depression (STAR*D) –part 2: study outcomes. *Journal of Psychosocial Nursing*, 46(10): 21–24.

Humble, M. (2010). Vitamin D, light and mental health. *Journal of Photochemistry and Photobiology*, 101: 142–149.

Jacka, F.N., Maes, M., Pasco, J., Williams, L.J. & Berk, M. (2012). Nutrient intakes and the common mental disorders in women. *Journal of Affective Disorders*, 141(1): 79–85.

James, M. (1974). Self-reparenting: theory and process. *Transactional Analysis Journal*, 4(3): 32–39.

James, M. (1981). *Breaking Free: Self-reparenting for a new life*. Reading, MA: Addison-Wesley.

Jan Conradi, H. & de Jonge, P. (2009). Recurrent depression and the role of adult attachment: a prospective and a retrospective study. *Journal of Affective Disorders*, 116: 93–99.

Joiner, T.E., Jr. (1997). Shyness and low social support as interactive diatheses, and loneliness as mediator: testing an interpersonal-personality view of depression. *Journal of Abnormal Psychology*, 106: 386–394.

Joiner, T.E. (2000). Depression's vicious scree: self-propagating and erosive processes in depression chronicity. *Clinical Psychology: Science and Practice*, 7: 203–218.

Joiner, T.E., Alfano, M.S. & Metalsky, G.I. (1993). Caught in the crossfire: depression, self-consistency, self enhancement, and the response of others. *Journal of Social and Clinical Psychology*, 12: 113–134.

Joorman, J. & Siemer, M. (2004). Memory accessibility, mood regulation, and dysphoria: difficulties in repairing sad mood with happy memories? *Journal of Abnormal Psychology*, 113: 179–188.

Kannan, D. & Levitt, H.M. (2013). A review of client self-criticism in psychotherapy. *Journal of Psychotherapy Integration*, 23(2): 166–178.

Kapur, R. (1987). Depression: an integration of TA and psychodynamic concepts. *Transactional Analysis Journal*, 17: 29–34.

Karpman, S. (1968). Fairy tales and script drama analysis. *Transactional Analysis Bulletin*, 7(26): 39–43.

Kazdin, A.E., Sherick, R.B., Esveldt-Dawson, K. & Rancurello, M.D. (1985). Nonverbal behavior and childhood depression. *Journal of American Academy of Child Psychiatry*, 24: 303–309.

Keller, M.B., Lavori, P.W., Endicott, J., Coryell, W. & Klerman, G.L. (1983). Double depression: two-year follow up. *American Journal of Psychiatry*, 140: 689–694.

Kendler, K.S., Hettema, J.M., Butera, F., Gardner, C.O. & Prescott, C.A. (2003). Life event dimensions of loss, humiliation, entrapment and danger in the prediction of onsets of major depression and generalised anxiety. *Archive of General Psychiatry*, 60: 789–796.

Kerr, C. (2013). TA treatment of emetophobia: a systematic case study. *International Journal of Transactional Analysis Research*, 4(2): 16–26.

Kessler, R.C., Berglund, P., Demler, O., Jin, R., Koretz, D., Merikangas, K.R., . . . Wang, P.S. (2003). The epidemiology of major depressive disorder: results from the National Comorbidity Survey Replication (NCSR). *Journal of the American Medical Association*, 289: 3095–3105.

Kiesler, D.J. (1996). *Contemporary Interpersonal Theory and Research: Personality, psychopathology, and psychotherapy*. New York: Wiley.

Klein, M. (1975). *Envy, Gratitude and Other Works*. London: Hogarth Press and Institute for Psycho-Analysis.

Kopta, S.M., Howard, K.I., Lowry, J.L. & Beutler, L.E. (1994). Patterns of symptomatic recovery in psychotherapy. *Journal of Consulting and Clinical Psychology*, 62(5): 1009–1016.

Krishnan, V. & Nestler, E.J. (2010). Linking molecules to mood: new insight into the biology of depression. *American Journal of Psychiatry*, 167: 1305–1320.

Lai, J., Moxey, A., Nowak, G., Vashum, K., Bailey, K. & McEvoy, M. (2012). The efficacy of zinc supplementation in depression: systematic review of randomised controlled trials. *Journal of Affective Disorders*, 136(1–2): e31–e39.

Lee, A. (1997). The drowning man, workshop presentation. In T. Tilney (ed.) *Dictionary of Transactional Analysis*. London: Wiley Blackwell.

Lee, A. (2006). Process contracts. In: C. Sills (Ed.) *Contracts in Counselling and Psychotherapy*. London: Sage.

Levenson, R.W. (1992). Autonomic nervous system differences among emotions. *Psychological Science*, 3: 23–27.

Levitt, H.M., Neimeyer, R.A. & Williams, D.C. (2005). Rules versus principles in psychotherapy: implications of the quest for universal guidelines in the movement for empirically supported treatments. *Journal of Contemporary Psychotherapy*, 35: 117–129.

Lewinsohn, P.M. (1974). A behavioral approach to depression. In: R.J. Friedman & M.M. Katz (Eds.) *The Psychology of Depression: Contemporary theory and research* (pp. 157–178). New York: John Wiley.

Lister-Ford, C. (2002). *Skills in Transactional Analysis Counselling and Psychotherapy*. London: Sage.

Little, R. (2013). The new emerges out of the old: an integrated relational perspective on psychological development, psychopathology and therapeutic action. *Transactional Analysis Journal*, 43(2): 106–121.

Lorant, V., Deliege, D., Eaton, W., Robert, A., Philippot, P. & Ansseau, M. (2003). Socioeconomic inequalities in depression: a meta-analysis. *American Journal of Epidemiology*, 157: 98–112.

Luborsky, L. (1984). *Principles of Psychoanalytic Psychotherapy: A manual for supportive-expressive treatment*. New York: Basic Books.

Maggiora, A.R. (1987). A case of severe depression. *Transactional Analysis Journal*, 17: 38–43.

Mahmoud, R.A., Pandina, G.J., Turkoz, I. *et al.* (2007). Risperidone for treatment-refractory major depressive disorder: a randomized trial. *Annals of Internal Medicine*, 147: 593–602.

Malouff, J.M., Thorsteinsson, E.B. & Schutte, N.S. (2007). The efficacy of problem-solving therapy in reducing physical and mental health problems: a meta-analysis. *Clinical Psychology Review*, 27: 46–57.

Maroda, K. (2010). *Psychodynamic Techniques: Working with emotion in the therapeutic relationship*. New York: Guilford Press.

Marroquin, B. (2011). Interpersonal emotion regulation as a mechanism of social support in depression. *Clinical Psychology Review*, 31: 1276–1290.

Marshall, M.B., Zuroff, D.C., McBride, C. & Bagby, R.M. (2008). Self-criticism predicts differential response to treatment for major depression. *Journal of Clinical Psychology*, 64(3): 231–244.

Matthews, A. & MacLeod, C. (2005). Cognitive vulnerability to emotional disorders. *Annual Review of Clinical Psychology*, 1: 167–195.

Matt, G.E., Vasquez, C. & Campbell, W.K. (1992). Mood-congruent recall of affectively toned stimuli: a meta-analytic review. *Clinical Psychology Review*, 12: 227–255.

McCullough, J.P. (2000). *Treatment for Chronic Depression: Cognitive behavioral analysis system of psychotherapy (CBASP)*. New York: Guilford Press.

McCullough Vaillant, L. (1997). *Changing Character: Short term anxiety regulating psychotherapy*. New York: Basic Books.

McGrath, C.L., Kelley, M.E., Holtzheimer, P.E., Dunlop, B.W., Craighead, W.E., Franco, A.R., Craddock, C. & Mayberg, H.S. (2013). Toward a neuroimaging treatment selection biomarker for major depressive disorder. *JAMA Psychiatry*, 70(8): 821–829.

McKay, M. & Fanning, P. (1992). *Self-esteem: A proven program of cognitive techniques for assessing, improving and maintaining your self-esteem* (2nd edn). Oakland, CA: New Harbinger Publications.

McLeod, J. (1998). *Introduction to Counselling* (3rd edn). Maidenhead: Open University Press.

McLeod, J. (2009). *Introduction to Counselling* (4th edn). Maidenhead: Open University Press.

McLeod, J. (2013). Process and outcome in pluralistic Transactional Analysis counselling for long-term health conditions: a case series. *Counselling and Psychotherapy Research*, 13(1): 32–43.

McLeod, J. & McLeod, J. (2011). *Counselling Skills*. Maidenhead: Open University Press.

McNeel, J. (1976). The parent interview. *Transactional Analysis Journal*, 6(1): 61–68.

McNeel, J. (2010). Understanding the power of injunctive messages and how they are resolved in redecision therapy. *Transactional Analysis Journal*, 40(2): 159–169.

Mearns, D. & Thorne, B. (2000). *Person-centred Therapy Today: New frontiers in theory and practice*. London: Sage.

Mearns, D. & Thorne, B. (2007). *Person-centred Counselling in Action* (3rd edn). London: Sage.

Mellor, K. (1980). Impasses: a developmental and structural understanding. *Transactional Analysis Journal*, 10(3): 213–222.

Mellor, K. & Schiff, E. (1975). Discounting. *Transactional Analysis Journal*, 5(3): 295–302.

Miller, W.R. & Rollnick, S. (2002). *Motivational Interviewing: Preparing people for change* (2nd edn). New York: Guilford Press.

Moiso, C. (1984). The feeling loop. In E. Stern (Ed.) *TA, The State of the Art: A European contribution* (pp. 69–75). Utrecht: Foris Publications.

Morley, T.E. & Moran, G. (2011). The origins of cognitive vulnerability in early childhood: mechanisms linking early attachment to later depression. *Clinical Psychology Review*, 31: 1071–1082.

Morrison, K.H., Bradley, R. & Westen, D. (2003). The external validity of controlled clinical trials of psychotherapy for depression and anxiety: a naturalistic study. *Psychology and Psychotherapy: Theory, Research and Practice*, 76: 109–132.

Morrow-Bradley, C. & Elliott, R. (1986). Utilization of psychotherapy research by practicing psychotherapists. *American Psychologist*, 48(2): 188–197.

Mothersole, G. (1996). Existential realities and no-suicide contracts. *Transactional Analysis Journal*, 26(2): 151–159.

Moussavi, S., Chatterji, S., Verdes, E., Tandon, A., Patel, V. & Ustun, B.J. (2007). Depression, chronic diseases, and decrements in health: results from the world health surveys. *Lancet*, 370(9590): 851–858.

National Collaborating Centre for Mental Health (2009). *Depression: The treatment and management of depression in adults (update)*. NICE Clinical Guideline 90. London: National Institute for Health and Clinical Excellence.

Navajits, L.M., Weiss, R.D., Shaw, S.R. & Dierberger, A.E. (2000). Psychotherapists' views of treatment manuals. *Professional Psychology: Research and Practice*, 51(4): 404–408.

Neff, K. (2003). Self-compassion: an alternative conceptualisation of a healthy attitude toward oneself. *Self and Identity*, 2: 85–102.

Newton, T. (2006). Script, psychological life plans, and the learning cycle. *Transactional Analysis Journal*, 36(3): 186–195.

Nolen-Hoeksema, S., Stice, E., Wade, E. & Bohon, C. (2007). Reciprocal relations between rumination and bulimic, substance abuse, and depressive symptoms in female adolescents. *Journal of Abnormal Psychology*, 116: 198–207.

Nolen-Hoeksema, S., Wisco, B.E. & Lyubomirsky, S. (2008). Rethinking rumination. *Perspectives in Psychological Science*, 3: 400–424.

Norcross, J. (2002). *Psychotherapy Relationships That Work: Therapist contributions and responsiveness to patients*. Oxford: Oxford University Press.

Norcross, J.C. (2011). *Psychotherapy Relationships that Work: Evidence-based responsiveness*. New York: Oxford University Press.

Office for National Statistics. (2000). *Psychiatric Morbidity Among Adults Living in Private Households in Great Britain*. London: Office of National Statistics.

O'Reilly-Knapp, M. & Erskine, R.G. (2010). The script system: an unconscious organization of experience. In: R.G. Erskine (Ed.) *Life Scripts: A transactional analysis of unconscious relational patterns* (pp. 291–308). London: Karnac.

Papakostas, G.I., Petersen, T., Denninger, J., Sonawalla, S.B., Mahal, Y., Alpert, J.E., Nierenberg, A.A. & Fava, M. (2003). Somatic symptoms in treatment resistant depression. *Psychiatry Research*, 118: 39–45.

Papakostas, G.I., Mischoulon, D., Shyu, I., Alpert, J.E. & Fava, M. (2010). S-adenosyl methionine (SAMe) augmentation of serotonin reuptake inhibitors for antidepressant nonresponders with major depressive disorder: a double-blind, randomized clinical trial. *American Journal of Psychiatry*, 167: 942–948.

Parrott, W.G. (1993). Beyond hedonism: motives for inhibiting good moods and maintaining bad moods. In D.M. Wegner & J.W. Pennebaker (Eds.) *Handbook of Mental Control* (pp. 278–308). Englewood Cliffs, NJ: Prentice Hall.

Parrott, W.G. & Sabini, J. (1990). Mood and memory under natural conditions: evidence for mood incongruent recall. *Journal of Personality and Social Psychology*, 59: 321–336.

PDM Task Force. (2006). *Psychodynamic Diagnostic Manual*. Silver Spring, MD: Alliance of Psychoanalytic Organizations.

Perlman, D. & Peplau, L. A. (1984). Loneliness research: a survey of empirical findings. In: L.A. Peplau & S.E. Goldston (Eds.) *Preventing the Harmful Consequences of Severe and Persistent Loneliness* (pp. 13–46). Rockville, MD: National Institute of Mental Health.

Philips, W.J., Hine, D.W. & Thorsteinsson, E.B. (2010). Implicit cognition and depression: a meta-analysis. *Clinical Psychology Review*, 30: 691–709.

Piccinelli, M. & Wilkinson, G. (1994). Outcome of depression in psychiatric settings. *British Journal of Psychiatry*, 164: 297–304.

Pope, H.G., Cohane, G.H., Kanayama, G., Siegel, A.J. & Hudson, J.I. (2003). Testosterone supplementation for men with refractory depression: a randomized, placebo-controlled trial. *American Journal of Psychiatry*, 160: 105–111.

Pulleyblank, E. & McCormick, P. (1985). The stages of redecision therapy. In: L.B. Kadis (Ed.) *Redecision Therapy: Expanded perspectives*. Watsonville, CA: Western Institute for Group and Family Therapy.

Quilty, L.C., Mainland, B.J., McBride, C. & Bagby, R.M. (2013). Interpersonal problems and impacts: further evidence for the role of interpersonal functioning in treatment outcome in major depressive disorder. *Journal of Affective Disorders*, 150(2): 393–400.

Ravitz, P., Maunder, R. & McBride, C. (2008). Attachment, contemporary interpersonal theory and IPT: an integration of theoretical, clinical, and empirical perspectives. *Journal of Contemporary Psychotherapy*, 38: 11–21.

Rector, N.A., Bagby, R.M., Segal, Z.V., Joffe, R.T. & Levitt, A. (2000). Self-criticism and dependency in depressed patients treated with cognitive therapy or pharmacotherapy. *Cognitive Therapy and Research*, 24: 571–584.

Retief, Y. & Conroy, B. (1981). Conscious empowerment therapy: a model for counselling adult survivors of childhood abuse. *Transactional Analysis Journal*, 27(1): 42–48.

Riley, W.T., Treiber, F.A. & Woods, M.G. (1989). Anger and hostility in depression. *Journal of Nervous and Mental Disease*, 177(11): 668–674.

Rocha, F.L., Fuzikawa, C., Riera, R., Guarieiro-Ramo, M. & Hara, C. (2013). Antidepressant combination for major depression in incomplete responders – a systematic review. *Journal of Affective Disorders*, 144: 1–6.

Rogers, C. (1951). *Client-Centered Therapy: Its current practice, implications and theory*. London: Constable.

Rogers, C. (1957) The necessary and sufficient conditions of therapeutic personality change. *Journal of Consulting Psychology*, 21(2): 95–103.

Ryle, A. & Kerr, I.B. (2002) *Introducing Cognitive Analytic Therapy: Principles and practice*. Chichester: John Wiley.

Sacher, J., Neumann, J., Fünfstück, T., Soliman, A., Villringer, A. & Schroeteret, M.L. (2011). Mapping the depressed brain: a meta-analysis of structural and functional alterations in major depressive disorder. *Journal of Affective Disorders*, 140(20): 142–148.

Sachs-Ericsson, N., Verona, E., Joiner, T. & Preacher, K.J. (2006). Parental verbal abuse and the mediating role of self-criticism in adult internalizing disorders. *Journal of Affective Disorders*, 93: 71–78.

Schiff, J.L., Schiff, A.W., Mellor, K., Schiff, E., Schiff, S., Richman, D., Fishman, J., Wolz, L., Fishman, C. & Momb, D. (1975). *The Cathexis Reader: Transactional analysis treatment of psychosis*. New York: Harper and Row.

Schlenker, B.R. & Britt, T.W. (1996). Depression and the explanation of events that happen to self, close others, and strangers. *Journal of Personality and Social Psychology*, 71: 180–192.

Segrin, C. (1998). Interpersonal communication problems associated with depression and loneliness. In: P.A. Andersen & L.K. Guerrero (Eds.) *Handbook of Communication and Emotion: Research, theory, applications, and contexts* (pp. 215–242). San Diego, CA: Academic Press.

Segrin, C. (2000). Social skills deficits associated with depression. *Clinical Psychology Review*, 20(3): 379–403.

Seligman, M.E., Steen, T.A., Park, N. & Peterson, C. (2005). Positive psychology progress: empirical validation of interventions. *American Psychologist*, 60: 410–421.

Seligman, M.E., Rashid, T. & Parks, A.C. (2006). Positive psychotherapy. *American Psychologist*, 61: 774–788.

Shahar, B., Carlin, E.R., Engle, D.E., Hegde, J., Szepsenwol, O. & Arkowitz, H. (2011). A pilot investigation of emotion-focused two-chair dialogue intervention for self-criticism. *Clinical Psychology and Psychotherapy*, 19(6): 496–507.

Shahar, G., Blatt, S.J., Zuroff, D.C. & Pilkonis, P.A. (2003). Role of perfectionism and personality disorder features in response to brief treatment for depression. *Journal of Consulting and Clinical Psychology*, 71(3): 629–633.

Sharpley, C.F. (2010). A review of the neurobiological effects of psychotherapy for depression. *Psychotherapy Theory, Research, Practice, Training*, 47(4): 603–615.

Shea, M., Widiger, T. & Klein, M. (1992). Comorbidity of personality disorders and depression: implications for treatment. *Journal of Clinical and Consulting Psychology*, 60: 857–868.

Sheline, Y.I., Gado, M.H. & Kraemer, H.C. (2003). Untreated depression and hippocampal volume loss. *American Journal of Psychiatry*, 160: 1516–1518.

Sifneos, P.E. (1980). Motivation for change. In H. Davanloo (Ed.) *Short Term Dynamic Psychotherapy*. New York: Jason Aronson.

Sills, C. (2006). *Contracts in Counselling and Psychotherapy*. London: Sage.

Skinner, B.F. (1937). Two types of conditioned reflex: a reply to Konorski and Miller. *Journal of General Psychology*, 16: 272–279.

Spalding, K.L., Bergmann, O., Alkass, K., Bernard, S., Salehpour, M., Huttner, H., Boström, E . . . & Frisén, J. (2013). Dynamics of hippocampal neurogenesis in adult humans. *Cell*, 153(6): 1219–1227.

Spence, S.H., Najman, J.M., Bor, W., O'Callaghan, M.J. & Williams, G.M. (2002). Maternal anxiety and depression, poverty and marital relationship factors during early childhood as predictors of anxiety and depressive symptoms in adolescence. *Journal of Child Psychology and Psychiatry*, 43(4): 457–469.

Spitz, R.A. (1946). Hospitalism; a follow-up report on investigation described in volume I, 1945. *The Psychoanalytic Study of the Child*, 2: 113–117.

Steiner, C. (1968). Transactional analysis as a treatment philosophy. *Transactional Analysis Bulletin*, 7(27): 63.

Steiner, C. (1974). *Scripts People Live*. New York: Grove.

Steiner, C. & Perry, P. (1999). *Achieving Emotional Literacy*. New York: Bloomsbury.

Sterba, S.K., Prinstein, M.J. & Cox, M.J. (2007). Trajectories of internalizing problems across childhood: heterogeneity, external validity, and gender differences. *Development and Psychopathology*, 19: 345–366.

Stern, D.N. (1985). *The Interpersonal World of the Infant: A view from psychoanalysis and developmental psychology*. New York: Basic Books.

Stewart, I. (1992). *Eric Berne*. London: Sage.

Stewart, I. (1996). *Developing Transactional Analysis Counselling*. London: Sage.

Stewart, I. (2006). Outcome-focused contracts. In: C. Sills (Ed.) *Contracts in Counselling and Psychotherapy*. London: Sage.

Stewart, I. (2007). *Transactional Analysis Counselling in Action* (3rd edn). London: Sage.

Stewart, I. (2010a). The theory of ego. *The Psychotherapist*, 46: 8–10.

Stewart, I. (2010b). The "three ways out": escape hatches. In R.G. Erskine (Ed.) *Life Scripts: A transactional analysis of unconscious relational patterns*. London: Karnac.

Stewart, I. (2014). *Transactional Analysis Counselling in Action* (4th edn). London: Sage.

Stewart, I. & Joines, V. (1987). *TA Today: A new introduction to transactional analysis*. Nottingham: Lifespace.

Stewart, I. & Joines, V. (2012). *TA Today: A new introduction to transactional analysis* (2nd edn). Nottingham: Lifespace.

Stuthridge, J. (2010). Script or scripture? In R.G. Erskine (Ed.) *Life Scripts: A transactional analysis of unconscious relational patterns* (pp. 73–100). London: Karnac.

Taylor, M.J., Freemantle, N., Geddes, J.R. et al. (2006). Early onset of selective serotonin reuptake inhibitor antidepressant action: systematic review and meta-analysis. *Archives of General Psychiatry*, 63: 1217–1223.

Toth, S.L., Manly, J.T. & Cicchetti, D. (1992). Child maltreatment and vulnerability to depression. *Development and Psychopathology*, 4: 97–112.

Tryon, G.S. & Winograd, G. (2002). Goal consensus and collaboration. In: J.C. Norcross (Ed.) *Psychotherapy Relationships that Work*. New York: Oxford University Press.

Tudor, K. & Widdowson, M. (2008). From client process to therapeutic relating: a critique of the process model and personality adaptations. *Transactional Analysis Journal*, 38(1): 218–232.

Ustun, T.B., Ayuso-Mateos, J.L., Chatterji, S., Mathers, C. & Murray, C.J. (2004). Global burden of depressive disorders in the year 2000. *British Journal of Psychiatry*, 184: 386–392.

van Rijn, B. & Wild, C. (2013). Humanistic and integrative therapies for anxiety and depression: practice-based evaluation of transactional analysis, gestalt and integrative psychotherapies and person-centred counseling. *Transactional Analysis Journal*, 43(2): 150–163.

van Rijn, B., Wild, C. & Moran, P. (2011). Evaluating the outcomes of transactional analysis psychotherapy and integrative counselling psychology within UK primary care settings. *International Journal of Transactional Analysis Research*, 2(2): 34–43.

Veale, D. (2008) Behavioural activation for depression. *Advances in Psychiatric Treatment*, 14: 29–36.

Vearnals, S. & Asen, E. (1998). Depression and expressed emotion. *In Session: Psychotherapy in Practice*, 4/3: 93–107.

Von Wolff, A., Holzel, L.P., Westphal, A., Harter, M. & Kriston, L. (2013). Selective serotonin reuptake inhibitors and tricyclic antidepressants in the acute treatment of chronic depression and dysthymia: a systematic review and meta-analysis. *Journal of Affective Disorders*, 144: 7–15.

Watson, J.C., Goldman, R. & Greenberg, L.S. (2007). *Case Studies in Emotion-focused Treatment of Depression: A comparison of good and poor outcome.* Washington, DC: American Psychological Association Press.

Watzlawick, P., Weakland, J. & Fisch, R. (1974). *Change: Principles of problem formation and problem resolution.* New York: W.W. Norton.

Weeks, D.G., Michela, J.L., Peplau, L.A. & Bragg, M.E. (1980). Relation between loneliness and depression: a structural equation analysis. *Journal of Personality and Social Psychology*, 39: 1238–1244.

Weiss, E. (1950). *Principles of Psychodynamics.* New York: Grune and Stratton.

Westen, D. & Morrison, K. (2001). A multidimensional meta-analysis of treatments for depression, panic, and generalized anxiety disorder: an empirical examination of the status of empirically supported therapies. *Journal of Consulting and Clinical Psychology*, 69(6): 875–899.

Widdowson, M. (2008). Metacommunicative transactions. *Transactional Analysis Journal*, 38(1): 58–71.

Widdowson, M. (2010). *Transactional Analysis: 100 key points and techniques.* Hove: Routledge.

Widdowson, M. (2011). Depression: a literature review on diagnosis, subtypes, patterns of recovery, and psychotherapeutic models. *Transactional Analysis Journal*, 41(4): 351–364.

Widdowson, M. (2012a). Perceptions of psychotherapy trainees of psychotherapy research. *Counselling and Psychotherapy Research*, 12(3): 178–186.

Widdowson, M. (2012b). TA treatment of depression: a hermeneutic single-case efficacy design study – 'Peter'. *International Journal of Transactional Analysis Research*, 3(1): 3–13.

Widdowson, M. (2012c). TA treatment of depression: a hermeneutic single-case efficacy design study – case two: "Denise". *International Journal of Transactional Analysis Research*, 3(2): 3–14.

Widdowson, M. (2012d). TA treatment of depression: a hermeneutic single-case efficacy design study – case three: "Tom". *International Journal of Transactional Analysis Research*, 3(2): 15–27.

Widdowson, M. (2013). *The Process and Outcome of Transactional Analysis Psychotherapy for the Treatment of Depression: An adjudicated case series.* Unpublished doctoral thesis, University of Leicester.

Widdowson, M. (2014a). TA therapy for a case of mixed anxiety and depression: a pragmatic adjudicated case study. *International Journal of Transactional Analysis Research*, 5(2): 66–76.

Widdowson, M. (2014b). Avoidance, vicious cycles, and experiential disconfirmation of script: two new theoretical concepts and one mechanism of change in the psychotherapy of depression and anxiety. *Transactional Analysis Journal*, 44(3): 194–207.

Williams, D.C. & Levitt, H.M. (2007). Principles for facilitating agency in psychotherapy. *Psychotherapy Research*, 17(1): 66–82.

Wisco, B.E. (2009). Depressive cognition: self-reference and depth of processing. *Clinical Psychology Review*, 29: 382–392.

Wissink, L.M. (1994). A validation of transactional analysis in increasing self-esteem among participants in a self-reparenting program. *Transactional Analysis Journal*, 24(3): 189–196.

Woollams, S. & Brown, M. (1979). *Transactional Analysis.* Dexter: Huron Valley Institute.

Young, J., Klosko, J. & Weishaar, M. (2003). *Schema Therapy: A practitioner's guide.* New York: Guilford Press.

Zinbarg, R., Lee, J.E. & Yoon, L. (2007). Dyadic predictors of outcome in a cognitive-behavioral program for patients with generalised anxiety disorder in committed relationships: a 'spoonful of sugar' and a dose of non-hostile criticism may help. *Behaviour Research and Therapy*, 45, 699–713.

Zuroff, D.C., Blatt, S.J., Sotsky, S.M., Krupnick, J.L., Martin, D.J., Sanislow, C.A. & Simmens, S. (2000). Relation of therapeutic alliance and perfectionism to outcome in brief outpatient treatment of depression. *Journal of Consulting and Clinical Psychology*, 68(1): 114–124.

Index

acceptance 128–9
affect-focused 65, 98
affect regulation/dysregulation 28–30, 32, 39, 44, 51, 62, 71, 86, 97, 102, 103, 117, 118, 123, 127–8, 146, 154–155
alliance rupture and repair 84, 109, 111, 115
amplification 61, 71, 72
anger 29–30, 51, 53
antidepressants 158–160, 162–4
antipsychotics 166–7
assertiveness 38, 53, 140, 146
attachment style 28
autonomy 17
avoidance 29, 30, 32–3, 37, 38, 39, 53

benzodiazepines 167
beta-blockers 167–8
between session contact 86
Biased Adult thinking 46–47, 145
brain 151–157

case formulation 45, 66, 90, 103–104, 108, 110
catastrophising 145
cognitive dissonance 114
complementary medicines 165–6
confirmation 60, 113–116
confrontation 58–9
contaminating process 112
contamination 45–6, 47, 105, 112
contingency planning 61, 109, 138, 147
contracting 16–17, 62–3, 83–4, 89–90, 98, 106, 135, 138, 139
countertransference 12, 69, 98, 122–3, 134
couples therapy 41, 81–2, 139

critical thinking 114
crystallisation 61

deconfusion 14, 18, 51, 53, 60, 97, 106, 140
decontamination 18, 19, 113–116
depression: affect 28–30; comorbidity 24–5, 79; diagnostic features and symptoms 21–2; natural course 22–3; patterns of recovery 23–4; prevalence and epidemiology 20; relapse rates 23
developmental factors 26–8
discounting 32, 106, 112, 114, 134, 143, 145, 191
domains of experience and change 64
drama triangle 41, 44, 140, 194
drivers 196–8
dual awareness 62

early scene work 72
effectiveness of TA therapy 77–8
ego states 10–12, 97, 123–4, 186–7; Adult ego state 10–11, 47 97, 131, 134, 186; Child ego state 10, 11, 14, 44, 97, 123, 186–7; functional model 40, 44, 123; Parent ego state 10–11, 44, 45, 123, 128, 186
electroconvulsive therapy 168
emotional literacy work 116–118
emotions 14, 28–30, 51–53, 98, 116; positive emotions in depression 118–119
empathy 87, 94, 97
enactment 99–100
enquiry 57–8, 84, 87, 88, 114
excessive reassurance seeking 40, 110, 145
experiencing self 97

explanation 59–60
explicit memory 68

fear 51, 53–4; of change 87, 95–96
forbidden feelings 53, 54, 118
frame of reference 31, 48–9, 115

games 14–15, 40, 42, 99, 194
general session structure 82–7
genetic factors 26–7, 156
Global Assessment of Functioning Scale 78
goal setting 95, 108, 109, 111, 137–8
grandiosity 32, 106, 191
grief 51, 53
guilt 28, 44, 51, 52

heighteners: see amplification
historical development of TA 9–10
homework 84, 106, 107, 108, 110, 132–4
humanistic basis of TA 96

illustration 59–60
injunctions 43, 50, 192–3
insomnia 21, 22, 142, 156 (also see sleep hygiene)
internal dialogue 12, 28, 43, 44, 105, 107, 123–6, 128, 130, 141, 187–8
internal nurturing parent 44, 97, 123, 128, 131
interpretation (as an intervention) 60
impasse 43
implicit learning 107–8, 118
implicit memory 13, 53, 68–73, 100
initial phase of therapy 87
internal dialogue 187–8
interpersonal problems 36, 37–41, 44, 108, 139
interpersonal relationships 37–41, 138–140
intolerance of uncertainty and ambiguity 31, 87, 128

key therapeutic tasks 105–6

life positions 13–14, 43
Life Script 13–14, 43, 48, 49–51, 66–7, 69, 84, 99, 191–2
limbic system 154
low energy 142–3

manual: development 77–8; effectiveness 77–8; suitability 78–9
maternal depression 26–7
medication 78, 79, 81, 158–165
memory enhancement effect 67
metacommunication 62, 99
mindfulness 113, 131–2, 183–5
mood-stabilisers 168
motivation 94–6, 109, 134, 136–7, 142

narrative 107–8
negative feedback seeking 40, 146
negative interpretation (of events) 31–4, 119
negative memory bias 32–4
neurotransmitters 151–3
normalisation 113, 116–117, 126, 128, 144, 148

observing self 97
optimal neutrality 101
outcome measures 82, 90–3

parent interview 36, 131
perfectionism 36, 110–112
permission 102
physical exercise 153, 156, 169, 180
physis 96
potency 101–2
principles for practice 106–9
primary emotion 42, 51, 195–6
problem identification 89, 135
problem-solving 134–8
process measures 85–86
prodromal symptoms 147–8
prognostic indicators 79
protection 103
protocol 13, 66, 68, 69, 70
psychoeducation 40, 42, 59, 65–6
psychological hungers 15–16

racket feelings 14, 42, 195–6
racket system: see script system
redecision 18–19, 36, 49, 69–72, 106
redecision therapy 36, 70, 72
referral 79
reframing 113
risk assessment: see suicidal ideation

role induction 87–8, 97–8
rumination 30, 33–4, 112–113

sadness 51, 53
secondary emotion 42, 51, 195–6
self-compassion: see self-nurturing
self-criticism 28, 34–36, 43, 44, 52, 53, 59, 97, 101, 105, 107, 110, 111, 115, 123–132
self-efficacy 95, 97, 135
self-image 31
self-nurturing 112, 123–132, 181–182
self-reparenting 35, 131
session bridging 82–83
session contract 83–85
script beliefs 31, 34, 40, 43, 47, 48, 49–51, 52, 61, 68, 70, 90, 105, 112, 125, 127–8, 141–2, 146
script narrative 66–67
script system/associative network 14–15, 32, 42, 47, 50–1, 52, 53, 54–5, 70, 105
shame 28, 44, 51, 52, 144
sleep hygiene 182–3
social contact 182
soothing 62

specification 58
stages of cure 17
state-dependent memory 53, 67, 195–6
strokes 16, 39, 40, 41, 43, 105, 130, 140, 147, 188–190
suicidal ideation 121–3
summarising sessions 85
supervision 79, 80–1
systematic experiential disconfirmation 67, 69–70, 99, 100, 107, 115, 132, 142

termination of therapy 146–8
therapist characteristics 101–2, 108
trading stamps 42
transference 12, 52, 100
treatment planning 109–110
therapeutic operations 57–61
therapeutic relationship 2, 18, 84, 96–103, 111, 129, 142
transaction 12, 37–8, 40, 41, 44, 58, 139
two-chair work 35, 131

unconditional positive regard 101

vicious cycles 33, 40, 41, 109, 119–120